Plate 1. Royal Crown Derby plaque, one of a series painted by Reuben Hague, this one showing
Queen Elizabeth II as a young girl. 10½ in. 1951.

Royal Crown Derby

John Twitchett F.R.S.A. and Betty Bailey F.R.S.A.
revised by John Twitchett

Antique Collectors' Club

ISBN 1 85149 057 4

First published in 1976 by Barrie & Jenkins Ltd.
Second edition 1980
Third edition published by Antique Collectors' Club 1988
Reprinted 1989

Published for the Antique Collectors' Club
by the Antique Collectors' Club Ltd.

British Library CIP Data
Twitchett, John
Royal Crown Derby.—3rd ed.
1. Crown Derby porcelain to 1987
I. Title   II. Bailey, Betty   III. Antique
Collectors' Club
738.2'7

Printed in England by the Antique Collectors' Club Ltd.
5 Church Street, Woodbridge, Suffolk

This book is dedicated to the men and women, too numerous to mention individually, who have worked in productive and non-productive jobs at Osmaston Road and without whom Royal Crown Derby could not have existed.

From an engraving of the Osmaston Road Manufactory, c.1878.
Royal Crown Derby Museum

Royal Crown Derby vase and cover, finely painted with roses on an almost ivory ground and signed by Richard Pilsbury. The vase bears the inscription 'First piece bearing Royal Arms, 1890' and carries the Royal Warrant arms for H.M. Queen Victoria.
Courtesy Bearnes Rainbow Torquay

CONTENTS

COLOUR PLATES

COLOUR PLATES

Preface

In 1972, after the Company had appointed me as Curator and my co-author Betty Bailey as Assistant Curator, the mammoth task of reconstructing the historical records of the King Street and Osmaston Road factories began. After the moving of much dust certain of the surviving records such as the Royal Warrants, original designs and other documentations were unearthed. Fortunately our industrial archaeology paid good dividends and it has proved possible to produce this book, which is the first comprehensive work on the two 19th-century factories, King Street and Osmaston Road.

It has been necessary to correct many erroneous beliefs; for instance the name 'Stevenson & Hancock' is a name frequently used for the later wares produced at the King Street factory which should be correctly known as Sampson Hancock, the former referring to the period 1863-66 only. Certain patterns have been previously published, in part, showing attributed painters rather than those authenticated by the Osmaston Road pattern books. In this work the complete list of named patterns is given for the first time and the complete shape book for Osmaston Road is also published for the first time.

The establishment of Open Days at the Royal Crown Derby Museum has enabled us to have contact with the general public and to meet former designers, painters and gilders and relatives of those who have worked both at King Street and Osmaston Road. The biographies of the designers, modellers, painters and gilders may seem, in some cases, rather brief, but it was thought that the mention of a name might result in some light being shed upon the person's stay at the respective factory.

It is the sincere wish of the writers that the book will prove enjoyable, as well as useful, to all lovers of Royal Crown Derby.

South Kensington January 1976   John Twitchett

Preface to the 3rd Revised Edition

It is now over a decade since the publication of the first edition in June 1976, and *Royal Crown Derby* is recognised as the standard work on the subject. When the Antique Collectors' Club approached me with the prospect of a new edition, I welcomed the opportunity to revise the original text in the light of my researches over the past twelve years, particularly in the chapter on Designers, Modellers, Painters and Gilders, and I have added a new chapter on design and three new appendices. Those familiar with the first edition will see that the book has been redesigned, and will find that some illustrations have been omitted, others replaced by photographs of superior quality and that there are many new ones, including for example, the fascinating series of designs by Donald Birbeck for a specially commissioned dinner service. There are now over sixty pieces illustrated in colour, all of which have been specially selected for the new edition.

As with the first edition, it is my hope that the many people who admire the wares of Royal Crown Derby, will find this book both a source of information and of pleasure.

June 1988   John Twitchett

Introduction: The First Derby China Works

The town of Derby has long been associated with the manufacture of china wares of the highest quality. This book tells the story of two of the three great china works at Derby, King Street and Osmaston Road. But china making in Derby goes back to the mid-eighteenth century, with the first of the china works at Nottingham Road.

There are Derby figures dating from 1750 of such a quality that one must assume that they were made by an established manufactory, and it is known that Andrew Planché, the son of Huguenot immigrants, was making small figures in Derby, c.1748. Although the exact site of Planché's works is unknown, it is thought to have been adjacent to Nottingham Road, the manufactory of Duesbury and, later, Bloor. William Duesbury was an independent decorator, well known in the trade in London where he painted wares of the leading European manufactories. Certainly Planché's work was known to him, and in 1756 he entered into an agreement with Planché from which the Nottingham Road factory was born.

It was under Duesbury's management that Derby's reputation grew, not only in England, but also abroad. In 1770 Duesbury purchased the Chelsea china works, thus bringing to Derby the prestige and clientèle of the London works, and the skills and technical knowledge of its workforce. He managed both establishments until 1784, when he closed down the Chelsea works. With ruthless determination, Duesbury eliminated his rivals; in the mid-1770s he bought up and closed down the Bow manufactory and the decorating establishment of James Giles. Joseph Lygo, Duesbury's London agent, reported that by opening a warehouse in Covent Garden in 1773, he was able to receive the Royal Warrant in 1775, and thereby the right to use the crown mark on Derby wares. On his death on 30th October 1786, he was succeeded by his son William II under whose direction Derby China continued to prosper. During this period artists of the calibre of Zachariah Boreman, William Billingsley, James Banford, Richard Askew, George Complin and the brothers Brewer were decorating sets of china with panels of landscapes, fruit, floral and figure subjects.

In 1795 William Duesbury II's health began to fail and he took the Irish artist, Michael Kean, into the firm, then styled Duesbury and Kean. In 1797 William II died and Kean married his widow, an alliance which caused family friction and long legal battles between Kean and the Duesburys.

Robert Bloor, a clerk at the china works, became its proprietor in 1811, and the factory, now styled Robert Bloor and Co., continued to produce fashionable decorative wares of a high quality. Artists employed at the time included William Pegg, the Quaker, Joseph Bancroft, Moses Webster and Thomas Steel. In 1826 Bloor had become insane, and under the management of James Thomason, the decorator John Haslem's uncle, the company's reputation began to suffer, and there was a general decline in the quality of the wares. In 1848 the Bloor family closed the Nottingham Road China works.

Workmen at the King Street factory about 1870. Fifth from left, Sampson Hancock.

Group of King Street small productions consisting of a dromedary, a cow, a miniature teapot, a bud vase with applied flowers and an incenser: all 20th century.
Royal Crown Derby and Private Collection

1 THE KING STREET FACTORY 1848-1935

After the close of the Nottingham Road factory in 1848, the last proprietor, Thomas Clarke, Robert Bloor's son-in-law, sold much of the plant and moulds to Samuel Boyle of Fenton, who removed them to Staffordshire. This, however, was not the end of the 'Derby' story, as is reported by Sampson Hancock: 'I succeeded Robert Bloor, transplanting the Nottingham Road works to my present factory — King Street. Six working men employed at the old factory put their wits together and started my works — William Locker, James Hill, Samuel Fearn, Samuel Sharp, John Henson and myself. We afterwards took George Stevenson into the concern.'

The original style of the company was Locker & Co. Late Bloor. Locker, having been the chief clerk at Nottingham Road, assumed control until his death in 1859 when, as stated, the remaining partners took George Stevenson, a draper, into the firm. The style then changed to Stevenson, Sharp & Company; later Stevenson & Co., then Stevenson & Hancock, whose initials S. & H., were adopted by Sampson Hancock in 1866 upon the death of Stevenson and were used until the merger with Royal Crown Derby in 1935.

After Sampson Hancock's death in 1895 the works were carried on by his grandson, Mr. James Robinson, until 1916, when a bid to take the small factory over by Royal Crown Derby failed. The works were then purchased by Mr. W. Larcombe, who the following year took Mr. F. Howard Paget[1] into partnership, purchased for Paget by his father when he was wounded during the First World War. During the last few years before the merger Howard Paget was in control, latterly with H. Werner as manager.

From the early years the production consisted mainly of patterns used at the old Nottingham Road factory. Dinner, dessert and tea services, as well as ornamental ware, continued to be decorated with the Japan patterns so typically Derby. Witches, Rose, Garden, and Old Japan were some of the names given to these patterns when they were first introduced at Nottingham Road towards the end of the eighteenth century.

Many of the Derby Sprig patterns were produced, and of course with two fine flower painters, Sampson Hancock and James Hill, it is not surprising that the flower painting was of a high standard. 'Hill's Flowered', and 'Hancock's Laurel' are both mentioned in an old costing book dating from 1861.

It is also known that a certain amount of white ware was sent to Courtney of Bond Street, but because of the small size of the factory, which it is believed never employed more than thirty-five hands at one time, it is not surprising to find invoices from Aynsley (1869), Minton & Co. (1869), Worcester Royal Porcelain Company (1874), Josiah Wedgwood (1870) and Coalport (1871), amongst other lesser known manufacturers, for white wares supplied to the King Street factory for decoration. One invoice from Coalport, John Rose & Co., June 15th 1871 shows:

3 Dishes 20 in. Derby embossed
24/.

White China	3	12
Gross	£3 – 12 – 0	
Cash 3/.	Nett £	3 – 0

But in spite of this the majority of the ware was potted at King Street.

It has been stated that Richard Ablott, a landscape painter from the old

1 Francis Edward Howard Paget, born 4-6-1886, was a member of the Anglesey family.

King Street group with all the charm of a rustic scene, modelled by Joseph Taylor. c.1914.
Courtesy Mrs. Myrtle Taylor

Nottingham Road factory, worked at King Street, but certainly some fine landscape services were decorated by Edwin Prince, who had also worked at the old factory, a good deal of his work being signed. James Rouse sen. returned to Derby to work for Sampson Hancock from 1875-1882, executing, with great skill, all kinds of subjects which he often signed. A service was got up of 'Newcastle pierced' plates (almost certainly from Aynsley, as an invoice stated '25 plates Newcastle Best White') decorated with Rouse centres of rustic figures and floral, fruit, and trophy vignettes upon the pierced borders. Joseph Broughton, who had been apprenticed at Nottingham Road in 1816, painted a good deal of the 'Japan' ware at King Street from 1848-1875. Rayworth, whose main claim to fame was the large number of plaques, chiefly on opaline, which he left signed before his death, has been stated to have been a flower painter at King Street.

John Haslem tells us that from an early date raised flower work was done on baskets, looking-glass frames and other ornamental ware. This work was undertaken by Shufflebotham, Stephan, and James Barnet. Haslem further lists in his collection 'No. 119 Pair of small bisque baskets, modelled flowers by James Barnet, 1878'.

Flower encrusted ornamental ware was continued until the merger with Royal Crown Derby in 1935.

Figure production was largely adopted from Nottingham Road: sets of Seasons, Elements, Fruit- and Flower-sellers, Gardeners, Shepherds, Tythe Groups and, of course, the Derby Dwarfs. John Whitaker's Peacock and numerous Edward Keys figures were continued at King Street until its closure.

It is very important to clear up two points about the King Street factory.

Firstly: in the very early days the old Nottingham Road mark was used as well as the listed marks. It was not in fact until Llewellyn Jewitt, the ceramic historian, suggested in 1862 that the S & H mark should be used, that this was adopted with a *variation* of the old mark, *crossed swords*, and not *crossed batons* as has previously been stated by other historians.

Secondly: dating of King Street productions requires a great deal of care as, unlike other factories, they did not adopt the 'England' mark in accordance with

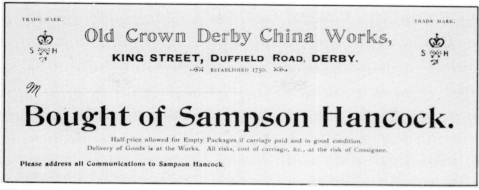

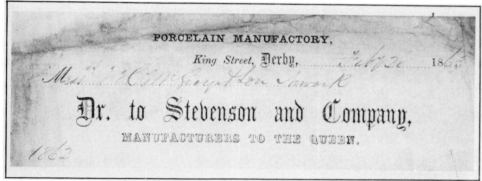

unlike other factories, they did not adopt the 'England' mark in accordance with the American McKinley Tariff & Trades Act, 1891. After 1862 the same mark was used unaltered until the merger in 1935. Much late King Street production is therefore offered for sale as nineteenth century, erroneously described as Stevenson & Hancock. The following list of partnerships is given to avoid future confusion.[2]

1848-1859	LOCKER & CO. LATE BLOOR
1859-1863	STEVENSON SHARP & CO., later
	STEVENSON & CO.
1863-1866	STEVENSON & HANCOCK
1866	SAMPSON HANCOCK
1895	SAMPSON HANCOCK (James Robinson)
1916	SAMPSON HANCOCK (William Larcombe & F. Howard Paget)
1935	SAMPSON HANCOCK purchased by ROYAL CROWN DERBY

As one can see from the bill heading reproduced above, 'Stevenson and Company, Manufacturers to the Queen', King Street enjoyed royal patronage, making replacements for the service got up at Nottingham Road in the closing years. A letter to the Editor of the *Derby Reporter* mentions the birth of the world-famous Royal Crown Derby, as well as Her Majesty's commands:

The Derby China Manufacture.

To the Editor of the Derby Reporter.

Sir, — In briefly announcing the starting of a new China Factory in Derby in last week's issue, you mention the dispersion of the workmen, moulds, &c., of the Old Derby China Factory, and lament that such a state of things did come to pass. Now anyone having the welfare of Derby at heart would naturally regret the collapse of any branch of industry that tends to the commercial prosperity of the town; however, in this case, a slight misunderstanding has arisen, in this wise, that although the old premises and materials were disposed of, six of the workmen, including myself, formed a combination to carry on the old Derby China Works and trade in another part of the town with the same artistic, if not so extensive a success, in proof of which many of

King Street figure of the 'Greenwich Pensioner'. Height 5in. 1900.
A similar figure was in the collection of the late Mrs. Doris Wyatt.
Mrs. Joan Neat Collection

2 The same mark was used from 1863 to 1935.

the articles made previous to 1848 by the old firm have been sent to us to match, including three separate commands from the Queen, besides many of the most eminent collectors and admirers of antique china. As my grandfather served his time with the old firm, and I still carry on the business, it leads me in common fairness to regard our place as the old Derby China Factory, because operations were never suspended.

I am, yours respectfully,

SAMPSON HANCOCK.

King Street, Derby, Sept 22nd. 1875.

Haslem supports Hancock's claim that 'operations were never suspended'. In his book *The Old Derby China Factory,* published in 1876 and, therefore, presumably written in 1875, Haslem says of the King Street factory 'for the last twenty-seven years the concern has been carried on', thus bringing us back to 1848 when the Nottingham Road factory closed.

The Hancocks were concerned with Derby porcelain from the time when John Hancock had been apprenticed to William Duesbury, and this long connection lasted until the death of Harry Sampson Hancock in 1934. With his cousin James Robinson he had moved to Derby to live with his grandparents so that Sampson Hancock might impart to them all the arts of the potter and decorator.

The Hancock family tree is shown opposite as a tribute to a remarkable family whose contributions to the ceramic industry have seldom been surpassed.

The Duesbury Throwing Wheel, illustrated above, was used at Nottingham Road in the 1780s and was in constant use at King Street until 1935 when it was removed to Osmaston Road.

During this century amongst the painters and gilders etc. who worked at King Street were: Annie Bailey *flowers,* Frank Bucknall *painter,* F.H. Chivers *fruit,* Albert Haddock *gilder,* H. Sampson Hancock *flowers, landscapes,* W. Hargreave *birds,* G. Jessop *flowers,* W. Jones *birds and flowers,* A. Machin *flowers,* W.E. Mosley *flowers, landscapes,* J. Ratcliffe *flowers,* F. Schofield *flowers,* Swainson *modeller,* Wencker *flowers.*

During the Larcombe-Paget administration, Paget was able to bring the King Street factory to a wider market, and a London showroom was opened at 16 Brook Street, Mayfair; and in June 1924 the company exhibited at the British Empire Exhibition, Wembley. An undated press cutting tells of the visit to the Old Crown

King Street baskets divided by a
boy sitting on a pedestal, and a rare
item. Width 7in. c.1860-70.
Mrs. Joan Neat Collection

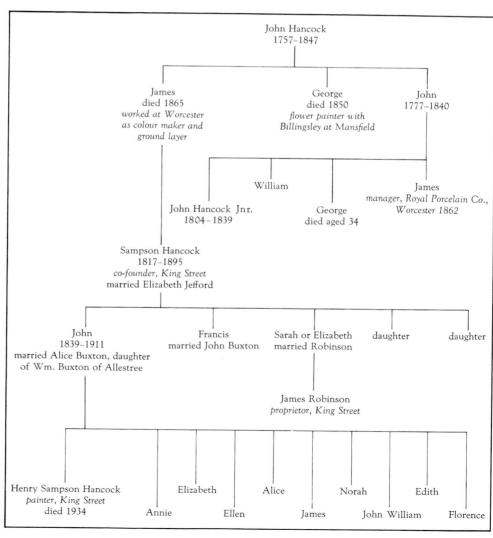

John Hancock
1757–1847

James
died 1865
*worked at Worcester
as colour maker and
ground layer*

George
died 1850
*flower painter with
Billingsley at Mansfield*

John
1777–1840

William

James
*manager, Royal Porcelain Co.,
Worcester 1862*

John Hancock Jnr.
1804–1839

George
died aged 34

Sampson Hancock
1817–1895
co-founder, King Street
married Elizabeth Jefford

John
1839–1911
married Alice Buxton, daughter
of Wm. Buxton of Allestree

Francis
married John Buxton

Sarah or Elizabeth
married Robinson

daughter

daughter

James Robinson
proprietor, King Street

Henry Sampson Hancock
painter, King Street
died 1934

Annie

Elizabeth

Ellen

Alice

James

Norah

John William

Edith

Florence

Oval dish, green groundlaid border with raised gilding, painting of Morley Church by
H.S. Hancock at King Street factory. Inscribed: 'Presented to Miss Boden by the parishioners of
Morley as a token of their esteem. 1883-1917.'
Private Collection

King Street plate with elaborate gilt border and painted with a view of 'Miller Dale Buxton' and
signed by Edwin Prince on the scene, which seems his usual custom. The verso with the red King
Street mark and a JW 12 in red. This JW appears on a pair of small covered vases with raised
gilding and enamel decoration. It nearly always accompanies Prince's signed work at King Street
and must surely belong to a gilder whose name, to date, we do not know. Diameter 10in.
c.1875-80.
John Twitchett Collection

Plate 2. King Street plate painted and signed by James Rouse sen. 10in. c.1875. A plate was sold in the C. Humphreys sale in June 1884 and was described thus: 'Plate blue frosted work border (gilding) centre and panels in border painted by J. Rouse Snr.'.
Private Collection

Plate 3. King Street pierced plate painted with a dog (Pomeranian?) and signed 'J. Rouse Sen.' King Street mark in red. 9½ in. c.1875.
Mr. and Mrs. Peter Budd Collection

King Street plate painted with a
view of Derby by Harry S. Hancock,
signed. c.1920.
Royal Crown Derby American Collection

Derby Works at King Street by the Duchess of Devonshire, accompanied by
several of her grandchildren. She was shown part of a tea service being got up for
Senor Liguia, former President of Peru. Also being prepared was part of a coffee
service for Ras Tafari, whose recent coronation as Emperor of Abyssinia had been
attended by the Duke of Gloucester. During the zeppelin raid on Derby, in 1916,
Larcombe was firing a kiln and he had all the ware from it painted with a crescent
moon, a zeppelin and a monogram W.L., as well as the normal factory mark. This
was indeed a most remarkable and unusual commemorative firing. (See plate 11,
p. 36.)

Pages from the King Street illustrated catalogue for 1934-35 and the price list
are reproduced on pp. 25-32, 34-35 and 38-44. This will afford the student an
opportunity to study the productions which had in fact been very similar over
quite a considerable length of time and which show the continued loyalty to the
traditional wares of the old Nottingham Road factory, adopted by the founder
partners on leaving the works in 1848.

The writers feel that they should, at this point, stress the quality of production of
figures, useful and ornamental wares coming from this little works, which they feel
were equal to anything got up at the old factory during the Robert Bloor ownership.

The competition with their more illustrious and famous neighbours on the
Osmaston Road finally ended with the purchase of the King Street factory by the
Royal Crown Derby Porcelain Company in 1935. A total of £4,100 was paid for
the company broken down as follows: stock, £1,280; property, £1,500; bad debts,
£70; trademark and goodwill, £1,280. This purchase forged the direct link with
the old Nottingham Road factory and validates the claim of china having been
made continuously, since about 1750, in the famous old town of Derby.

Plate 4. King Street plate with central fruit and floral group painted and signed by James Rouse sen. 10¼ in. Dated 1879 in puce script. This is rare and highly important in dating Rouse's stay at King Street. *Mr. and Mrs. Peter Budd Collection*

King Street, wall pocket.
King Street Museum

King Street gadroon shaped plate
with elaborate gilt border and
central landscape, by Harry S.
Hancock, signed on verso. Inscribed
'Littleover Hollow, Nr. Derby'
c.1920. A tray with the same view
is shown in plate 5, overleaf.

King Street plate of embossed daisy shape, painted with a rare moonlight scene, signed Edwin Prince and named Rhuddlan Castle. Diameter 8¾ in. 1875-80. The King Street mark is both impressed and painted which is unusual.
Courtesy David John Ceramics

King Street plate, gadroon shape, painted with 'Old Japan' by Sampson Hancock, signed, red mark, 8¾ in. c.1885. This is one of the very few signed pieces by one of the founders of the King Street works in 1848. His grandson Harry Sampson Hancock's work is often found signed.
King Street Museum

Plates 5a and b. King Street pair of small trays painted with views of 'Old Silk Mill, Derby' and
'Littleover Hollow, Derby' by Harry S. Hancock, signed. 5¾ x 3¾ in. c.1920. A plate with a view of
'Littleover Hollow' is shown on p. 22.
Mr. and Mrs. R. J. Williams Collection

King Street figure of Dr. Syntax,
puce mark. Height 5¼ in. c.1920.

PRICE LIST to King Street Catalogue 1934-35

				£	s.	d.
Page	3	Large size centrepiece comport ..	(Not illustrated)	16	16	0
	18	The Virgins awakening Cupid ..	(Not illustrated)	6	14	6
No.	1	Gardener ..		2	10	6
	2	Companion Gardener ..		2	10	6
	3	Syntax Sketching..		1	16	0
	4	Syntax up Tree ..		2	10	6
		Syntax on Horseback ..	(Not illustrated)	3	7	6
		Syntax Walking ..	(Not illustrated)	0	15	0
		Syntax at Calais ..	(Not illustrated)	1	0	0
	5	French Shepherd..		2	10	6
	6	French Shepherdess ..		2	10	6
	7	Dessert Plate. Flowers ..		3	7	6
	8	'No. 8' Boy ..		1	16	0
	8	'No. 8' Girl ..		1	16	0
	9	Dessert plate. Ground laid border ..		2	0	0

Flower Groups by various artists

			£	s.	d.
No.	10	Tea and saucer ..	0	14	0
		Coffee and saucer ..	0	12	6
		Breakfast and saucer ..	0	19	0
		4 in. plate..	0	8	6
		5 in. plate..	0	9	0
		6 in. plate..	0	10	5
		7 in. plate..	0	14	0
		Cream jug ..	0	14	0
		Sugar ..	0	14	0
		Cake plate ..	1	8	0
		Hot water jug ..	0	19	9
		Open jug, 1 pint ..	0	14	0
		Open jug, 1½ pints ..	0	16	10
		Open jug, 2 pints ..	0	19	9
		Tea pot or coffee pot, 1 pint ..	1	5	3
		Tea pot or coffee pot, 1½ pints ..	1	10	9
		Tea pot or coffee pot, 2 pints ..	1	16	3
		Tea set, 21 pieces ..	10	2	6
		Tea set, 40 pieces ..	18	17	0
		Morning set, 2 persons ..	4	10	3
		Breakfast set, 29 pieces ..	16	15	0
	11	Three-handled loving cup ..	3	7	6
	12	Dog flower holder ..	1	13	6
	13	Incensor. Rose Trellis ..	1	13	6
		Incensor. Flowers ..	1	8	0
	14	Altar vase. Large size, 9 in. ..	1	16	0
		Altar vase. Medium size, 7 in. ..	1	8	0
		Altar vase. Small size, 4½ in. ..	1	0	0
	15	Small Bouquet ..	4	0	0
	16	Large Bouquet ..	8	0	0
	17	Flower Spray ..	0	17	0
	18	Basket of Flowers ..	2	10	6
	19	Violet Basket ..	1	0	0
	20	Derby Peacock ..	6	0	0
	21	The Seasons: Spring ..	3	7	6
	22	Summer ..	3	7	6
	23	Autumn ..	3	7	6
	24	Winter ..	3	7	6
		Fitted with electric flame light, complete, as Nos. 23 and 24, each figure extra ..	1	1	0
	25	Heart-shaped dessert dish. Flowers ..	2	10	6
		8 in. gadroon dessert plate. Flowers ..	2	2	0
	26	The Elements: Earth ..	2	16	0
	27	Air ..	2	16	0
	28	Fire ..	2	16	0
	29	Water ..	2	16	0
	30	Snuff-taker ..	1	16	0
	31	Tinker ..	2	16	0
	32	Companion Tinker ..	2	16	0
	33	The Cobbler ..	3	12	0
	34	Scalloped dish. Game ..	3	7	6
	35	Scalloped dish. Chelsea Birds. Ground laid border ..	2	12	0
	36	8 in. gadroon dessert plate. Landscape ..	3	7	6
Page	3	8 in. gadroon dessert plate. Fruit ..	3	7	6
		8 in. gadroon dessert plate. Fruit and Flowers ..	3	7	6
		8 in. gadroon dessert plate. Fish ..	3	7	6
		8 in. gadroon dessert plate. Game Birds ..	3	7	6
		8 in. gadroon dessert plates. Seascapes ..	3	7	6

No. 2.
Companion Gardener.

No. 3.
Syntax Sketching.

No. 1.
The Gardener.

No. 4.
Syntax up Tree.

No. 6.
French
Shepherdess.

No. 5.
French Shepherd.

Page from the King Street Catalogue 1934-35.

No. 7.
Dessert Plate.

No. 11.
Three-handled
Loving Cup.

No. 12.
Dog
Flower Holder.

No. 25.
Heart-shaped Dessert Dish.

No. 13.
Incensor.
Rose Trellis.

No. 14.
Altar Vase.

No. 9.
Dessert Plate.

No. 10.
Tea and Saucer.

Page from the King Street Catalogue 1934-35.

No. 15.
Small Bouquet.

No. 19.
Violet Basket.

No. 17.
Flower Spray.

No. 16.
Large Bouquet.

No. 20.
Derby Peacock.

No. 18.
Basket of Flowers.

Page from the King Street Catalogue 1934-35.

Page 3	8 in. gadroon dessert plates. Garden Scenes	3	7	6
	8 in. gadroon dessert plates. Cottage Gardens	3	7	6
	Low comports and dishes	4	0	0
	Tall comports	6	0	0
	Bon-bon dishes. Shell or leaf shape	2	5	0
	8 in. dessert plates. Flower sprays and gold (Not illustrated)	0	19	0
	Low comports and dishes. Flower sprays and gold			
	(Not illustrated)	1	2	9
	Tall comports. Flower sprays and gold (Not illustrated)	1	14	0
	Bon-bon dishes. Shell or leaf shape. Flower sprays and gold			
	(Not illustrated)	0	12	6
	8 in. Salad Bowls. Roses and gold leaves (Not illustrated)	2	16	0
	8 in. Salad Bowls. Flowers .. .. (Not illustrated)	3	7	6
No. 37	Square dish. Flowers. Ground laid border	2	16	0
38	8 in. dessert plate. Bird and flower panels. Ground laid border	2	16	0
	Low comports and dishes. Bird and flower panels. Ground			
	laid border .. .. (Not illustrated)	3	7	6
	Tall comports. Bird and flower panels. Ground laid border			
	(Not illustrated)	5	0	0
No. 39	The Hairdresser	5	0	0
40	The Tythe Group	6	14	6
41	The Thrower	3	0	0
42	Toby jug	0	4	6
43	Laughing Philosopher	1	16	0
	Crying Philosopher .. .. .. (Not illustrated)	1	16	0
44	'Morning'	0	12	6
45	'Night'	0	12	6
46	African Sall	0	15	0
47	Billy Waters	0	15	0
52	Pot pourri. Fruit	2	4	0

OLD CROWN DERBY PATTERNS

Witches. Rose. Garden. Old.

No. 48	Heart-shaped dessert tray	2	0	0
49	Oval dessert dish	2	0	0
50	Shell gadroon dish	2	4	0
	Dessert plate	1	13	9
	8 in. salad bowl	3	7	6
	Bon-bon dishes. Shell or leaf shape	1	2	6
51	Bottle vase	4	0	0
53	Tea and saucer	1	0	0
59	Tea and saucer	1	0	0
61	Tea and saucer	1	0	0
62	Tea and saucer	1	0	0
87	Coffee and saucer	0	18	6
88	Coffee and saucer	0	18	6
	Breakfast and saucer	1	8	0
53	4 in. plate	0	12	6
59	4 in. plate	0	12	6
61	4 in. plate	0	12	6
62	4 in. plate	0	12	6
	5 in. plate	0	13	6
	6 in. plate	0	15	6
	7 in. plate	1	0	0
	Cream jug	1	0	0
	Sugar	1	0	0
	Hot water jug	1	8	0
	Open jug. 1 pint	1	0	0
	Open jug. 1½ pints	1	4	0
	Open jug. 2 pints	1	8	0
86	Coffee pot or tea pot. 1 pint	1	16	0
	Coffee pot or tea pot. 1½ pints	2	4	0
	Coffee pot or tea pot. 2 pints	2	12	0
	Cake plate	2	0	0
	Tea set, 21 pieces	14	13	0
	Tea set, 40 pieces	27	6	0
	Morning set, 2 persons	6	9	6
	Breakfast set, 29 pieces	24	5	0
54	Square tray	0	7	9
55	Octagonal tray	0	10	0
60	Octagonal tray	0	10	0
56	Toy watering can	0	12	6
57	Cigarette box	1	0	0
58	Pastille	2	10	6
	Small size Gipsy kettle	0	12	6
	Small size pot pourri	0	8	6

No. 21.
Spring.

No. 24.
Winter.

No. 22.
Summer.

"No. 8"
Boy.

"No. 8"
Girl.

No. 23.
Autumn.

Page from the King Street Catalogue 1934-35.

30

No. 26.
Earth.

No. 30.
Snuff Taker.

No. 27.
Air.

No. 31.
Tinker.

No. 32.
Companion Tinker.

No. 28.
Fire.

No. 33.
The Cobbler.

No. 29.
Water.

Page from the King Street Catalogue 1934-35.

				£	s	d
No. 58	Small size vase			0	7	6
	Round powder or trinket box			1	0	0
85	Bridge set, in case. (4 coffees and saucers, 4 ash trays, cigarette box)			6	17	6

Old Crown Derby Bramble

				£	s	d
No. 89	Coffee and saucer			0	14	0
	Tea and saucer			0	15	6
	Breakfast and saucer			1	1	3
	4 in. plate..			0	9	6
	5 in. plate..			0	10	0
	6 in. plate..			0	11	8
	7 in. plate..			0	15	6
	Cream jug			0	15	6
	Sugar			0	15	6
	Hot water jug			1	1	9
	Open jug, 1 pint			0	15	6
	Open jug, 1½ pints			0	18	9
	Open jug, 2 pints			1	2	0
	Tea pot or coffee pot, 1 pint			1	8	0
	Tea pot or coffee pot, 1½ pints			1	14	3
	Tea pot or coffee pot, 2 pints			2	0	0
	Cake plate			1	11	0
	Tea set, 21 pieces			11	5	0
	Tea set, 40 pieces			20	19	0
	Morning set, 2 persons			4	19	9
	Breakfast set, 29 pieces			18	12	6
63	Coffee's Season, 'Spring'			2	8	0
64	Coffee's Season, 'Autumn'			2	8	0
65	Small size Chelsea Fruit Seller			1	8	0
66	Small size Chelsea Flower Seller			1	8	0
	Medium size French Fruit Seller	(Not illustrated)		3	7	6
	Medium size French Flower Seller ..	(Not illustrated)		3	7	6
	Small size Fisher Boy	(Not illustrated)		1	8	0
	Small size Flower Girl	(Not illustrated)		1	8	0
	Small size Fisher Boy	(Not illustrated)		1	8	0
67	Roman Lamp			1	0	0
68	Paul Pry			1	8	0
69	Mother Gamp, match holder			0	11	9
70	Falstaff			3	12	0
71	English Shepherd			2	10	6
72	English Shepherdess			2	10	6
73	Welch Tailor			4	4	0
74	Welch Tailoress			4	4	0
75	Cow cream jug			1	0	0
76	Cabinet cup. Rose trellis			1	0	0
77	Pot pourri. Rose trellis			0	10	0
78	Green vase, 7 in. Flowers			1	0	0
79	Spills, 4½ in.			1	0	0
	Spills, 3¼ in.			0	16	9
80	Pastille. Flowers			2	4	0
81	Gipsy kettle, raised flowers			0	9	0
	Gipsy kettle, raised flowers, small size.. ..			0	6	6
	Gipsy kettle, small size, painted flowers ..			0	9	0
82	Menu holder. Flowers and butterflies			0	10	6
	Menu holder. Pair, in case			1	4	0
	Serviette ring. Flowers	(Not illustrated)		0	7	6
	Serviette ring. Pair, in case			0	19	0
83	Round powder or trinket box. Flowers			1	8	0
	Round powder or trinket box. Flower posies			1	0	0
84	Small vase. Flowers			0	8	6

Butterflies

				£	s	d
No. 90	Coffee and saucer			0	12	6

Green Star, or Purple Star

				£	s	d
No. 91	Coffee and saucer			0	12	6
	Tea and saucer			0	14	0
	Breakfast and saucer			0	19	0
	Tea set, 21 pieces			10	2	6
	Morning set, 2 persons			4	10	3
	Breakfast set, 29 pieces			16	15	0

Duesbury Sprig and Border

				£	s	d
No. 92	Coffee and saucer			0	11	8

A print of 'Belper Joe' from *Derbyshire Gatherings*, 1866. The King Street model was based on this print (see plate 8). Belper Joe was in fact Joseph Houghton, a harmless simpleton. He was born in Derby and went to Belper where he would do odd jobs, such as distributing news sheets, etc. Sadly no one mourned him when he died in the Belper Workhouse.
Royal Crown Derby Archives

King Street price list continued

Plate 6 (top left). King Street match holders. Left: 'Elizabeth Fry', 4¼ in. Red King Street mark. Right: 'Mother Gamp', 4¼ in. (no mark).
David Holborough Collection

Plate 7 (above). King Street pair of figures carrying panniers on their backs. Man 5½ in., woman 5 in., c.1880.
Mr. and Mrs. R.J. Williams Collection

Plate 8. Three small popular King Street figures, 'Billy Waters', 3¾ in. 'Belper Joe', 4½ in. and 'African Sall'. Billy Waters and African Sall mark in puce, Belper Joe in red. c.1920. African Sall was originally modelled as a pair to 'Dusty Bob' by Edward Keys, each costing 4/-. Billy Waters was also modelled by Keys, and later at King Street came to be paired with African Sall. A print, probably published during the 1830s by the Bailey of Fleet Street, shows the original pair dancing. The characters appear in Moncrieff's 'Tom and Jerry', with William H. Walborn appearing as 'Dusty Bob' and Saunders as 'African Sall' at the Adelphi Theatre, London, November 26th, 1821. Walborn and Saunders were celebrated in the roles and appeared at many fairs.[3]
David Holborough Collection

Plate 9. King Street pair of figures representing 'Spring' from the Seasons. King Street mark in puce. 6½ in. c.1925.
David Holborough Collection

3 Information supplied by Mrs. Delia Napier, who is researching Staffordshire porcelain figures, and by the Theatre Museum at the Victoria and Albert Museum.

No. 34.
Scalloped Dish.
Game.

No. 35.
Scalloped Dish.
Chelsea Birds.
(Ground laid border.)

No. 36.
Dessert Plate.
Landscape.

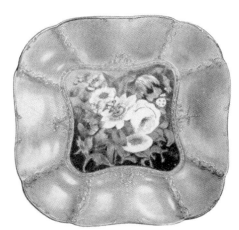

No. 37.
Square Dish. Flowers.
(Ground laid border.)

No. 38.
Dessert Plate.
Bird and Flower Panels.
(Ground laid border.)

Page from the King Street Catalogue 1934-35.

No. 42.
Toby Jug.

No. 43.
The Laughing Philosopher.

No. 39.
The Hairdresser.

No. 45.
"Night."

No. 44.
"Morning."

No. 40.
The Tythe Group.

No. 46.
African Sall.

No. 47.
Billy Waters.

No. 41.
The Thrower.

Page from the King Street Catalogue 1934-35.

Plate 10. A very rare King Street group of Polish dancers. 8¾in. c.1884. A biscuit version was sold in Mr. W.W. Winter's sale on 27 June 1884, catalogued 115, 'DERBY BISQUE DANCING GROUP in Polish costume, about 11in. high, under glass shade'.
David Holborough Collection

Plates 11a and b. Two views of a King Street bottle and stopper painted and signed by Harry Sampson Hancock. Marked with the rare zeppelin commemorative mark as well as the normal mark in red. 1916 (see p. 20). Sketches of the birds painted on this vase have now come to light.
Royal Crown Derby Museum

Plate 12. Pair of King Street baskets, each individual flower being added separately, with butterflies perched upon the basket edges. c.1930.
Royal Crown Derby Museum

Plate 13. King Street figures of the 'Welch Tailor' and his 'Wife' taken from Nottingham Road models which in turn came from a Meissen source. Puce mark. 5½ in. c.1910-20.
David Holborough Collection

No. 48.
Heart-shaped Dessert Tray.
Old Crown Derby Witches.

No. 51.
Bottle Vase.
Old Crown Derby Witches.

No. 52.
Pot Pourri. Fruit.

No. 50.
Shell Gadroon Dish.
Old Crown Derby Rose.

No. 49.
Oval Dessert Dish.
Old Crown Derby Witches.

Page from the King Street Catalogue 1934-35.

No. 58.
Pastille.
Old Crown Derby Witches.

No. 59.
Tea, Saucer and Plate.
Old Crown Derby Rose.

No. 53.
Tea, Saucer and Plate.
Old Crown Derby Witches.

No. 60. Octagonal Tray.
Old Crown Derby Rose.

No. 54.
Square Tray.
Old Crown Derby Witches.

No. 55. Octagonal Tray.
Old Crown Derby Witches.

No. 61.
Tea, Saucer and Plate.
Old Crown Derby Garden.

No. 56.
Watering Can.
Old Crown Derby Witches.

No. 57.
Cigarette Box.
Old Crown Derby Witches.

No. 62.
Tea, Saucer and Plate.
Old Crown Derby.

Page from the King Street Catalogue 1934-35.

39

No. 92	Tea and saucer	..	..	..	..	..	..	0 12 6
	Breakfast and saucer	..	..	..	..	..	..	0 16 9
	Tea set, 21 pieces	..	..	..	..	..	..	9 0 0
	Morning set, 2 persons	..	..	..	..	..	..	4 0 0
	Breakfast set, 29 pieces	..	..	..	..	..	..	14 17 6

Purple Scroll

No. 93	Coffee and saucer	..	..	..	..	..	..	0 15 3
	Tea and saucer	..	..	..	..	..	..	0 18 0
	Breakfast and saucer	..	..	..	..	..	..	1 5 0
	Tea set, 21 pieces	..	..	..	..	..	..	13 2 6
	Morning set, 2 persons	..	..	..	..	..	..	5 16 0
	Breakfast set, 29 pieces	..	..	..	..	..	..	21 15 0

Rose Barbeau

No. 94	Coffee and saucer	..	..	..	..	..	..	0 18 6
	Tea and saucer	..	..	..	..	..	..	1 0 0
	Breakfast and saucer	..	..	..	..	..	..	1 8 0
	Tea set, 21 pieces	..	..	..	..	..	..	14 13 0
	Morning set, 2 persons	..	..	..	..	..	..	6 9 6
	Breakfast set, 29 pieces	..	..	..	..	..	..	24 5 0

Sprig and Star

No. 95	Coffee and saucer	..	..	..	..	..	..	0 10 10
	Tea and saucer	..	..	..	..	..	..	0 14 0
	Breakfast and saucer	..	..	..	..	..	..	0 19 0
	Tea set, 21 pieces	..	..	..	..	..	..	10 2 6
	Morning set, 2 persons	..	..	..	..	..	..	4 10 3
	Breakfast set, 29 pieces	..	..	..	..	..	..	16 15 0

Bloor Rose. (*Not illustrated*)

	Tea and saucer	..	..	..	..	..	..	0 14 0
	Breakfast and saucer	..	..	..	..	..	..	0 19 0
	Tea set, 21 pieces	..	..	..	..	..	..	10 2 6
	Morning set, 2 persons	..	..	..	..	..	..	4 10 3
	Breakfast set, 29 pieces	..	..	..	..	..	..	16 15 0

Roses and Forget-me-nots. (*Not illustrated*)

	Coffee and saucer	..	..	..	..	..	..	0 12 6
	Tea and saucer	..	..	..	..	..	..	0 14 0
	Breakfast and saucer	..	..	..	..	..	..	0 19 0
	Tea set, 21 pieces	..	..	..	..	..	..	10 2 6
	Morning set, 2 persons	..	..	..	..	..	..	4 10 3
	Breakfast set, 29 pieces	..	..	..	..	..	..	16 15 0

Rose Trellis. (*Not illustrated*)

	Coffee and saucer	..	..	..	..	..	..	0 18 6
	Tea and saucer	..	..	..	..	..	..	1 0 0
	Breakfast and saucer	..	..	..	..	..	..	1 8 0
	Tea set, 21 pieces	..	..	..	..	..	..	14 13 0
	Morning set, 2 persons	..	..	..	..	..	..	6 9 6
	Breakfast set, 29 pieces	..	..	..	..	..	..	24 5 0

Roses and Gold Lines. (*Not illustrated*)

	Coffee and saucer	..	..	..	..	..	..	1 6 6
	Tea and saucer	..	..	..	..	..	..	1 8 0
	Breakfast and saucer	..	..	..	..	..	..	1 19 3
	Tea set, 21 pieces	..	..	..	..	..	..	20 18 0
	Morning set, 2 persons	..	..	..	..	..	..	9 3 3
	Breakfast set, 29 pieces	..	..	..	..	..	..	33 19 6

| Fitted case for six coffees and saucers | .. | .. | .. | .. | 0 12 6 |

A collection of small animals, including dogs, pigs, cows, calves, lambs, etc. .. .. .. each (*Not illustrated*)	0 4 6
Greyhound, on base .. .. .. (*Not illustrated*)	1 0 0
Fox (sitting), on base .. .. (*Not illustrated*)	1 0 0
Stirrup cups. Dog or Fox Head .. (*Not illustrated*)	1 0 0
Christening mug. Flowers. With initial in flowers (*Not illustrated*)	1 1 0
Christening mug. Flowers. With name in flowers (*Not illustrated*)	1 4 0

No. 63.
Coffee Season.
Spring.

No. 67.
Roman Lamp.

No. 68.
Paul Pry.

No. 66.
Chelsea.
Flower Seller.

No. 64.
Coffee Season.
Autumn.

No. 69.
Mother Gamp.

No. 65.
Chelsea.
Fruit Seller.

Page from the King Street Catalogue 1934-35.

No. 71.
English.
Shepherd.

No. 70.
Falstaff.

No. 72.
English
Shepherdess.

No. 74.
Welch Tailoress.

No. 73.
Welch Tailor.

No. 75.
Cow Cream Jug.

Page from the King Street Catalogue 1934-35.

No. 76.
Cabinet Cup.
Rose Trellis.

No. 78.
Green Vase.
Flowers.

No. 79.
Spills.

No. 77.
Pot Pourri.
Rose Trellis

No. 80.
Pastille.
Flowers.

No. 81.
Gipsy Kettle.
Raised Flowers.

No. 14.
Altar Vase.
Flowers.

No. 82.
Menu Holder.

No. 83.
Trinket Box.
Flowers.

No. 84.
Small Vase.
Flowers.

Page from the King Street Catalogue 1934-35.

No. 85.
Bridge Set in Case.
Old Crown Derby Witches.

No. 87.
Coffee and Saucer.
Old Crown Derby Garden.

No. 88.
Coffee and Saucer.
Old Crown Derby Rose.

No. 90.
Coffee and Saucer.
Butterfly.

No. 91.
Coffee and Saucer.
Green Star.

No. 92.
Coffee and Saucer.
Duesbury Sprig and Border.

No. 93.
Coffee and Saucer.
Purple Scroll.

No. 86.
Coffee Pot.
Old Crown Derby Witches.

No. 94.
Coffee and Saucer.
Rose Barbeau.

No. 89.
Coffee and Saucer.
Old Crown Derby Bramble.

No. 95.
Coffee and Saucer.
Sprig and Star.

Page from the King Street Catalogue 1934-35.

2 THE DERBY CROWN PORCELAIN COMPANY 1875-1890

In 1875 Edward Phillips, who was a Staffordshire potter, and William Litherland of the Liverpool china and glass retailers, decided to leave Worcester where they had been concerned with the foundation of the modern Royal Worcester Company and in September of that year, according to Sampson Hancock's letter (p. 15), announced the setting up of the Derby Crown Porcelain Company.

It is interesting to note that the ambition to create an entirely new factory in the Arboretum at Worcester, which was thwarted by the lack of finance, was made reality at Derby. The old Derby workhouse set in the Derby Arboretum was purchased, but the proposition to construct the new works on Osmaston Road was strongly opposed by the Litchurch Local Board, who were concerned about the effect of 'innocuous [sic] fumes of his sky-high chimneys' upon the paupers, and the trees of the arboretum. Very possibly, if it had not been for the aid of the press and strong expression of feeling displayed at a public meeting held in Litchurch on March 22nd 1876, the works would have been built elsewhere. The company purchased in June 1875 an acre and a half adjoining the Derby workhouse on the Osmaston Road, on which a mill, slip-houses etc. were shortly erected. On December 15th 1876 the workhouse and extensive grounds were sold by auction and purchased by the company for £9,150. Modelling was done at premises rented from Messrs Bemrose & Sons in Chetwynd Street in August 1876, removing to Osmaston Road one year later, and thus after considerable delay, production got under way in 1877.

The limited liability company was formed with a capital of £67,850; the original directors were:

William Litherland	20	shares
Edward Phillips	15	,,
John McInnes	20	,,
Henry Litherland	20	,,
John Litherland	2	,,

Henry & Walter Evans, H.W. and Will Bemrose, Fred Robinson and C.E. Newton 1 share each.

Jewitt writes in *Ceramic Art of Great Britain,* 2nd. Ed. 1883, p. 355:

'1877 Present company formed by Mr. Phillips. 3 Biscuit and 3 Glost Ovens.

The works now employ some 400 hands. Productions are:— China, Parian, and vitrified stoneware. In china all the usual services — Dinner, Tea, Breakfast, Toilet, Trinket and Dejeuner and a variety of other useful articles are made, as are vases of every conceivable design....In Parian:— Busts, Statuettes and Groups are produced in considerable variety. Specialities are vases, principally of Persian and Indianesque character...with a profusion of raised gilt ornament... The eggshell china cups and saucers thus decorated being far beyond those of other houses.'

Cassell's *Magazine of Art* reported in 1884:

'The showroom of the ''Crown Porcelain Works'' at Derby is such a resplendent repository of art, that for a space the eye is bewildered with an embarras de richesses, kaleidoscopical in its changes of contour and colour...while the promoters of the revival[4] of the manufacture of Derby china have respected with becoming reverence the artistic

4 This is an error which many writers have perpetuated, the King Street factory of Sampson Hancock and his partners having produced china since 1848.

45

Plaque with a portrait painted by G. Landgraf. c.1880, signed.
Courtesy Sotheby's Belgravia

tradition of the "old Derby" school, and reproduced its more famous patterns, they have not been content to remain mere plagiarists in porcelain...The plaques are larger than those attempted at the old works, those from the pencil of Mr. Landgraf being paintings of exceptional delicacy of drawing and colouring. The figures too, of the new factory are larger than those of the past, and modelling more correct. While the old quaint and grotesque patterns,[5] such as Dr. Syntax, the Mansion House Dwarfs, etc., have been revived, something more than reputation in this direction is aimed at. For instance, there is an original series of statuettes, representing Tribulation, Supplication, Resignation and Adoration, with one or two spirited essays in the classic, and certain droll illustrations of "Force" and "Persuasion" in which a monk and a mule are the leading characters.

5 Figures not patterns.

Derby Crown pair of large and impressive vases and covers painted with maidens in classical style by Landgraf and signed; the verso by Bier decorated with floral subjects and signed. The vases gilt and groundlaid with robin's-egg blue. Height 27½ in. c.1880.
Courtesy Sotheby's New York.

'In decoration "modern" Derby altogether distances the productions of the past. Raised gold work is a favourite form of decoration of the present factory. It combines nearly all the porcelain decorator's methods of gaining richness of effect; opulent ground-colour, gold, burnished and dead, gem-like enamelling, and so forth. This raised gold treatment is applied to dinner and teaware and dessert services; but it is displayed with the most lavish advantage in the luxurious fish and game plates, of which the Americans are the largest purchasers. . . The mere catalogue description, "fish and game plates" conveys no adequate idea of these elaborate pictures in porcelain framed in gold. The pictures are of fish and wildfowl, Landseer-like suggestions of stag and moorland, dainty seascapes lit up with a snowy bit of far-off sail; dreamy bits of river scenery where the kingfisher flies like a patch of rainbow over voiceful stream — alluring sketches of the haunts of the grouse, partridge, the pheasant and the blackcock — the birds painted feather, with naturalistic minuteness.

'Prominent are services of raised gold dessert plates enriched with Venetian vignettes, the design of which, I should note, is due to Mr. Richard Lunn, the Art Director of the company. Another style of decoration which separates the "Old Derby" from the new is the rich Persian decoration which entirely covers the surface of the article decorated. Divers schemes of colouring are brought into requisition, and intricate ornament is in raised gold, sometimes jewelled. "Egg-shell" is still another pattern,[6] the delicate fragility of the ware being well described by that designation. "Ivory" ware is a dainty imitation of the material it assimilates, while perforated china, graceful and basket like, is another happy departure from conventionalism. The Derby works today have also achieved a creditable triumph in "stained bodies" of delicate mauves and greens. The art directorate of South Kensington[7] has encouraged the Derby factory by ordering

6 Egg-shell is a china body and not a pattern.
7 Now the Victoria & Albert Museum

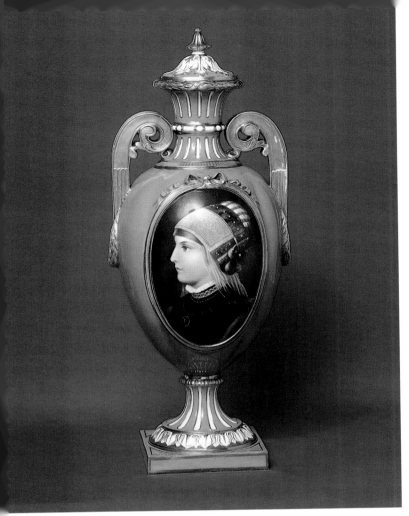

Plate 14. Derby Crown vase and cover, pink groundlay decorated with the head and shoulders of a girl and signed by Landgraf. Verso painted by Bie▮ with flowers. Height 21¾ in. 1882.
Royal Crown Derby Museum

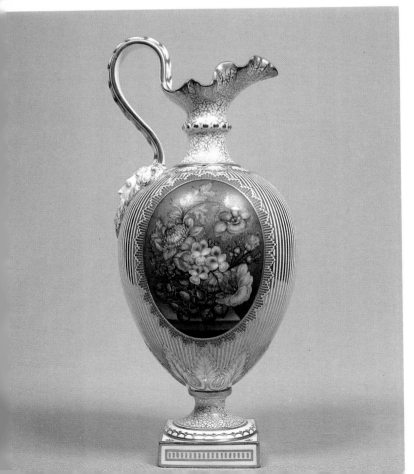

Plate 15. Derby Crown 'Kedleston' shaped ewer, signed, finely painted b▮ James Rouse sen., with an oval panel of flowers reserved upon white gro▮ with vertical gilt stripes. Shape 350. 10¼ in. 1884.
Mr. and Mrs. Peter Budd Collection

Derby Crown 'Crown Earthenware' plaque painted and signed by Landgraf. Impressed crown and mark no. 4. Width 15½ in. c.1880. This subject has long been admired by other artists who have a high opinion of the skill displayed in the painting of hair and natural skin tones.
Private Collection

reproductions of blue Rhodian and Persian rice dishes, bottles and other objects. Such reproductions have been attempted in Germany and France, but the authorities of South Kensington are best satisfied with the Derby transcripts.'

With such a start to its life it was no wonder that the future promised and indeed fulfilled so much, for during the next ninety years many more triumphs were to be enjoyed.

James Platts painted *figures*, Count Holtzendorf *figures and landscapes*, W.N. Statham *landscapes*, H.H. Deakin *fish and other subjects*, J.P. Wale *landscapes, birds and flowers*, Bier *flowers*, James Rouse *flowers and general subjects*, Landgraf *figures*, Tom Bradley *sea views;* much *raised and enamel work* was done by George Lambert, T. Gadsby did *flowers*, J.J. Brownsword *flowers* and Edwin Trowell *landscapes*. These painters were predominant during the Derby Crown Porcelain period. Although they are included in the biographical section, a list is given here of other Derby Crown Porcelain painters with their main subjects:

Bednall S. *raised and chased sprays (gilder)*
Corden Joseph *birds, flowers, shells etc.*
Flowerdew *flowers*
Hartshorn *birds, fish, animals etc.*
Keene A.J. *animals, figures etc.*
Marsh *Japanese flowers etc.*
Peach A. *alpine and other flowers*

Piper *raised jewelling*
Radford *flowers*
Rouse C. *gilder*
Smith G. *animals and marine subjects*
Storer *flowers*
Wright *flowers, leaves etc.*

Plate 16. A rare Derby Crown cologne bottle with pierced cover decorated with vertical stripes. 7¾ in. 1880.
Mr. and Mrs. L.C. Prosser Collection

Plate 17. A rare Derby Crown figure of a lady billiards player. Height 12¼ in. 1880. The base is very interesting as it shows how the modeller Herbert Warrington Hogg has used her dress for support, an innovation at Derby.
Royal Crown Derby Museum

Plate 18. Derby Crown pair of figures 'Blindman's buff'. Height 7½ in. This charming pair of figures would seem to have been modelled by William Stephan c.1878-80.
Mrs. Joan Neat Collection

Plate 19. Derby Crown knife rest modelled in 'Crown Earthenware'. Shape 351 'Knife and fork rest'. 1885. It is perhaps not surprising that very few of these have survived. One pair is known.
Courtesy Mrs. Jeanne Sorensky Missouri, USA, and John Twitchett Collection

Plate 20. Derby Crown plate with pierced rim, painted with a foral centre and radiating with ten reserves of alternating flowers and insects, and signed 'Rouse Senr. Derby'. 8¾in. c.1882. Derby.
Mr. and Mrs. Peter Budd Collection

Plate 21. Derby Crown plate of 'Devon' shape, painted with a shore view and signed by Statham. 9in.
Private Collection

Plate 22. Derby Crown plate of 'Devon' shape, the centre of which is painted with a young boy wearing a hat. Painted and signed by James Platts. 9in.
George Woods Collection

White figures of Friar Tuck (No. 57), 12in., and Robin Hood (No. 57), 12in. to top of pipe.
c.1878-80.
Royal Crown Derby Museum and Private Collection

White figures of Don Quixote (No. 56) and Sancho Panza (No. 57). c.1878-80.
Royal Crown Derby Museum

Plate 23. Derby Crown plate, a replica of the celebrated Gladstone Service, the centre painted with a view of Dale Abbey Church and Guest House signed by Holtzendorf with the initials GH. The small oval panels of flowers painted by James Rouse sen. 9¼ in. 1883.
Mr. and Mrs. R.J. Williams Collection

Plate 24. Derby Crown plate, 'Harrow' shape, painted with a full central view on the Dove by Edwin Trowell. 8¾ in. 1888.
Mr. and Mrs. R.J. Williams Collection

Plate 25. Derby Crown 'eggshell' coffee cup and saucer, 'Duchess' shape, pattern 1294 by George Lambert. Cup 2¼ in. high. 1884.
Mr. and Mrs. Arthur Sansom Collection

Plate 26. Left: Derby Crown toy sugar and cover in repoussé ware, height 2¼ in. 1889. Made for American retailer Wright Key & Co., Detroit. Right: heartshaped box and cover *en suite,* height 1⅛ in. 1888. Made for American retailer Burley & Co., Chicago. 'Repoussé Wares' appear in the Shape book between numbers 634-647, 635 being 'heart shaped box' and 645 'Teapot, *sugar* and cream, small, round'. The wares were moulded to give the impression of metal repoussé work.
Mr. and Mrs. Arthur Sansom Collection

'Victoria' pierced dessert plate, richly gilt and painted with Cupid figure subject by Count George Holtzendorf, initialled G.H. 1884.
Ronald William Raven Room
Royal Crown Derby Museum

Derby Crown plate painted and signed by Henry Deakin. Monochrome, slate blue upon a pink ground, with orchids and exotic plants. 9in. 1885.
Royal Crown Derby Museum

Plate 27. A prize winning Derby Crown plate decorated in Persian style. Designed by Richard Lunn and painted by G. Hemstock. Several painters including G. Hemstock, W. Smith and Mrs. E. Bird won prizes for their entries in competitions staged in Derby by the Art Gallery committee during 1885-86.
Private Collection

Plate 28. Derby Crown oval dish, crown earthenware, decorated with 'Imari' style pattern no. 198. Impressed crown mark as well as printed mark. Width 15¼ in. 1880.
Mr. and Mrs. W.L.C. Prosser Collection

Royal Crown Derby vase and cover modelled on a four footed base, shape 1640 incised. The scene of Matlock High Tor is finely painted by Cuthbert Gresley and although his signature has been obscured in the firing, the vase is without question typical of this painter's work. Height 9in. 1918.
Mr. and Mrs. W.L.C. Prosser Collection

3 THE ROYAL CROWN DERBY PORCELAIN COMPANY 1890-1975

The title 'Royal' (and the use of the Royal Arms) was granted in 1890 by Queen Victoria. A contemporary report in *The Gentlewoman* stated (December 5th, 1891):

'Her Majesty had been graciously inclined, at the solicitation of the venerable Duke of Devonshire, K.G., Lord Lieutenant of the County and Lord High Steward of Derby, to confer upon these works the title of "Royal" (and the use of the Royal arms) in January 1890.'

Thus the style of the company was changed, and was henceforth known as the Royal Crown Derby Porcelain Company.

It is perhaps not coincidental that Mr. Richard Lunn, appointed Art Director in May 1882, had designed in 1887 a fine pair of vases, 20in. high, which were presented to Queen Victoria by the Ladies of Derby to commemorate her Jubilee. The vases were decorated on a mazarine blue ground with raised and chased gold. Also presented was a plaque painted with a portrait of the Queen in the centre surrounded by the Garter and the Quarterings of the Royal Arms.

Many of the fine vase shapes had been designed and modelled by Warrington Hogg, and some were featured in the above-mentioned article in the 1891 *Gentlewoman:* 'A visit to the Royal Crown Derby Museum will afford the student with the opportunity to study the "Baroda Jar" (see illustration p.115) and other Persian and Indianesque Vases designed by him.' Of the other modellers employed on the new figures and vase shapes the names R.G. Morris, W.R. Ingram, Bourne and Stephen are mentioned. It would appear that Stephen should read Stephan, and it is quite possible that he was the modeller mentioned by Haslem, in his collection catalogue, as having modelled flowers at King Street.

In the Sale catalogue of founder-director William Bemrose's collection, March 1909, appeared 'Lot 559 FINE VASE, painted in flowers by Pilsbury, Derby Royal Factory. The first piece bearing the Royal Arms; 17in. (see illustration p.6).

'Lot 1053 CROWN DERBY porcelain jug, white and gold, with inscription — "One of the first dozen manufactured at the Crown Porcelain Works, Derby: February 7th, 1878"; and a plate, border perforated, raised gold flowers and insects in six panels, centre painted flowers, inscription similar.'

The granting of the Royal Warrant in 1890 was to be a reward to a company whose factory was probably the most modern in Europe. By 1878 everything was in full production, and we have quoted contemporary notices which show how successful the dream of Edward Phillips and William Litherland had become.

We quote again from the *Gentlewoman* of December 5th, 1891:

'Our pleasant flow of information is checked by our entering the spacious and well designed showroom [now the Royal Crown Derby Museum]. Here are glass cases filled with vases of every conceivable hue and lovely outline. Colour indeed! We were informed that the Crown Derby body admits of a treatment of colour unattainable elsewhere. Here are vases of the noted "Derby blue", there are plates of rose du Barri, with the most delicate painted roses in white enamel. What lovely egg-shell cups and saucers, with their delicate tracery and dotwork of raised gold — fit for an Emperor! So they are, for "Crown Derby" is in use in all parts of the earth. In 1777 Dr. Johnson and Boswell visited the old Derby China Works, and left a record that the

Plate 29. Royal Crown Derby plate of 'Argyle Pierced' shape, the full centre of which is coral pink groundlaid and decorated by Leroy with white enamel and signed. 9¼ in. 1901.
Mr. and Mrs. R.J. Williams Collection

china made there was very beautiful, but cost as much as silver. If he could revisit this world, and pay a visit to the Royal Works, he would find that a coffee can and saucer, in egg-shell, now fetch their weight in gold; for a can and saucer were so gossamer-like as to weigh only two ounces.

'These apparently very fragile articles are mostly decorated in schemes of gold and various bronzes, of the daintiest possible designs, thoroughly in keeping with the body they decorate; and to obtain these admirable results the pieces have to pass through the fire several times.

'We were particularly pleased with an egg-shell chalice,[8] of exquisite design, in which were introduced eight grotesque figures, that must be unique as a masterpiece of the potter's skill. Although the chalice is only 10¼ in. high, and weighs 5 oz., between eighty and ninety different moulds were required to produce this marvellous piece of china. The decoration was in various shades of gold most delicately pencilled.'

1890 saw the arrival at Osmaston Road of Désiré Leroy whose contributions to the ceramic world are the subject of a special chapter in this book. The report in the *Gentlewoman* continues: 'Amongst other beautiful examples we must mention the plates, &c, in Old Sèvres and Old Chelsea styles, by Monsieur Leroy, who hails from Sèvres, and whose fine painting in white enamels on cobalt grounds much resemble pâte sur pâte.'

The production of Japan patterns, or Imari, as they were to become known at Osmaston Road, was greatly increased, there being many new patterns added to the traditional ones first produced at the old Nottingham Road factory at the close of the eighteenth century. Perhaps the most famous of all the patterns which were designed at the new factory is '1128', in common with all such patterns known simply by number. 'Witches' Japan was allocated 6299; as a glance at the shape book at number 465 will indicate: 'Vase 3¼ in. Patt. no. 6299 and 1128 only'.

Many copies have been made of the much celebrated Derby Japans, chiefly in Staffordshire; but most, on inspection, show the use of inferior gold and lack the workmanship of the Royal factory. Any piece which does not bear the factory mark, as listed in Appendix II, cannot be accepted as genuine.

The type of decoration served equally well for dinner, dessert and teaware as well as other useful and ornamental ware and is as popular today. Indeed some are still in current production: 383 (Old Japan), 1128, and 2451 for example.

From the onset of the twentieth century the French influence, always in evidence at Derby, became stronger, and obviously the presence at the factory of Désiré Leroy led to the production of much fine ornamental ware, as the illustrations in this book show.

Printing on china was used to help increase production and in 1891 a new wing was completed for this work. For this process a pattern was engraved upon a copper plate, which was then covered with a specially prepared colour, then the surface cleaned, the transfer colour being left in the engraved parts. The impression was then taken by means of a press on prepared transfer paper. It would then be carefully cut and fitted to the plate or other object, and rubbed down; shortly after, the paper was moistened and peeled off, leaving the pattern printed or transferred on the surface, to be passed on through the kiln. In modern times silk screen printing[9] has largely replaced the more traditional method.

8 Summercoates Museum, Bournemouth. A later reproduction of this may be seen in the Royal Crown Derby Museum. See illustration p. 150.
9 See pp. 71-72.

It must be clearly stated, so as not to mislead readers, that the use of printing was largely for the further adornment of services and vase shapes. The majority of ware was hand ground laid, painted and gilt.

In 1904 Toy shapes were introduced which have become well known to collectors of miniatures. These included teapots, sugar boxes and creams, cups and saucers, irons, saucepans, fish kettles, coal buckets, watering cans, milk churns, vases, tea caddies, triple trays, baskets, coffee pots etc. These pieces, made entirely for ornament, are much sought after today, fetching high prices. They are usually decorated with patterns 6299, 2451 and 1128, but were also introduced with slighter Imari style and other patterns. The production of these had mainly ceased by the 1940s.

Until his death in 1919 John Porter Wale was in charge of the men who worked in the painters' room and listed below are painters with their main subjects.

Barratt R. *flowers*
Birbeck D. *birds, fish, animals*
Clark E. *birds, flowers, landscapes*
Dale J. *gilder*
Darlington G.W. *flowers etc.* in the manner of M. Leroy
Dean W.E.J. *ships, landscapes*
Gregory A. *flowers*
Gresley *flowers, landscapes*

Hague R.E. *flowers, figures*
Harris C. *birds, flowers*
Hemstock G. *gilder*
Jessop G. *flowers*
Marple F. *flowers*
Mosley W.E. *flowers, landscapes*
Taillandier, P. *figures, cupids*
Williams F. *birds, flowers, fish*
Wood A.F. *flowers*

It is interesting to note that the company exhibited at the Toronto National Exhibition in 1925[10] and at the Paris Exposition des Arts Décoratifs. Among the exhibits at the Paris Exposition was 'new Japan pattern no. 9571'.

10 See p. 86.

The Litherland-McInnes family administration of Osmaston Road came to a
conclusion when, in 1929, H.T. Robinson of Cauldon purchased a large number
of shares in Royal Crown Derby and thus forged the Robinson family control
which continued until 1961. H.T., as he was always known, remained as
chairman until his death in 1953.

During the difficult recession of the thirties Albert Gregory, perhaps the best
natural flower painter to have worked at Osmaston Road, Cuthbert Gresley and
Billy Dean were responsible for the hand-painted ware, which they usually signed.

The Imari type patterns were done by the women painters, gilders and
burnishers, many of whom gave long years of service to the company, and from
the early days to modern times, are too numerous to mention individually.

Figure production was increased in the late twenties and early thirties, some
interesting new models being made by M.R. Locke and Tom Wilkinson, who was
destined to become head modeller. The earlier series of figures, first produced in
the 1880s, was re-introduced: 'Pickwick', 'Sam Weller', 'Oliver Twist', 'Little
Dorrit' (earlier produced in Parian as well as china), 'Don Quixote', 'Sancho
Panza', 'Falstaff', 'Mistress Ford', 'Robin Hood', 'Friar Tuck', and so on. (See
illustrations on pp. 52-53.)

During the difficult war years, 1939-1945, production was maintained, but
mostly useful ware was made. In the postwar period, production was back to
normal in a short time. It was at this time that the company were fortunate to
obtain the services of a very talented modeller from Riga, Latvia, Arnold Mikelson.
It was he who was responsible for the modelling of the life-like birds and animals,
which are still very popular amongst collectors. Later in the fifties Phillip, H.T.'s
son, became chairman. The middle fifties were to see the now famous services got
up for Middle Eastern royalty and heads of state and which were to cause the
company to export 85 per cent of its wares. These, together with the earlier royal

View of Royal Crown Derby Porcelain Co. stand at the British Industries Fair 1956.

and other celebrated productions, are reported in detail in chapter 7.

In February 1956 the company had a magnificent stand at the British Industries Fair at Earls Court; they were the only representative of the Fine China Association exhibiting (see illustration above).

In 1961 Mr. Phillip Robinson resigned from the company, which was taken over by a financier, Mr. A.T. Smith. In 1964 Royal Crown Derby became a member of Allied English Potteries Limited, a subsidiary company of S. Pearson & Co. Ltd, the family company of Lord Cowdray. Under the auspices of A.E.P., Derby had again become a respected part of England's heritage, and in 1967 the Royal Crown Derby Museum was opened by Her Grace the Duchess of Devonshire. Mr. A.L. Thorpe, Curator of the Derby Borough Museum, advised in the setting up of the collection. In 1972 the company appointed the writer as its first curator, with his co-author as assistant. It was at this time that 'Open Days' were started giving the public the chance to see what was, by that time, a fine collection, and which illustrates the progressive production of useful and ornamental porcelain and china from 1748-1988. At the time of writing the Museum 'open days' are held on the first Tuesday in each month, when the Curator is present from 10 a.m. to 4 p.m. to discuss with the public any pieces which they own, but wish to have more knowledge about.

In 1972 the company held a celebration luncheon at Kedleston Hall, by kind permission of Viscount and Viscountess Scarsdale. The celebration was to launch the new 'Queen's Gadroon' shape, named in honour of Her Majesty Queen Elizabeth the Queen Mother, who visited the factory on June 8th 1971 and commissioned the shape by impressing her cypher upon some plates and casting a cream jug in 'Queen's Gadroon'. The new shape was designed by Brian Branscombe, Des. R.C.A., Chief Designer to the company. The six patterns chosen for the new shape were 'Brocade', 'Prince Consort', 'Caliph', 'Imperia', 'Aquitane' and A.962. Also, a new Royal Crown Derby Connoisseur Collection was issued, the first pieces being a series of plates hand-painted with Derbyshire views by Michael Crawley, and the second a series of six coffee cans and stands in the new shape painted with birds by John McLaughlin (see illustration p. 144).

Royal Crown Derby pair of covered urns decorated with birds in landscape; right hand by C. Harris, signed, 1906; left by C. Gresley, signed, 1913.
Courtesy Julie Asbridge Antiques

On Thursday October 18th 1973 the company were hosts to the American Study Group in their second 'English Pottery & Porcelain Seminar' which ran from 5th to 18th October. The Curator joined the distinguished faculty which included R.J. Charleston, Arnold R. Mountford, Bernard Watney, Brian Loughbrough, Hugh Tait, Ian Lowe, Henry Sandon, W.J. Grant-Davidson, Sir Leslie Joseph, Miss Mellanay Delhom, F.R.S.A. and Dewey Lee Curtis who was the director of the seminar. Following a lecture entitled 'The History of Derby Porcelain', given by John Twitchett, F.R.S.A., the seminar concluded with a work-study in the Royal Crown Derby Museum.

On Wednesday 27th November 1974, Her Royal Highness The Princess Anne visited Osmaston Road. During her tour of the factory the company directors and various heads of departments were presented. Princess Anne was able to see 'Derby Green Panel' in production, a service of which was given to her and Captain Mark Phillips as a wedding present from the British Ceramic Manufacturers Association. The tour concluded with the Chairman of the Royal Crown Derby Porcelain Company, Mr. John Bellak, escorting H.R.H. to the Museum, where she signed the Distinguished Visitors' Book. Then the Mayor of Derby asked Her Royal Highness to sign the Distinguished Visitors Book of the Borough. The Princess was presented with six hand-painted plates of Derbyshire views, from the Connoisseur Series. These were later auctioned at Leicester, where they were sold in aid of the Save the Children Fund and fetched £1,350. The Chairman then presented the directors' wives and the writers, after which Her Royal Highness and party toured the Museum Collection and refreshments were served.

The company having overcome the problems of the middle of this century, and having been given stability by the Allied English Potteries, has even greater backing today than in 1972. Pearsons acquired Royal Doulton Ltd and the tableware interests of this company were merged with the A.E.P., the Royal Crown Derby Porcelain Company becoming a member of the resultant Royal Doulton Tableware Ltd. The company continues to make fine china in the best traditions of its forbears.

4 PARIAN BODY

The eighteenth-century Derby biscuit body is justly famous and is characterised by its remarkably soft, white and waxen appearance, but owing to the formula being lost, the body degenerated, becoming merely unglazed china. John Mountford, who had been apprenticed at Derby as a figure modeller, is said to have invented Parian body whilst trying to recapture the famous old Derby biscuit. This was during his time at the Copeland and Garett factory, and it seems likely that Thomas Battam, Art Director, and Spencer Garrett took the credit for the discovery.

The marble-like qualities of the body were emphasised and the suitability for figure making could not be stressed strongly enough. The name Parian was given to this body because of the resemblance to the ivory tinted marble quarried on the Island of Paros. Although the use of Parian is largely remembered because of the enormous quantity of figures and groups marketed by the leading ceramic firms in the second half of the nineteenth century, it was of course used for much ornamental ware. Vases were often made in this body, except where the use of cobalt blue was involved in the decoration; brooches were produced with applied floral groups, baskets and numerous items. The body was cheap to produce and easy to use. Sometimes figures were made in Parian to act as supports to elaborate centre pieces, such as those made by Copeland and Minton and exhibited at the 1851 Exhibition.

In L. Jewitt's reference to the Derby Crown Company (see p. 45) he says 'In Parian:— Busts, Statuettes and Groups are produced in considerable variety.'

'Little Dorrit' and a small medallion showing Christ crowned with thorns, the latter bearing the mark of the company, are examples of Parian products. The medallion has a glazed rim to allow the use of gold for a simple edge.

It seems very strange that in spite of Jewitt's report, only a few pieces, of which two are illustrated here, have been authenticated. In the year 1880, Thomas Hough, a boy of thirteen years, began to work in the mill at Osmaston Road. The head miller at that time was a Mr. Thomas Aines, a man of some 65 years of age who had come from the Potteries a short time previously to help get the works started. Also working at that time was Mr. John McInnes (1808-1896). This elderly gentleman, a chemist of the old school, almost an alchemist, had left his colour works in Cheshire, and was using his knowledge and experience to put the manufacturing side of the works on its feet. Taking a fancy to young Thomas Hough, he took him into the laboratory with him and it was under the tuition of these two elderly men, Mr. Aines and Mr. McInnes, that Thomas Hough was to acquire his knowledge of the manufacture of china and Parian, and the making of colours to decorate it. The figure of 'Little Dorrit' came from the collection of his daughter, Miss Elsie Hough, who worked at one time at the factory, before making music her career. She possessed other interesting pieces, mostly modelled by Samuel Swan, including a group of animals and a finely modelled basket of flowers, manufactured in the thinnest Parian body. All these pieces form a small but very important collection.

Thomas Hough's notebook contains a formula for glost oven Parian slip: 9 lbs Spar, 6 lbs China Clay, 8 lbs Glass, 1 lb Antwerp Frett.

The gradual decline in the demand for Parian wares at the end of the nineteenth century probably accounts for the considerable rarity of factory-marked Derby Parian pieces.

A Parian figure of 'Little Dorrit'.
This rare figure came from the
collection of the late Thomas
Hough. No mark.
Royal Crown Derby Museum

Parian medallion showing the head of Christ (above). The outer rim is
glazed and gilt. The reverse of the medallion (below) shows the Royal
Crown Derby stamp.
Royal Crown Derby Museum

5 TECHNIQUE OF GILDING

From the end of the eighteenth century gilding has been an important method of decoration in most china manufacture. Generally the medium used was 24 carat gold, mercury and a small quantity of flux. The mercury, when added to the gold, immediately turned it grey and began to break it down into smaller granules. The mixture was ground in water for 24 hours, dried out and then ground for a further 8 hours in turpentine, drying then to a fairly solid consistency which could be weighed into individual measures of one penny weight.

An apprentice training to become a gilder spent at least nine months arduously practising strokes, lines and shapes before being allowed to move on to patterns, and a further six months before touching gold. Every trace of gold had to be accounted for and a method of measurement was devised. One penny weight of gold should be sufficient to decorate the edges of sixteen teacups and saucers and sixteen five-inch tea-plates. Any apprentice consistently using more than this would be removed from gilding. The vessels holding the turpentine and oils necessary to make the gold sufficiently fluid had to be frequently cleaned; the rags employed in cleaning were all collected, as were the old brushes, and from time to time sent to the smelting company. The amount of gold reclaimed was credited to Royal Crown Derby. During firing the oils evaporate, and the flux fuses gold and glaze, leaving the decoration firmly fixed. At this stage the gold colour is dull

Royal Crown Derby pair of pink groundlaid vases with three colour gilding. Height 5½ in. 1891.
Courtesy David John Ceramics

Plate 30. Royal Crown Derby plate painted and signed by Leroy, with a central birds in landscape theme, popular at all the Derby China Works. 'Royal Gadroon' shape, with the Royal Warrant mark of Queen Victoria. Initial TB on verso rim. 8¾in. 1891.
Mr. and Mrs. W.H. Mordecai Collection

Plate 31. Pair of Royal Crown Derby vases finely painted with fruit and flowers and gilded by Désiré Leroy, signed, shape 1520 and Leroy pattern 531. 5in. 1906.
David Holborough Collection

and requires burnishing — a very skilled and time-consuming operation. Firstly the burnisher needs very fine grain silver sand, a small bowl of water and a piece of cloth. The cloth is wound round the index finger which is dipped first into the water, then into the sand, and then rubbed with a firm, even, pressure over the gilt surface. This operation is followed by the actual burnishing, for which a bloodstone or agate is used. Again a firm pressure over the surface of the gold decoration is applied, which will bring it to a very high degree of polish. At the same time great care must be taken when using a burnishing stone or the resultant brown scratches on the white of the china are almost impossible to remove.

Another aspect of gilding is the raising and re-raising so popular during the late nineteenth and early twentieth century. The medium used was made up from ground enamel colour, flux and glaze frits, mixed with turpentine. The pattern to be raised was either sketched or smoke printed depending on the style, then the paste was applied with a very fine sable brush. Where necessary for added depth, an extra stroke of paste could be applied after drying and before firing, but as a general rule the first coat was fired through the enamel kiln and then further decoration added. Finally the whole of the raised paste was covered with gold. A very good example of this technique is the service made for Tiffany in 1910, the raising and gilding being carried out by George Darlington.

Royal Crown Derby dessert plate decorated with an exercise in the art of gilding. The border has small panels of pink roses. Painted and signed by Leroy. 1901.
Mr. and Mrs. P.J. Williams Collection

6 PRINTING

Printing was one of the first and perhaps one of the more important of the early forms of decoration used at Osmaston Road. Firstly, it could produce an extremely fine design, if done correctly, which needed just a little attention from an enameller and was then a creditable pattern. The first pattern book contains many such border designs which were used quite frequently on Crown Earthenware,[11] a body produced from the beginning of the factory until 1914, mainly for dinnerware, although there is evidence of large plaques being made in the same body. There were also very many printed designs which stand on their own merit and were still being produced as late as 1945, e.g. 'Wilmot', 'Victoria', 'Peacock' etc.

Secondly, printing was used to great advantage in an attempt to save the senior artists' time and to enable the slightly less experienced painters to produce work of a similar quality. This was done by printing a very fine outline for them to work to; again an outline proved to be a tremendous help to gilders — saving hours of time which would have been used in sketching the designs on the work before actually gilding.

The making of a print was regarded as a man's job but the team who worked for him were once again women and girls: usually there were four to a team, the printer, the transferer and two apprentices. A printer's colour is always used warm, hence the printer's stove, a piece of equipment equally useful for boiling the lunchtime egg or kettle. The warm colour is applied to a copperplate engraving

11 Crown Earthenware is quite easily identified by the *impressed* crown on the back.

H. Short engraving the 'Mikado' pattern.

Plate 32. Royal Crown Derby vase of 'Majestic' shape. One of a pair with gilt and coloured flowers on a deep green groundlay, and clearly the work of the finest decorators. Made for Maples. Date mark for 1890.
Private Collection

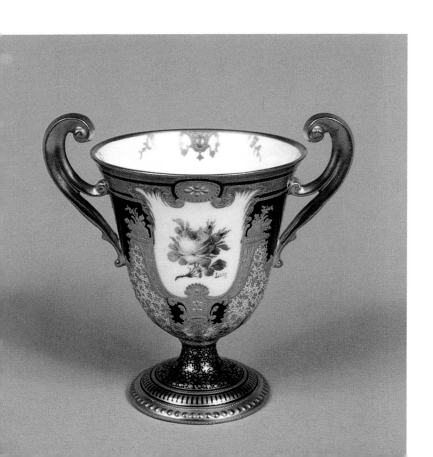

Plate 33. Royal Crown Derby loving cup, shape 1416, painted and signed by Leroy. 4½ in. 1890.
Private Collection

with a spatula, forcing the colour into the engraving, but wiping away all surplus colour. The plate is then covered with soap-dampened tissue paper, stretched across, and the whole passed between the felt-covered rollers of the press which squeezes the moisture from the paper and forces the pattern on to it. The printing shop often resembled a laundry with the prints hanging up to dry. Applying the transfer print is next done by the transferer, making sure of the fit, which calls for considerable skill. The next member of the team rubs the print down quite firmly before putting the piece aside to wait for the final washing off in a bath of clear water. This last stage involves the removal of the tissue paper under water after the required waiting time has elapsed. Before leaving the subject of printing, credit must be given to hundreds of people who have worked as printers or transferers at Osmaston Road. One or two names immediately come to mind: E. Bradshaw, R. Russell, F. Cartledge, W. Brough, S. Eardley (printers), Mrs. Brain, Z. Pearson, C. Pearson, M. Adams, H. Eardley (transferers). This type of printing has now been largely superseded by the more up-to-date method of screen printing.

Most of the silk screen transfers used are produced at the Osmaston Road factory. This department, known as Graphic Process, first began at Derby in 1964, and under the guidance of Antonio Burrell, Technical Manager, and Brian Branscombe, Art Director, has become an integral part of Royal Crown Derby.

Because of the size of the earlier printing department an engraver was permanently employed at Osmaston Road, generally with an apprentice. The illustration on p. 71 shows H. Short engraving the 'Mikado' pattern. (A 'Mikado' teapot, teabowl and cream jug are illustrated on p. 171.) Mr. Short was another who spent his entire working life at the factory, clocking up more than fifty years, and during that time he became union representative, a position he held for many years. Working with him as his apprentice he had Walter Lowndes, who has now turned to the art of silversmith and has held several successful exhibitions.

Original design for 'Mikado' dated 1894 and drawn by Thomas Reed.
Courtesy the late Thomas Amos Reed's family

Sample plate for the Gladstone service, with central landscape of the old Derby Silk Mill by Count Holtzendorf, and miniature floral reserves by James Rouse Sen. The service is still in the possession of the Gladstone family.
Derby Museum and Art Gallery

Important watercolour of the Free Library Derby, the subject of one of the plates in the 'Gladstone' service, signed on the verso by Count Holtzendorf.
John Twitchett Collection

7 SPECIAL PRODUCTIONS

Unfortunately, owing to the lack of satisfactory records, it has proved impossible to give details of all the Special Productions that have been made at Osmaston Road. However, an effort has been made, after research through remaining records, contemporary notices and press cuttings to record some of the major ones.

We have described in detail the pair of vases and plaque made for Queen Victoria (p. 59) in 1887. In the same year *The Illustrated London News* reports the reception of the British Mission to the Emperor of Morocco: 'After dinner, which was served in the middle of the day, came tea and coffee, both excellent, in charming little cups of Crown Derby.' The cups were egg-shell, part of the Emperor's service. In 1883 the Derby Liberals decided to present Mr. Gladstone, the aged Prime Minister, with a memento of his 50 years' service. Richard Lunn designed the service which consisted of twenty-six pieces. (See Appendix VI.) Each plate or dish depicted a Derbyshire view by Count G. Holtzendorf and oval panels of beautifully painted flowers by James Rouse sen. Before completing his work Rouse suffered a paralytic stroke and the last few plates had to be painted by others. We have been informed that this service is still at Hawarden Castle, Chester. (See illustrations opposite and plate 23, p. 54.)

In 1893 the citizens of Derby gave a service of dessert plates to Princess May of Teck and the Duke of York, on the occasion of their marriage. The service was designed and largely decorated by Désiré Leroy. The plates were of Royal Gadroon shape, the embossed edges of which were finished with turquoise and raised gold work, from which depended exquisitely painted flowers with medallions and the heraldic badge of the House of York. In the centre was introduced a floral monogram, 'G.M.', the first letter raised and chased gold. Leroy was assisted by F. Williams, Jack Dale, George Hemstock and J. Rogers. About the year 1901 Sir Henry Howe Bemrose was presented with a set of plates and dishes to celebrate his Unionist victory in Derby of 1895. (See illustration on p. 89). These were decorated most beautifully by Charles Harris.

During the reign of Edward VII the Royal Warrant was renewed and orders were placed for the Royal Yacht *Victoria and Albert*. (See illustration overleaf.) It is interesting to note that similar orders were received about 1886 for the Royal Yacht *Osborne*.

In 1891 a fine vase was ordered by the Derby Corporation for presentation to Mr. Felix Joseph, the donor to the Art Gallery of the Felix Joseph collection of Old Derby porcelain and china. In a panel on one side are the arms of the borough, which form a landscape of 'A buck in the park'. On the reverse are Mr. Joseph's initials 'F.J.', entwined, surmounted by a crest, and below, as a pendant, is the Order of a Knight of the Royal Order of Isabella of Spain, of which order Mr. Joseph was a Knight.

There is a large vase in the Topkapi Palace at Istanbul, which was presented to Abdul Hamid II by Queen Victoria in 1901 to celebrate his Silver Jubilee. The vase carries a portrait of Her Majesty.

In 1911 Mr. James Deering, the well-known American businessman, commissioned Royal Crown Derby through Tiffany's to produce an elaborate dinner service with raised and chased gold work consisting of 120 pieces. Mr. Deering had engaged the services of Paul Chalfin, former Curator of the Boston Museum of Fine Arts, to advise him in setting up his remarkable palace, Vizcaya, about

Teacup and saucer made for King
Edward VII. 1903.
Brian Quinn Collection

four miles from Miami in Florida. It is interesting to note that a telegram from Tiffany's in the archives confirms the order duly 'Chalfinated'.

In 1912 Herbrand, 11th Duke of Bedford, ordered several services for use on his yacht. The breakfast service, tea service and coffee service were for the use of twelve persons. Also there were six mocha coffee cups and saucers of Old Derby shape. These, together with a Wedgwood dessert service, were specially made to fit into a sideboard. Examples of the Derby services are displayed in the Royal Crown Derby Museum; the decoration, chiefly garlands of roses, was mostly painted by Cuthbert Gresley, but not signed.

To celebrate the marriage of the Princess Royal in 1922 an inkstand was commissioned.

In 1926 orders were received from the Governor General and Prime Minister of Australia for use at functions connected with the Australian Houses of Parliament at Canberra. It should of course be recorded that the company has made china for many royal houses, presidents and embassies during the last ninety years or so.

The Borough of Derby has commissioned many Freedom Caskets to be presented to distinguished people who have been granted, over the years, the Freedom of the Borough of Derby. (See illustration on p. 167.)

A teaset was designed by Donald Birbeck for presentation to H.R.H. Princess Margaret in 1934, bearing her monogram and a coronet in raised gold, with a renaissance design in green and gold with an ivory ground-lay. The cups were of a smaller size than usual.[12] Birbeck also designed the flowers for William Edwin Mosley's painting on a dessert service for an Indian Prince. The Prince had decided that all the pieces should be painted with English flowers, save for one which was to be painted with a lotus flower. The service was completed in 1941. The designs are shown on pp. 90-94.

In 1947 Princess Elizabeth was presented with a Derby puce scroll pattern tea service, known as 'Princess', on the occasion of her marriage to Prince Philip. In 1952 the citizens of Derby were presented with a portrait of the royal couple, painted by Reuben Hague, and which now hangs in the mayor's parlour. William

12. The set was displayed at an exhibition to celebrate the Empire Tea Centenary. Another set was made by Copelands for Princess Elizabeth. The Fine China and Earthenware Manufacturers' Association had joined with the Empire Tea Growers to stage the exhibitions and a ballot had been held to select the companies to make the presentation tea services for the two princesses. Royal Crown Derby and Copelands were the winners.

Edwin Mosley was also responsible for the decoration of a pair of traditional Derby Dwarfs, which were presented to Her Majesty the Queen. One of his last tasks was to paint a christening mug on the birth of H.R.H. Prince Charles.

The British Pottery Manufacturers' Federation commissioned an heraldic vase for the coronation, an example of which was presented to the Queen and to representatives of the countries of the United Kingdom and Commonwealth, and the separate parts of which were supplied by the leading fine china manufacturers in the country. Derby contributed a pair of Queen's beasts (1953).

The *Pottery Gazette* of March 1956 reported the Canadian Pacific Railways were supplied with a banqueting service for use at the Royal York Hotel, Toronto.

In February 1956 Royal Crown Derby received the Pakistan Official Warrant for supplying special banqueting services for the official use of the Governor General, Major-General Iskander Mirza.

The ruler of Qatar in the Persian Gulf, Sheikh Ali Bin Abdullah Al-Thani, ordered a service consisting of 3,000 pieces, which was to include twelve large size bowls capable of holding rice and a whole roast sheep. Yet another order was for Sheikh Jabir Abdullah Al-Sabah of Kuwait, for a service of 1,200 pieces. It is not surprising that the overseas director, Mr. Peter de Waller, was kept busy!

In 1957 the Derby Corporation presented the Queen with a service in the new 'Royal Pinxton Roses' pattern, consisting of 120 pieces.

In 1956 the company secured an order from Sir John Kotelawa, Prime Minister of Ceylon, for official use. This service of 1,500 pieces was decorated with the coat-of-arms of Ceylon.

In 1957 a further banqueting service, consisting of 600 pieces, was made for King Saud of Saudi-Arabia and was reputed to have cost £15,000.

The *London Evening News* in March 1957 reported that the Shah of Persia had ordered a 200-piece service for use in his private aircraft.

In 1960 a dinner service was produced for Princess Margaret to commemorate her marriage.

Mr. Harold Macmillan, whilst on a visit to Russia in 1959, presented an Imari type Crown Derby tea service, consisting of 40 pieces, to Mrs. Nina Khrushchev, wife of the Soviet leader.

A Shakespeare service was presented to Princess Alexandra to celebrate the opening, by her, of the Chichester Festival Theatre in 1961. The service was decorated with scenes from the bard's plays.

In 1965 the company produced a service for H.M. Queen Elizabeth the Queen Mother. Her Majesty had a plate which had been made for the Prince of Wales at the end of the eighteenth century by the Derby factory. She asked to have it copied, and this was done, except that the feather emblem of the Prince of Wales was replaced by the Queen Mother's monogram, designed by Laurence Whistler. This service consisted of 48 dinner plates and the same number of soup plates.

In 1971 the company presented Her Majesty with an octagonal bowl to match the service on the occasion of her visit to the factory. As previously mentioned it was then that Her Majesty honoured the Royal Crown Derby Porcelain Company by commissioning a new bone china shape to be known as 'Queen's Gadroon'.

In 1973 The British Ceramic Manufacturers' Federation presented a dinner and coffee service to Princess Anne and Captain Mark Phillips on the occasion of their marriage. This consisted of 134 pieces of 'Derby Green Panel'.

A comport to commemorate the visit by Her Majesty The Queen to Japan in May 1975. Limited edition.

The Bell, produced in a limited edition of 500 to commemorate the Investiture of H.R.H. The Prince of Wales in 1969.
Royal Crown Derby Museum

8 COMMEMORATIVE ISSUES

The company does not seem to have produced much commemorative ware, in contrast to the Special Productions, and the records are almost non-existent. However an effort has been made to record examples that have been authenticated. It is known that services, or at least dessert dishes, were produced in 1897 with a printed portrait of Queen Victoria, after Bassano, and a beaker with this print was exhibited in 1972 at the Woburn Exhibition of Commemorative Wares.

It is thought possible that some productions were made for the coronation of Edward VII. Small mugs and blue and white fern pots are known to have been produced to commemorate the coronation of George V in 1911.

A small mug was made for the uncrowned Edward VIII and in 1937 two trays were issued with respective portraits of King George VI and Queen Elizabeth.

An urn was also made, which had eagle handles and on the front a double portrait of the King and Queen. The reverse showed an eagle and a shield, but it is not known, however, whether it was issued as a limited edition.

Another tray was issued in 1953, with a printed portrait of Her Majesty, and also a double handled loving cup with a portrait of the Queen. This cup was issued as a limited edition of 250.

Reuben Hague painted eighteen out of a series of twenty-five plaques which were painted with portraits of Her Majesty the Queen (see plate 1, p. 2).

To commemorate the Investiture of H.R.H. The Prince of Wales, at Caernarvon Castle in 1969, the company produced two items, a dragon and a bell. The College of Arms granted permission to use the badge of the Royal Dragon of Wales and the Prince's ostrich feather badge. A model dragon was produced in a limited edition of 250 and a hand bell, decorated with the Prince's badges, was issued as a limited edition of 500 (see opposite). These were designed by Brian and June Branscombe.

On July 20th, 1972 a small tray was given to each of the guests assembled at Kedleston Hall, to launch the Queen's Gadroon shape. These were part of a limited edition of 250. Each had a view of Kedleston Hall and a Queen's Gadroon border (see overleaf).

To celebrate Benjamin Britten's 60th birthday on November 22nd, 1973, the Aldeburgh Festival promoted, together with two music publishers, Boosey & Hawkes Ltd and Faber Music Ltd, the publishers of Benjamin Britten's operas, a service of 500 limited sets. Each service consisted of 14 pieces, twelve 9¼ in. plates and two 11½ in. bowls (see overleaf).

Sporting commemoratives were made for various organisations, including the Football Association and Derbyshire County Cricket Club.

A comport, shape 1821, was issued as a limited edition of 100 to commemorate H.M. The Queen's visit to Japan in 1975. The decoration was pattern number 1128 with a central inscription (see opposite).

Tray, five petal shape; a limited edition of 250 was produced to commemorate the launching of the Queen's Gadroon shape June 1972.
Royal Crown Derby Museum

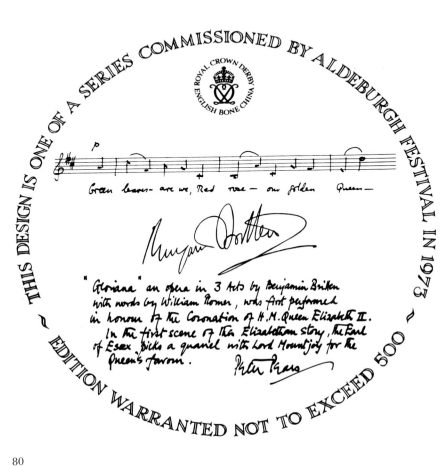

Reverse side of Aldeburgh Festival plate, see opposite.

GLORIANA

FIRST PERFORMED
AT THE
ROYAL OPERA HOVSE
COVENT GARDEN

8th JVNE 1953

BENJAMIN BRITTEN

Plate from a set of twelve commissioned by Aldeburgh Festival to commemorate the sixtieth birthday of
Benjamin Britten, each one depicting an opera. c.1974. The reverse is shown opposite.

Plate 34. Royal Crown Derby ewer, shape 1134 (incised), decorated with turquoise scroll and blue cornflowers, signed Leroy. 9¾ in. 1896.
John McCabe Collection

Plate 35. Royal Crown Derby ewer, shape 1020 (incised), decorated with exotic birds on dark blue and turquoise ground, signed by Leroy. Height 7in. 1896. Retailer's mark for Phillips, Mount St., London.
Private Collection

Plate 36. Royal Crown Derby pair of vases of campana shape, shape 1201 (incised), painted with floral panels on deep green ground, signed by Leroy. 5in. 1898.
John McCabe Collection

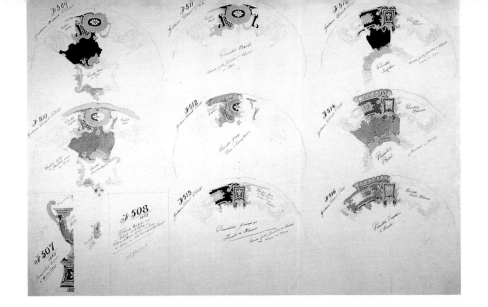

Plate 37a, b and c. Designs drawn by
Désiré Leroy.
Royal Crown Derby Museum Archives

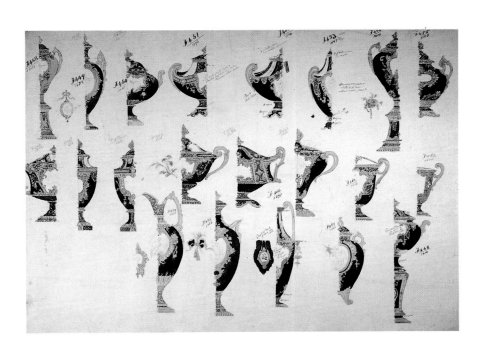

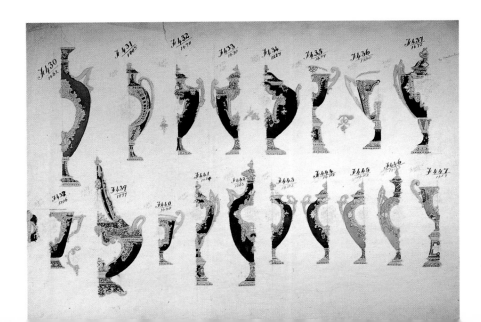

9 DÉSIRÉ LEROY, DESIGNER AND ARTIST

Désiré Leroy was born in 1840 at Les Loges, Commune d'Arrou, Eure et Loire, France.

He was apprenticed at the famous Sèvres factory at the age of eleven, and it was here that the most distinguished designer-artist in the history of Crown Derby was to commence his artistic career. In his own words his aim was to 'become a clever artist and leave behind a name which would not be soon forgotten'. His talents must have been so obvious and his progress so great that at the age of twenty-two he was hailed as a leading artist in the ceramic world.

He came to England in 1874 to accept an engagement with the firm of Minton. The 1878 Paris Exhibition afforded him an opportunity of showing his very great ability and, as an ambitious young man, he excelled in the work he undertook.

The contemporary *Report of the Society of Arts* comments:

> 'There is a flower painter, D. Leroy, whose work is deserving of great praise, as instanced in a couple of card trays with groups of flowers in the centre. These for neatness, delicate manipulation, and artistic refinement, cannot be surpassed, and this is the character of all his work.'

Monsieur Leroy executed many important services and other works whilst with the same factory, and then in the year 1890 he was engaged by the Royal Crown Derby Porcelain Company where he remained until his death in 1908.

At Derby he had his own studio, where he worked with Jack Dale and George Darlington as his assistants. It was at Osmaston Road where the majority of his most remarkable talents were shown to the greatest advantage.

Possibly the most striking successful contribution was his use of white enamel upon ground colours such as the Derby blue, turquoise or rose du barri grounds. (See plate 40, p. 109.)

In Chapter 12 a list, sadly incomplete, is given showing the designs by this great artist to be painted on plates and vases etc. These special designs do not appear in the general pattern books, and were numbered separately with the prefix 'F' (see illustration opposite). To add to the confusion for the Derby collector, 'F' was also used as a prefix for figures. Leroy's designs show a remarkable use of colours that most ceramic artists could hardly dare to attempt to use together. Also they show the versatility of design. The influence obviously is that of the Sèvres factory, but more particularly it is the interpretation of a true artist that may never be equalled. The designs are lavish, but however restrained is one's taste, one cannot afford to dismiss the works of Désiré Leroy lightly. The student will examine specimens of his work and notice the groundlaying, always brilliantly executed with an even finish, the minute jewelling, so much more delicate than the original Sèvres pieces, and of course the painting contained in reserved panels. The subjects were usually birds in landscapes, fruit and flowers, musical trophies and occasionally figures, as can be seen from the many illustrations of his work throughout this book.

The beautiful shapes manufactured at Osmaston Road afforded a unique opportunity for the display of his art as a porcelain decorator and some remarkable specimens are to be seen in many parts of the world. Indeed some extremely fine examples are exhibited in the Royal Crown Derby Museum.

Interesting combination of design book and actual vase decorated by Leroy. The book reads 'F. 528 Shape I470 Height 6 in Ground Colour Dover Green'.
Courtesy David John Ceramics and Royal Crown Derby Museum Archives

A writer in *The Pall Mall Magazine* for December 1906 said:

'There can hardly be two opinons but that D. Leroy's work is that of a great artist. Every line of it is harmonious, even when the colour scheme is daring and unconventional; every detail of the rich, but never overweighted ornamentation, from the heavy gold chasing to the tiny turquoise jewelling, of which he seems especially fond, is his own work. His floral medallions might serve to illustrate a lecture on botany; every flower, down to the smallest bud, is true to nature and grouped by the eye of an artist. There can be little doubt that when his work is ''antique'' it will be worth its weight in gold, for everything that comes from his cunning hand is a unique gem of art in itself.'

Leroy had designed the fine service consisting of 18 dessert plates to be presented to Princes May of Teck (later Queen Mary) on the occasion of her wedding to H.R.H. The Duke of York. Much of the decoration of the service was done by himself although he was assisted by F. Williams, J. Dale, G. Hemstock and J. Rogers. It has been stated that Leroy only used painters other than Darlington when engaged upon large services.

In January 1894 P. Taillandier joined Derby from Coalport to work with Leroy. In the list of Special Production plates and vases (see pp. 199-201) it can be seen that a few patterns were actually given to this fine figure painter, reported to have been a descendant of the Sèvres flower painter. Taillandier's work is rare because he seems only to have remained at Osmaston Road for a very short time.

The earlier reference to Leroy's work becoming worth its weight in gold is made clear by Tiffany's invoice of which details are given here,[13] showing the cost, to the retailer, of two pairs of vases and a service of plates in 1909. It should be remembered that the body used by Leroy was extremely light.

Messrs Tiffany & Co., New York   June 4th, 1909

Service of 15 Dessert Plates,
'Royal Gadroon'; richly
   decorated & painted by   £35 per plate.
      Leroy. F.509-F.520.

1 Crater Vase, by Leroy. F.533
1   do   do   F.534   £120 the pair
1 pair Vases   do   F.543   £120 the pair

Mr. Charles Jackson, now living in America, and who had been apprenticed at Osmaston Road in 1904, visited our Museum in 1973 and gave us a verbal picture of this talented man. We were told of Leroy's arrival at the factory in a cab wearing a silk hat and carrying a cane — a truly aristocratic figure who apparently worked only two or three days a week. In spite of this, we know that he was not too proud to play whist with the other painters and workpeople at the factory. He was, in fact, a member of the Works Institute, and is listed in its membership in 1905. Later illness prevented him from working fully, but again he was known to have been working shortly before his death on another special service of fifteen plates, which he designed and executed throughout. The plates were painted with flowers, exotic birds and trophies, all being framed with finely executed ornament, in raised and chased gold, in jewelled work on grounds of rich mazarine blue or of greens of different hues, and no two plates were alike.

Désiré Leroy died on a Sunday night, May 17th 1908, and was buried in Old Normanton Cemetery, Derby.

Sixteen years after his death an assortment of his work was sent to the Toronto National Exhibition of 1925, on a sale or return basis agreed with the Canadian agents, Messrs. Cassidy. It would therefore appear likely that some of the exhibits must have found homes in Canada and the U.S.A.

13 Interpreting this invoice one must first realise that the Custom House at New York was exacting 60% duty.

10 DERBY CROWN AND ROYAL CROWN DERBY SHAPES

Normally on hollow-ware shape numbers are incised on the base, but after 1890 the shape number usually appears in fractional form below a pattern number usually applied by the gilder. This should not be mistaken for impressed stamped marks which indicate the year of potting, see Appendix II. During the early 'Derby Crown' period some early shapes were soon discontinued and destroyed and are sometimes missing from the shape lists. The use of 'Sèvres' or 'Danish' is to indicate the shape; where otherwise used it describes a style.

1	Dish, shell shape, with figure of seated boy
2	Dish, shell shape, with figure of seated girl
3	Wall vase
4	Vase, square, with cover
5	Wall vase
6	Vase, with cover
7	Vase, twin
8	Vase, twin
9	Vase, on shell plinth
10	Vase, triple, with handle and butterfly
11	Vase, twin, with handle
12	Vase, tall, footed, with four cherubs, cover also with cherub
13	Vase, with two cherubs
14	Vase, with claw feet and cover
15	Vase, tall, footed, with cover
16	Dish, fluted, resting on seahorse tail
17	Vase, with cherubs
18	Vase, with three classical figures
19	Vase, tall
20	Vase, tall, tulip shape
21	Vase, flask shape
22	Urn, footed, with cover
23	Sauce boat
26	Dish, shell shape, supported by dolphin
27	Vase, footed, with ram's head at neck
28	Basket, small
29	Vase, dolphin and shell shape
30	Cornucopia, supported by dolphins
32	As 27
33-1	Vase, large, shell shape, supported by seahorse
33-2	Vase, large, shell shape, supported by dolphin
34	Box, gourd shape, with handle, and applied flower on cover
35	Jardinière, with swans
36	Bowl, with stand
37	Similar to 27
38	Vase, triple
39	Vase, large, with cover *1 ft 3 in.*
40	Vase, with claw feet *9 in.*
41	Vase, with claw feet *9 in.*
42	Vase, twisted cone shape, with dolphin support
43	Jardinière, footed, with masque handles
44	Vase *10¾ in.*
45	Vase, with four feet *7½ in.*
46	Vase, footed *8 in.*
48	Vase, large, lions at base *1ft 2¼ in.*
49	Vase, footed, with cover *10 in.*
50	Dolphin, with shell and figure
51	Seahorse, with shell and figure
52	Vase, footed, with masque handles
53	Violet basket
54	As 49 but *1ft 5 in.*
55	Vase, footed and embossed *9¾ in.*
56	Tazza, with dolphin supports
57	Vase, footed, with masque handles *11½ in.*
59	Bowl, round, pedestal, with two figures on rim
61	Jug, owl shape
62	Wall vase
64	Vase, with masque handles and cover
65	Vase, with handles *4½ in.*
66	Vase *6¾ in.*
67	Vase *3¼ in.*
68	Vase, with feet *4¾ in.*
69	Vase *3½ in.*
72	Vase, with masque handles *6 in.*
73	Vase, with leaf handles *6¾ in.*
74	Vase, with elephant head handles *11¾ in.*
76-1	Vase, fluted *6¼ in.*
76-2	Vase, fluted and embossed *6¼ in.*
77	Wall vase
78	Candelabra
79	Fern pot, basketwork
80	Vase, swans at neck, and foliage handles *1 ft 2¼ in.*
81	Wall vase
82	Wall vase
83	Vase, tall, footed, with classical figure handles and domed cover
84	Squirrel *7¾ in.*
85	Swans *6 in.*
86	Urn, classical *1 ft 0¾ in.*
87	Wall vase
88	Bowl, small, with claw feet
90	Vase
94	Vase, with swan and reeds
95	Candelabra
96	Vase, with cover
97	Wall vase
98	Jardinière
99	Jardinière
100	Vase, with four swans
101	Vase, with claw feet
102	Comport, shell shape, with handle
103	Vase, low
104	Vases, twin, shell shape
105	Candelabra
106	Child, on dolphin
107	Basket
108	Vase, with figure on cover
109	Vase, with cover
111	Wall vase
112	Vase, with masque handles
113	Vase, low
114	Vase, with cover
117	Vase, tulip shape
119	Vase, flask shape
120	Bowl, with cover
121	Jardinière

Royal Crown Derby dish of 'Royal' shape with a central panel of garden flowers painted and signed by Albert Gregory. Width 11in. 1934.
Courtesy David John Ceramics

Royal Crown Derby plate of 'Royal' shape with a central floral group painted and signed by Albert Gregory. 8¾in. 1922.
Mr. and Mrs. W.L.C. Prosser Collection

Royal Crown Derby plate of 'Royal Gadroon' shape from the service presented to Sir Henry Howe Bemrose in 1902 to celebrate his election victory in 1895 and as elected member 1895-1900.
Courtesy M.K. Nielsen Antiques

122 Candlestick, branched	187 Tray, triple, with handle
123 Vase, tulip shape	189 Jardinière
124 Basket	190 Jardinière
126 Vase, with elephant head handles	191 Vase, classical, with domed cover $11\frac{3}{4}$ in.
127 Vase, $5\frac{3}{4}$ in.	192 Vase, shell shape, with dolphin base *1 ft*
131 Vase, with fluted top and heavily embossed *9 in.*	194 Vase, small
	195 Fern stand
132 As above but *1 ft 0½ in.*	196 Vase, ornate, footed, with handles and domed cover *1 ft 8½ in.*
135 Vase, with four feet $5\frac{1}{2}$ in.	
138 Card holder	197 Bowl, small
139 Dish, leaf shape, with handle	198 Bowl, small
140 Vase, with elaborate embossed or pierced handles	199 Bowl, small, with handle
	201 Bowl, small
146 Vase, with animal handles $8\frac{1}{2}$ in.	204 Vase *10½ in.*
148 Vase, with lion feet $7\frac{1}{2}$ in.	209 Jardinière
149 Jardinière, small, with ram heads	216 Vase $9\frac{1}{2}$ in.
150 Vase, with lion heads $7\frac{1}{2}$ in.	219 Vase, hexagonal shape, with cover $10\frac{1}{2}$ in.
151 Vase, with cover $4\frac{1}{2}$ in.	220 Vase, with conical cover $9\frac{3}{4}$ in.
152 Vase, embossed *6 in.*	221 Vase, with handles *5 in.*
155 Vase, with foot, rope handles and cover *1 ft 7 in.*	223 Vase, with handles and cover
	225 Vase, with hexagonal base and round neck with applied flower motif $6\frac{3}{4}$ in.
158 Wall vase	
159 Vase, ornate, with four feet, pierced handles and neck *10 in.*	226 Vase, with hexagonal base $7\frac{3}{4}$ in.
	227 Vase, ornate, with pierced handles and domed cover $11\frac{3}{4}$ in.
164 Vase, with straight sides $3\frac{3}{4}$ in.	
165 Vase, classical, with claw feet and kneeling figure on cover *1 ft 0½ in.*	229 Vase, footed, with handles $7\frac{3}{4}$ in.
	231 Vase, narrow necked $6\frac{1}{2}$ in.
168 Jardinière	232 Vase, low, round
171 Basket, footed, with two small handles	242 Bowl, low, with four feet
173 Vase, with shells and seaweed *6 in.*	244 Vase, with pierced handles and plain domed cover $5\frac{1}{4}$ in.
174 Vase, with pierced handles *7 in.*	
175 Spill vases, three sizes	247 Vase, hexagonal shape, with flower handles $6\frac{1}{2}$ in.
182 Toast rack	
184 Menu stand	248 Vase, with pierced handles $7\frac{1}{2}$ in.
185 Jardinière, with claw feet and lion heads	250 Vase, with pierced handles $6\frac{3}{4}$ in.
186 Basket, violet leaf shape, with stem handle	253 Vase, ovoid shape, fluted, with cover
	254 Vase, with apple branch handle

Donald Birbeck designs for the service commissioned by an Indian prince just at the outbreak of the Second World War. The thirty plate centres were to be painted by William Mosley. See page 76.
Royal Crown Derby Archives

Donald Birbeck designs for the service commissioned by an Indian prince just at the outbreak of the Second World War. The thirty plate centres were to be painted by William Mosley. See page 76.
Royal Crown Derby Archives

256 Spill vase, funnel shape, with three pierced feet and fluted neck
257 Jardinière, with four claw feet and pierced round top
258 Vase, Newcastle or locket
259 Tray, triple
260 Vase, tall, with forked handle
261 Ewer, old Roman style, with handle across top
262 Vase, with handle and knob
263 Vase, plain, tall
264 Vase, with double body
265 Vase, globe shape, with six holes round the shoulders
266 Bottle, octagonal shape, pierced
267 Water bottle, embossed
268 Caddy, square, with cover
269 Vase, with key border round top and handle
270 Vase, pierced and flowered
271 Vase, with key handle, wide top and open foot
272 Vase, square, with cover, four handles and feet
274 Inks, round and octagonal shape
275 Vase, globe shape
276 Ginger jar, with pierced cover
277 Bracket, plain, for ribbon
278 Vase, with bamboo handle
279 Vase, with pierced top, four claw feet and key handle
280 Vase, with pierced top, handle, and pierced rose and leaves
281 Dish, oval, for flowers
282 Cupid, with cornucopia on back

283 Jardinière, with square handle and claw feet
284 Duck, on toadstool stalk
285 Dish, round and deep, with sitting cupid
286 Vase, with cover, key handles and bow
287 Neptune, with seahorse
288 Baskets, in three sizes, one size with pierced handle
289 Lamps, ten shapes
290 Vase, globe shape, with pierced shoulders and neck
291 Trinket box, crescent shape
292 Comport, double, with handle
293 Vase, large, with embossed and beaded neck and cover
294 Vase, large, with long handle
295 Flower holder
296 Wall vase or bracket
297 Basket, rustic, with bow
298 Vase, large, with cover
299 Vase, plain, with bell top
302 Marmalade, Bamboo
303 Vase, large, ship shape
304 Vase, large, square, with two different handles
306 Vases, plain, with scalloped top, two sizes
307 Vases, globe shape, bead round neck, four sizes
308 Salt, Elkington
309 Pepper, Elkington
310 Vase, covered, eight flutes on body
311 Vases, fluted, with cover, three sizes

315 Candlestick, with octagon shaped pedestal and pierced handles
316 Menu stand, with tree stump and sheaf of wheat
323 Menu stand, easel shape
324 Vase, with pierced handles and embossed neck
325 Cover, to ginger jar lamp
326 As 64 but with well for lamp
327 Horn, to beer set (Mr Lunn's design)
328 Ewer, Derby, (smallest) reproduction of Old Derby
329 Vase, Kedleston
330 Basket, Old Derby
331 Menu, vase shape
334 Menu, cupid holding a book
336 Vase, Japanese style
337 Vase, plain
338 Vase, plain
339 Vase, oak leaf shape, small
340 Jar, large, for Japan
341 Jug, to beer set (Mr Lunn's design)
342 Vase, plain
343 Vase, footed
344 Cover, pierced and embossed, to jar shape
345 Vase, with bell shaped top
346 Vase (copy of Mr Lunn's)
347 Flower holder, small
348 Toilet set (nine complete pieces, Mr Lunn's design)
349 Thimble
350 Ewer, Kedleston, L *1 ft 3½ in.* M *1 ft 2 in.* S *10 in.*
351 Knife and fork rest

352 Vase, small shape, with pierced knob
353 Vase, small shape, without pierced knob
354 Vase, very small, with pierced cover
355 Knob, small shape, pierced
356 Vase, small, with pierced cover
357 Vases, narrow necked, three sizes
358 Menu stand, with archery accessories
359 Card tray
360 Menu stand, shell shape, on pedestal
361 Card tray, saucer shape, with four trefoil piercing
362 Card tray
363 Vase, small, octagonal body
364 Vase, with embossed top and embossing between handle
365 Vases, plain shape, with frilled top of neck, two sizes
366 Vase, small, with flat cover
367 Vase, narrow necked
368 Vases, with small foot, narrow top, three sizes
369 Drinking horn, salmon head shape
370 Vase, with globe shaped body
371 Vase, plain, with wide top (Mr Lunn's design)
372 Vase, footed, globe shape with wide neck, and two handles
373 Vase, with octagonal foot, globe shaped body, and narrow neck
374 Bowl, with pierced rim (Mr Lunn's design)
375 As 365 but with leaves
376 Dish, oval, fluted, with pierced handles

Donald Birbeck designs for the service commissioned by an Indian prince just at the outbreak of the Second World War. The thirty plate centres were to be painted by William Mosley. See page 76.
Royal Crown Derby Archives

377 Vase, footed, with embossed top
378 Vase, large, footed, and with wide fluted top
379 Sweetmeat dish
380 Sweetmeat tray, oval
381 Vase, large, heavily embossed, with pierced handles and cover *3 ft 4 in.*
382 Vase, with embossed foot and neck
383 Vase, small, globe shape, with embossed neck
384 Vase, bottle shape, narrow neck, with wide top
385 Ewer
386 Vase, small
387 Vase, small, Persian style, with two handles, narrow neck and small cover

388 Vase, with cover
389 Sweet, round, fluted
390 Dish, fluted
391 Pen tray
392 Vase, tall, footed, with cover
393 Dish, oval, with fluted edge
394 Vase, Kedleston, revised, L *1 ft 3 in.* M *1 ft 0¾ in.* S *10 in.*
395 Dish, low, fluted, with two handles
396 Vase, wide necked
397 Vase, narrow necked, with small fluted cover
398 Tray, double, with handle
399 Vase, fluted, with domed cover
400 Unidentified
401 Tray, small, hexagonal shape

Above left:
Derby Crown porcelain vase with pierced cover and handles, pattern 689, shape 322, decorated with pale yellow and bright red groundlay, heavily gilt in Persian style. Derby Crown mark. 13¾in. c.1880.
Courtesy David John Ceramics

Above right:
Derby Crown Persian style vase of elaborate shape, pierced, with rich raised gilding on ivory ground. Shape 381. Height 40in. 1886.
Royal Crown Derby Museum

Plaque painted by J. Rouse jun. of Mr. and Mrs. Samuel Gilbert and their daughter Edith. c.1887. Mr. Gilbert was the founder of Gilbert's Drapery Warehouse, 50 Queen Street, Derby, subsequently A.E. Moult Ltd.
Private Collection

402 Breakfast cruet
403 Trays, tiered, two round, one oval
404 Tray, small
405 Trays, tiered, one round, one oval
406 Bowl, with standing figure of boy
407 Tray, fan shape
408 Vases, globe shape, three sizes
409 Ewer, globe shaped base, with slender neck and ornate handle
410 Two trays and figure
411 Vase, plain
412 Water carrier
413 Figure, with bowl
414 Vase
415 Stand, dragon and lotus leaf
416 Two trays and figure
417 Companion to 412
418 Reading boy on stump, with two oval and one round tray
419 Girl companion to 418
420 Girl companon to 413

421 Comport, dragon, low
422 Boy, kneeling, beside fluted bowl
424 Figure supporting vase
426 Vase, with handle
427 Vases, with embossed neck, two sides
428 Vase, globe shape
429 Similar to above but with embossed base
430 Vase, with handles
431 Centrepiece (*The Lovers*), large sweet, on top boy with mandolin
432 Vase
433 Vase, with handle
434 Vase, small, with two handles
435 Vase, plain
436 Sweet dish
437 Vase, with frilled neck
438 Vase, with embossed neck and small domed cover
439 Sweet dish
440 Sweet dishes, fluted, five sizes

Royal Crown Derby 'Hastings' shape plate, groundlaid in pale yellow and painted with a group of roses signed by Charles Harris. 8½ in. 1898.
Courtesy David John Ceramics

441 Vase, small, globe shape, with tall narrow neck
442 Similar to above but embossed on shoulder and neck
443 Vase, with embossed shoulder and reeded neck
444 Similar to 438 but without cover
445 Vase, small
446 Vase, embossed on neck and shoulder
447 Vase, with two handles and cover
448 Vase, plain 7¼ in.
449 Vase, small
450 Vase, Persian style, with two handles and a cover
451 Vase, Persian style, with two handles and a cover
452 Vase, low, with cover
453 Vase, small
454 Vase, with two handles and domed cover 10¼ in.
455 Top part as 393 but on tall foot
456 Bowl, with handles
457 Bowl, with fluted edge
458 Vase, ewer shape
459 Vase, plain
460 Vase, with handles
461 Vase, with handle
462 Vase, with handle
463 Urn, globe shape, with four feet, two pierced handles and cover
464 Pen tray
465 Vase 3¼ in. patterns 6299 and 1128 only
466 Drinking horn
468 Vase, ewer shape, on foot with embossed neck 11 in.
469 Vase, plain, with narrow neck
470 Sugar and cream

471 Vase, with wide top
472 Kneeling figure, by tree trunk, round fluted dish on top
473 Companion to 472
474 Salt cellar, octagonal shape, embossed
475 Ginger jar, with cover
476 Dish, oval, plaited, with stand
477 Vase, plain
478 Vase, with handle
479 Vase, embossed
480 Vase, with handle
481 Vase, with handles
482 Vase, globe shape, with two handles and cover
483 Vase 392 (Mr Lunn's design), without handles
484 Vase, large, footed, with handles and cover
485 Vase, large, footed, with handles and cover
486 Vase, small, plain
487 Vase, with wide base and narrow embossed neck L and S 3 in.
488 Bowl, ribbed, with fluted edge
489 Strawberry set, bowl, sugar and cream
490 Vase, globe shape, with narrow neck and wide top
491 Centrepiece, boy and girl either side of a fluted bowl
492 Marmalade jar, plain, with straight flutes
Sardine box and stand, plain, with straight flutes
Butter tub, plain, with straight flutes
Biscuit box, plain, with straight flutes
Honey pot, plain, with straight flutes
493 Vase, large, with winged handles and cover

Left. Ewer, shape 328. Painted with pendant chain of flowers by W.E. Mosley, signed. Height 7¼in.
1903. *Private Collection*
Right. Small ewer, decorated in Sèvres manner and signed by Leroy. Height 7in. 1895. *Private Collection*

Derby Crown pair of vases, rose pompadour ground with raised gold floral motif and panels of formal gilding. Height 7in. 1887.
Courtesy Sotheby's Belgravia

494 Side comport, to centre 491 boy
495 Side comport, to centre 491 girl
496 Sweets, to centre 491, two sizes
497 Vase, with fluted top
498 Vase, plain
499 Vase, with slightly embossed top
500 Jar, without cover
501 Jar, without cover
502 Salt, made to a wooden pattern
503 Box, low, with tall cover 5¼ in.
504 Jar, covered, L 6¾ in.
505 Vase, large, globe shape, with handles and cover
506 Jar, round, covered, L–M 6 in. S 3⅞ in.
507 Vase, plain
508 Vase, plain, L 9½ in. S 7½ in.
509 Vase, low, round, with handles
510 Sugar and cream, fluted, similar to 470
511 Sugar and cream, fluted up to frilled edge
512 Vases, footed and with cover, two sizes
513 Similar to above but without foot
514 Vase, small, with narrow neck
515 Figure, Algerian, female
516 Vase, footed, with handles and large domed cover
517 Coffee pot, with straight sides and ribbed cover
519 Mustard spoon, plain
520 Vase, tall, footed, urn shape
521 Vase, ewer shape 6 in.
522 Vase, globe shape, with small domed cover
523 Vase, tall, footed, ovoid shape, with small domed cover

524 Vase, large, round, with hexagonal shape stand and two handles
525 Pepper pot, for mounting
526 Pickle jar, with reeded cover
527 Regent dejeuner set, teacup and saucer, teapot, sugar and cream, slop and tray to match, with fluted base and plain edge
528 Vase, small, with round, fluted base and straight neck
529 Honey pot, similar to above
530 Jar, large, with embossed cover
531 Vase, Persian style, with round base, slender neck with handles and incorporated small, embossed, domed cover
532 Glass, for lamp
533 As 516 but with pointed knob
534 Vase, small, round, with pierced neck and cover fitting inside
535 Vase, tall, footed, with handles
536 Vase, small, globe shape, neck ⅝ in. wide
537 As 478 but without embossing
538 Vase, Greek style, as 584 but without embossing
539 Vase, tall, bottle shape, with embossed neck and shoulder 1 ft 0½ in.
540 Flower holders, basket weave, two sizes
541 Vase, ovoid shape, embossed on neck and shoulder, plain top
542 Vase, with round, fluted base, elongated neck and small embossed cover
543 Vase, Greek style, with cover, no handles
544 Jar, large, round, fluted, with embossed cover and knob

Royal Crown Derby pair of vases and covers with large 'bird and landscape' panels reserved on cobalt blue ground painted and signed by George Darlington.
M.K. Nielsen Antiques

545 Vase, with hexagonal shape foot, heavily embossed handles, and small cover L *1 ft 9 in*. S *1 ft 4 in*.
546 Vase, round, with embossed handles and neck
547 As 574 but with flat cover
548 Vase, tall, ovoid shape, with domed cover and small knob
549 Jugs, 'Bass' shape, with straight sides and pointed lip, eleven sizes Sugars, five sizes
550 Vase, tall, with fluted foot, embossed, round, wide neck and plain cover
551 Vase, tall, with handles on shoulders and domed cover with knob
552 Vase, round, with slender neck with handle
553 Vase, round, ribbed, with domed cover fitting inside neck *1 ft*
554 Vase, large, with small embossed foot, handles and cover with knob
555 Similar to 553 but *6 in*.
556 Vase, large, oriental, heavily embossed, with handles and cover
557 Trinket set, six pieces

558 Pot pourri, similar shape to 555 *5½in*.
559 Jar, round, ribbed, with embossed neck and cover
560 Dessert plate, 'Lichfield' shape, with fluted and embossed border Dessert comports, 'Lichfield' shape, tall and low
561 Ginger jar, small, with cover
562 Dessert plate, 'Durham' shape, with embossed border and plain edge Dessert comports, 'Durham' shape, tall, low, oval, shell and square
563 Candlestick, with tiered foot, tapering middle and slightly embossed top
564 Vase, with round base, narrow neck and square embossed handles
565 Cream jug, small
566 Dessert plate, 'Harrow' shape, fluted Dessert comports, 'Harrow' shape, tall, low, oval, shell and square
568 Vase, ovoid shape, with embossed neck and stopper
569 Bottle, round, twisted flute shape, with stopper

Royal Crown Derby vase and cover with some applegreen groundlay and floral painting on the white ground. Pattern 6900. 1901.
Courtesy M.K. Nielsen Antiques

570 Bottle, round, plain shape with twisted flute stopper $7\frac{3}{4}$ in.
571 Egg-shell can
572 As 569 but with plain stopper $6\frac{1}{2}$ in.
573 Violet holder $3\frac{1}{2}$ in. to top of handle
574 Vase, body as 547, cover embossed L $5\frac{1}{2}$ in. S $4\frac{1}{2}$ in.
575 Jug, small, fluted
576 Pot pourri, with curved, pointed handles 7 in.
577 Vase, large, heavily embossed on cover and neck L 1 ft 6 in. S 1 ft 1 in.
578 Vase, double gourd shape, partially embossed 8 in.
579 Teacup and saucer, base fluted, top plain and tapered (made for Mr Owen)
580 Vase, round, with embossed neck and twisted flute body
581 Similar to 580 but with straight flute
582 Fern pots and stands, three sizes
583 Vase, fluted, bottle shape, with embossed neck and stopper $11\frac{1}{2}$ in.
584 Vase, small, plain, with two looped handles 5 in.

585 Vase, plain, with embossed neck and two small handles $6\frac{1}{4}$ in.
586 Vase, with fluted body and domed cover with knob
587 Vase, round, with narrow neck and square handle from shoulder to neck
588 Similar to 586 but with round body L and S
589 Vase, cover as 588 but with ovoid shape body $11\frac{3}{4}$ in.
590 Jug, decorative, $8\frac{1}{2}$ in.
591 Milk jug
592 Drinking cup, with cover $7\frac{1}{2}$ in.
593 Vase, wide base, with narrow neck and two small handles
594 Similar shape to 593 but without handles and with embossed edge
595 Ewer, large, with fluted body and elaborate handle
596 Vase, small, with fluted top and two small handles
597 Vase, large, with fluted, embossed neck and double lip top
598 Vase, tall, with elaborate embossed foot, neck and handles

Derby Crown plate of 'Harrow' shape painted in a manner so obviously influenced by Count Holtzendorf, by Edwin Trowell. The scene is 'Pickering Tor' and the five small panels on the border are also scenes in Dovedale, Derbyshire. 8¾ in. 1887.
W.H. Lowe Collection

599 Vase, low, round, with elaborate neck, handles and stopper
600 Vase, large, round, with embossed shoulder and handles 11½ in.
601 Vase, tall, with embossed foot and handles similar to 600 L 1ft 7¼in.
602 Vase, ewer shape, with twisted handle L 8¼in. S 6¾ in.
603 Vase, tall, fluted, with narrow neck and wider embossed top
604 Inkstand, square
605 Sugar and cream similar to 591
606 Jugs, 'Derby' shape, four sizes
607 Menu holder?
608 Vase, with round base, square handles from neck to shoulder 11 in.
609 Vase, tall, with heavily embossed neck, handles and top 1ft 1¼ in.
610 Clock case
611 Vase, plain, with two handles 8¼ in.
612 Vase, large round base, embossed neck and handle 10 in.
613 Vase, plain, ovoid shape, with two small handles L 10 in. S 8½ in.
614 Vase, plain, with two small handles curving from the edge
615 Vase, unusual
616 Vase, broad based, with two small handles on embossed shoulder, and fluted neck
617 Similar to 616 but with looped handles from longer neck to shoulder

618 Vase, plain, with fluted top L 8 in. M 7in. S 6¼ in.
619 Vase, large, small foot, embossed handles and neck, plain top 1ft 3in.
620 Similar to 608 9¼ in.
621 Tea and breakfast ware, 'Surrey' shape, fluted shape with twisted flute handle
622 Milk, small, straight sides, fluted at base, sparrow lip
    Sugar basin to match
623 Creams, 'Buxton' shape, round base, straight neck and lip, four sizes
624 Dessert, 'Rugby' shape, ribbed border
    Comports, 'Rugby' shape, oval, shell and tall
625 Lamp, classical shape, ribbed to shoulder, small foot
626 Ramekin, ovoid shape
627 Lamp, similar to 625
629 Jugs, 'Hop' shape, three sizes
630 Sugar, plain, to match cream 623
631 Sugar, 'Derby' shape, to match jug 606
632 Vase, round, embossed, with tall ribbed neck 7 in.
633 Vase, slender, embossed, and cover 5½ in.
634 Box, small, round, embossed repoussé
635 Box, heart shape, embossed repoussé
636 Box, oblong, embossed repoussé
637 Vase, small, globe shape, embossed repoussé 3½ in.

Royal Crown Derby plate of 'Clarence' shape painted with a view 'Near Aberfoyle, Scotland, and signed by Cuthbert Gresley. 8½ in. 1919.
David John Ceramics

638 Box, small, round, domed, embossed repoussé all over
639 Vase, ovoid shape, repoussé *4½ in.*
640 Vase, small, round, with round cover, repoussé
641 Similar to 637
642 Similar to 632
643 Vase, round, with thin neck, repoussé
644 Similar to 640 but with ribbed knob on cover, repoussé
645 Teapot, sugar and cream, small, round
646 Vase, small, plain shape, repoussé, with cover
647 Vase, small, globe shape, with fluted neck, repoussé
648 Sugar basin, plain, to 629
649 Sweet dishes, 'Surrey' shape, fluted, seven sizes
650 Sweets, oblong, fluted, six sizes
651 Drinking cup, small, with cover
652 Vase, large, Persian type, with embossed handles, shoulder and cover
653 Vase, classical, with plain foot and embossed rim to cover *6¼ in.*
654 Teacup, 'Bedford' shape, straight fluted with twisted flute handle
655 Similar to 654 but with small foot
656 Stand, small (modelled for Mr McInnes)
657 Teapot, sugar and cream, 'Dublin' shape, plain boat shape with domed cover

658 Baskets, small, trellis embossed, three sizes
659 Vase, pot pourri, with embossed handles and cover
660 Vase, large, with embossed handles, foot and cover
661 Similar to 577
662 Similar to 581 but embossed repoussé *1 ft.*
663 As 662 but with plain top
664 Vase, with same neck as 597, repoussé *1 ft 1 in.*
665 Similar to 637, repoussé *8½ in.*
666 Vase, plain, with fluted top, repoussé *11 in.*
667 Vase, with narrow neck and two small handles, repoussé *10 in.*
668 Jar, large, with cover, repoussé
669 Vase, with embossed shoulder and handle *11½ in.*
670 Vase, plain, with small foot
671 Malt jug, as 629 but taller
672 Vase, round, similar to 521
673 Cup and saucer, small, embossed
674 Similar to 647
675 Vase, slightly embossed in middle of neck L S *8¼ in.*
676 Vases, plain, with fluted top, three sizes
677 Vase, fluted, with elaborately embossed neck and handle *7½ in.*

Derby Porcelain 'Bute' shape coffee
cup and saucer, eggshell china, flat
gold with turquoise, pink and white
jewelling and miniatures painted by
James Rouse sen. c.1884.
Royal Crown Derby Museum

678 Sweets, 'Rugby' shape, fluted, two
shapes
680 Vase, with two handles, embossed on
domed cover, top of body and foot
681 Dessert, 'Stafford' shape, fluted
Comports, 'Stafford' shape, oval, shell
and square
682 Vases, large, with heavily embossed
cover, neck and handles, two sides
L 1 ft 7 in.
683 Vase, plain, with handle 8 in.
684 Dessert, 'Portland' shape, fluted
Comports, 'Portland' shape, oval, shell
and square
685 Vase, with slightly embossed neck and
top of body, and small handle L 6¾ in. S
686 Vase, with fluted neck and top of body
L 11½ in. S 9 in.
687 Vase, with embossed neck and handle,
688 Vase, with plain body and fluted top
4¼ in.
689 Vase, small, plain, similar to 585 L 5¼ in.
S 4 in.
690 Vase, small, plain, with two small
handles 5¼ in.
691 Jar, round, with cover L 6 in. S 4½ in.
692 Vase, small, ewer shape, embossed
shoulder 4½ in.
693 Vase, plain 6 in.
694 Vase, small, neck as 597
695 Vase, similar shape to 577 7¼ in.,
patterns 6299 and 1128
696 Vase, small, with embossed domed
cover 5½ in.
697 Similar to 587 4½ in.
698 Vase, globe shape, with two small
handles 3¾ in., patterns 6299 and 1128

699 Similar to 521, patterns 6299 and 1128
700 Vase, plain, patterns 6299 and 1128
701 Vase, small, with gadroon foot and edge
of cover 4½ in.
702 Vase, plain, with handle
703 Tea and breakfast sets, 'Vernon' shape,
plain shape
704 Sweet, 'Surrey' shape, footed 6 in. wide
705 Flower bowl, 'Surrey' shape 9 in. wide,
3½ in. high
706 Biscuit jar, straight sided S 6¾ in.
707 Sweet, 'Portland' shape, fluted, square
and oval
708 Boxes, 'Bamboo' shape, four sizes
709 Vase, with shaped foot, heavily
embossed neck and handles 10¼ in.
710 Vase, plain, with embossed top
L 1 ft 0½ in. S 8½ in.
711 Boxes, 'Bamboo' shape, hexagonal
shape, three sizes
712 Box, 'Bamboo' shape, rectangular,
shallow
713 Basket, 'Bamboo' shape
714 Bouillon cup and stand, 'Vernon' shape
715 Bouillon cup and stand, 'Surrey' shape
716 Ice cream tray and stand, oblong, fluted
717 Oyster shell, scalloped
718 Luncheon tray, triple, scallop fluted
719 Vase, similar to 683, with embossed
neck
720 Vase, large, with heavily embossed foot,
base, handles, neck and cover
721 Ramekin, with pointed flutes
722 Sugar and cream, small, with fluted base,
plain top, and plain sugar
723 Similar to above but plain cream
724 Eggcup and stand with looped handle

Lamp base, shape 742, cobalt blue with raised golds and enamel. c.1900.
Royal Crown Derby Museum

725 Lamp?
726 Flower holder, plain, oblong
727 Flower holders, curved, rustic, two sizes
728 Fern pot and stand, rustic
729 Punch bowl, fluted, and on fluted foot
730 Vase, very small, Old Derby
733 Teacup, 'Essex' shape, low, as 621
734 Vase, ovoid shape, with embossed shoulder, neck and cover with knob 10½ in.
735 Jar, with small foot, embossed shoulder and domed cover
738 Vase, ovoid shape, with embossed shoulder, neck and top
739 Jar, with embossed shoulder, cover and knob
740 Vase, low, ewer shape
741 Hot water jug, shape as 722
742 Lamp, with base fluted, centre stem with Greek style top
743 Vase, similar in shape to 738 but with different embossing 8 in. and 6 in.
744 'Toby Jugs', plain shape, eight sizes
745 Vase, similar to 710, with embossed neck
746 Butter and stand
747 Flower stand, rustic, with three holders
748 Flower stands, rustic, tree trunk shape, three sizes
749 Basket, on four small feet
750 Sweet dish, fluted, shape as 729
751 Jugs, 'Romford' shape, straight sided, ribbed, eight sizes
752 Sweet dish, round, scalloped and fluted
753 Tea and breakfast services, 'Clarence' shape, fluted and embossed
754 Dessert plates and oval, shell and square comports, 'Clarence' shape 4½ in. tall

755 Lamp, rustic
756 Flower holder, rustic, quarter circle shape
757 Vase, with handle, embossed neck and top 7 in.
758 Vase, fluted, with embossed neck and top L 7½ in. S 6 in.
759 Vase, urn shape, slightly embossed top, with handle 7½ in.
760 Similar to 759 but with embossed shoulder, neck and handle 8¼ in.
761 Sweets, 'Rouen' shape, oval, heavily embossed, six sizes
762 Sweets, 'Rouen' shape, round, heavily embossed, six sizes
763 Sweets, 'Rouen' shape, square, heavily embossed, six sizes
764 Dejeuner set, 'Paris' shape, large embossed edge tray
    Teapot, sugar box, cream and four cups and saucers, twisted flute
765 Vase, plain, with embossed neck
766 Vase, with embossed shoulder, neck and stopper 8 in.
767 Vase, plain, with two small handles
768 Vase, unusual
769 Biscuit box, ribbed, L and S
770 Vase, ewer shape, embossed neck, shoulder and handle 9¾ in.
771 Sugar, 'Romford' shape, shape as 751
772 Dish, plain, oval, footed
773 Dinnerware, 'Clarence' shape, as 753
774 Teaware, 'Paris' shape, as 764
775 Vase, with small foot, embossed shoulder, handle and top
776 Jar, with embossed cover and knob L 9½ in. S 7¾ in.

Royal Crown Derby cup and saucer decorated with City of Liverpool arms. It seems that in 1898 some additions for the civic service were made at Osmaston Road. It is hardly surprising as the Litherlands were from Liverpool and would have had many connections, especially as they were china and glass retailers in that city. The basic ground colour is orange with the coat of arms repeated in the bottom of the saucer. Shape 890.

Bernard and Nancy Wilson Collection

777 Vase, embossed, with wide neck L 9½ in. S 7½ in.

778 Milk jug, 'Wrexham' shape, twisted flute, plain handle

779 Vase, similar in shape to 652, but without knob 7½ in.

780 Vase, with embossed base, narrow embossed neck with two small handles and plain top

781 Dessert, 'Rouen' shape, shape as 761 Comports, 'Rouen' shape, oval and shell, shell on foot

782 Vase, ewer shape 7¾ in.

783 Vase, tall, heavily embossed foot and base, shoulder and narrow neck, with possible small stopper

784 Candlestick, 'Rouen' shape, low

786 Vase, 'The Empire' shape, large, with twisted embossed handles and neck, and embossed domed cover and knob L 1ft 3in. S 11½ in.

789 Vase, with top similar to 786 but without handles and with embossed foot 8¾ in.

790 Vase, ewer shape, with embossed shoulder and neck and plain handle

792 Vase, classical, embossed on foot and shoulder, and two small handles

793 Vase, tall, with twist handles and straight embossed neck

794 Teapot, 'Surrey' shape

795 Salad bowl, 'Rouen' shape

796 Syrup pitcher and stand, 'Rouen' shape

797 Ink stand, 'Rouen' shape

798 Toothpick holder, with fluted top

799 Dinnerware, 'Surrey' shape, as 621

800 Flower holder, half circle shape, fluted and embossed L and S

801 Flower holder, similar to 800

802 Toothpick holder, vase shape with embossed shoulder and neck

803 Toothpick holder, with broad base and narrow neck 2¼ in.

804 Dessert, 'Argyll' shape, pierced border, ninety holes

805 Vase, small, twisted flute neck 2¾ in.

806 Flower holder, quarter circle L and S

807 Flower holders, oblong, three sizes

808 Vase, globe shape, applied flowers on handles and edge

809 Vase, low, embossed and with applied flowers L and S

810 Mocha coffee and saucer, twisted flute

811 Fern pot, with embossed base and fluted top

812 Toast rack, three embossed bars on stand, used with 817

813 Flower basket, triple tray with curved handle, embossed

814 Teapot stand, plain, round

815 Flowerpot, heavily embossed

'Devon' dessert plate, golden fawn groundlaid border. Central figure subject by J. Platts, signed. 1882.
Victor Spenton Collection

816 Flower holder, curved and with handle
817 Bouillon set, with embossed tray, toast rack, salt and pepper
Bouillon cup with embossed cover, handles as 840
818 Vase, large, with small foot, fluted shoulder and neck, twisted leaf handles

819 Vase, large, classical, with tall foot, fluted base to vase, inverted flute neck, plain domed cover with knob
820 Vase, globe shape, narrow neck, small fluted top, two twisted leaf handles $6\frac{1}{2}$ in.
821 Vase, ovoid shape, with embossed neck and top, small foot L $7\frac{3}{4}$ in. S $6\frac{1}{2}$ in.

Rare scent bottle, turquoise blue
ground with raised gold and
jewelling, heart-shaped inset of
flowers. Painted by R. Barratt,
signed. Shape 860. c.1900.
*Royal Crown Derby Museum
Donated by the late Molly Barratt
(R. Barratt's daughter)*

822 Vase, globe shape, with embossed neck,
shoulder and small top L 5½ in. S 4½ in.,
patterns 6299 and 1128

823 Ewer, ornate, globe shape, with twisted
leaf handle *11 in.*

824 Vase, shape as 824 but without handle
L 10 in. S 8 in.

825 Flower holder, rustic, treble

826 Jar, with cover 5½ in., patterns 6299 and
1128

827 Teacup and saucer, 'York' shape,
twisted flute with straight top

828 Teacup and saucer, 'Fife' shape

829 Jar, with small foot, narrow neck and
cover 6 in.

830 Vase, globe shape, with wide embossed
neck 5¼ in.

831 Vase, ewer shape, fluted body 6½ in.

832 Vase, slender, with narrow neck and
wider embossed top 6 in.

833 Vase, with narrow embossed neck 5 in.

835 Vase, with flat base, embossing and
handles similar to 818 10¼ in.

836 Vase, small, with round embossed top

837 Ewer, ornate, with flat base, heavily
embossed neck and handle 8¼ in.

838 Vase, with straight sides and small
handles

839 Comb tray, oblong, with embossed
border

840 Bouillon cup and stand, twisted flute
shape with handle as 817

841 Vase, plain, with handle, narrow neck
and fluted top 4⅝ in.

842 Flower holder, four shell shapes

843 Vase, ewer shape, twisted flute 9½ in.

844 Vase, ewer shape, with winged handles
1 ft 1 in.

845 Coffee cup, 'Seine' shape, with straight
sides, plain saucer

846 Flower holder, rustic, double

847 Flower holder, rustic, single

848 Sweet dish, coiled, fluted shape

849 Sweet dish, round, fluted shape

850 Vase, large, oriental style, with heavily
embossed foot, handles, neck and
domed cover *2 ft*

851 Candle snuffer, 'Rouen' shape, twisted
flute and small handle

852 Figure, *My Pretty Jane*

853 Figure, *Sally in our Alley*

854 Tea and breakfast sets, 'Dover' shape

855 Candlestick, 'Rouen' shape, with
twisted flute column 7½ in.

856 Vase, tall, classical, footed, with plain
body and fluted neck L 1 ft S 9 in.

857 Figure, 'The Flower Queen', *1 ft 0¼ in.*

858 Vase, large, with plain foot, ovoid shape
body with decoration, embossed neck
and fluted top *1 ft 3 in.*

859 Matchbox, plain, round

860 Scent bottle, small, plain

861 Dessert plate, 'Brighton' shape,
embossed border
Dessert comports, 'Brighton' shape,
oval, shell and tall

862 Vase, tall, with embossed foot and base,
shoulder and neck L *1 ft 4½ in.*,
S *1 ft 1¾ in.*

863 Teacup and saucer, 'Cope' shape, fluted

864 Dessert plate, 'Hastings' shape
Dessert comports, oval, shell and tall,
scalloped

865 Vase, with embossed neck and top

866

867 Vase, globe shape, with small embossed
neck L 5¼ in. S 4 in.

Plate 38. Royal Crown Derby
'Argyle' pierced plate decorated and
signed by Désiré Leroy with a
central panel of flowers on a marble
ledge and border panels alternating
with flowers and musical trophies,
pattern 7283. Royal Warrant mark
for King Edward VII. 9in. 1901.
Private Collection

Plate 39. Royal Crown Derby
'Kedleston' shaped ewer, shape
1194, painted and signed by Leroy.
6in. 1890.
Private Collection

Plate 40. Royal Crown Derby vase
and cover painted and signed by
Leroy with white enamel decoration
on cobalt blue ground. 6⅛in. 1898.
Mr. and Mrs. R.J. Williams Collection

Vase shape 877, shell neck, rope entwined, painted in natural colours with shipping by W.E.J. Dean.
c.1897.
Royal Crown Derby Museum

Loving cup, 'Rouen' shape 884, green groundlaid borders with flower painting by G. Jessop, signed. 4½ in. x 4½ in. 1922.
Private Collection

868 Teacup and saucer, 'Crescent' shape, fluted
869 Figure, 'A Love Letter'
870 Figure, 'A Love Song'
871 Vase, large, ovoid shape, with heavily embossed foot, handles and neck *1 ft 1½ in.*
872 Vase, globe shape, with flat base and narrow neck
873 Vase, tall, with embossed foot, neck and top *1 ft 1¾ in.*
874 Vase, unusual
875 Vase, large, with plain body, embossed foot, shoulder and neck L *1 ft 6 in.* S *1 ft 2½ in.*
876 Vase, ovoid shape, with two small handles and narrow neck L *10¾ in.* S *8¾ in.*
877 Vase, globe shape, with shell neck L *9¾ in.* S *8 in.*
878 Vase, with wide base, embossed foot and base and fluted top L *1 ft 2 in.* S *11 in.*
879 Vase, plain, with small embossed foot, and embossed shoulder and top *11¼ in.*
880 Vase, plain, with embossed neck and fluted top L *9½ in.* S *7½ in.*
881 Vase, plain, with small foot, wide embossed shoulder, and plain top *7½ in.*
882 Vase, with flat base, globe shape, narrow neck and wider top L *6½ in.* S *5¼ in.*
883 Vase, ovoid body, slender neck, embossed *1 ft 1 in.*
884 Loving cups, with two embossed handles,

also available with one or three handles, three sizes *6 x 6 in.*, *5 x 5 in.* and *4½ x 4½ in.*
885 Vase, globe shape, with small foot and fluted top *6¼ in.*
886 Biscuit box, globe shape, fluted, for mounting
887 Pepper box, as 886
888 Salad bowl, as 886
889 Vase, large, with tall embossed foot, embossed shoulders, handles and domed cover *1 ft 7 in.*
890 Cup and saucer, Liverpool Corporation
891 Jardinière, embossed L *1 ft 3 in.* across top, *6 in.* high, S *10 in.* across top, *4½ in.* high
892 Vase, small, ewer shape, *5½ in.* high, patterns 6299 and 1128
893 Vase, plain, with fluted shoulders, neck and top L *6¾ in.* S *4¾ in.*
894 Fern pot, plain, with two handles
895 Biscuit box, 'Rouen' shape
896 Teapot, sugar and cream, hexagonal shape, for mounting
897 Trinket set, 'Fife' shape, tall box, low box, matchbox, pin tray, ring stand, comb tray, candlestick, taper candlestick, and scent bottle
898 Object, rectangular
899 Dish, oval, fluted, for fruit
900 Pepper and salt cellar
901 Jugs, 'York' shape, flat base, embossed top and lip, eleven sizes
902
903

Plate 41. Royal Crown Derby pair of vases, with domed covers, decorated all over by W.E.J. Dean with blue and white marine views, pattern 4613, shape 695. 7 1/4 in. 1897.
Private Collection

904 Vase, ewer shape, with frilled neck 7 in. high, patterns 6299 and 1128

905 As 904 but without handle 6¼ in., patterns 6299 and 1128

906 Tray, triple, fluted, no handle

907 Vase, footed, with cover 7½ in.

908 Teacup and saucer, 'Whitby' shape, plain

909 Coffee pot, cream and sugar for mounting

910 Vase, slender, with embossed neck 7¼ in. high, patterns 6299 and 1128

911 Dessert plate, 'Thames' shape, with fluted and embossed border

912 Drinking cup, no handle, embossed, similar to 911

913 Ashtray, oblong, embossed

914 Vase, Persian style, with one large and one small handle and embossed domed cover 1 ft 1½ in. high

915 Vase, unusual

916 Vase, plain, with embossed shoulders and top L 1 ft 2 in. S 10½ in.

917 Vase, double curved, with embossed base, twisted flute handle and frilled neck 11½ in. high

918 Vase, small, plain L 5½ in. S 4½ in.

919 Vase, globe shape, plain 2½ in.

920 Scent bottle, fluted, with embossed stopper 5 in.

921 Vase, Persian style, with embossed foot, shoulder, domed cover and knob L 1 ft 11 in. S 1 ft 6 in.

922 Vase, small, plain 4¼ in.

923 Trinket tray, 'Princess' shape, octagonal shape, without well

924 Vase, ribbed 5 in.

925 Similar to 922 4½ in.

926 Vase, fluted, with embossed shoulder, narrow neck and wider scalloped top 6 in.

927 Hand bell, with embossed base, shoulder and hexagonal handle 6¾ in.

928 Vase, globe shape, plain, with two handles L 6¾ in. S 5½ in.

929 Sweet dishes, 'Chelsea' shape, shell shape, heavily embossed, six sizes

930 Sugar, 'York' shape, to go with 901

931 Tea caddy, quarter pound, ribbed, with cover 4¾ in.

932 Teacup and saucer, 'Sefton' shape

933 Drinking cups, with fluted top, two sizes

934 Vase, globe shape, with narrow neck 3⅞ in.

935 Dessert plate, 'Exeter' shape, scalloped and fluted
Dessert comports, 'Exeter' shape, oval, shell and tall

936 Dessert plate, 'Warwick' shape, scalloped and fluted
Dessert comports, 'Warwick' shape. oval, square and oblong

937 Coffee pot, plain shape, embossed round middle, for mounting

938 Vase, footed, with embossed base, narrow ribbed neck and fluted top

939 Bell, oval, with shallow handle 4¾ in. overall

940 Tea caddy, half a pound, embossed on two sides, shoulder and cover 6½ in.

941 Knife handle, embossed

942 Vase, ribbed, with fluted neck 4½ in.

943 Slab, small, heart shape, possibly for mounting

944 Slab, small, round, possibly for mounting

945 Knife handle, small

946 Knife handle, large

947 Plate, Old Derby, 'Bow' shape

948 Vase, ewer shape, with wide base, slender neck and handle 5½ in.

949 Vase, with broad base, twin fluted necks, and curving embossed handle 1 ft 0¼ in.

950 Vase, classical, with embossed foot, base and top 7½ in.

951 Vase, plain, with narrow fluted neck 5¼ in.

952 Vase, globe shape, 4 in.

953 Similar to 952, with tapered neck 6⅛ in.

954 Bouillon and stand, fluted, with round knob on cover

955 Vase, double, with handles

956 Unidentified

957 Vase, large, with small embossed foot, broad base, and embossed shoulder and neck L 1 ft 6 in. S 1 ft 2½ in.

958 Vase, small, plain, with inverted flute neck L 7 in. S 6 in.

959 Teacup and saucer, plain, 'Derby and Leicester Midland' shape

960 Vase, large, with wide frilled top

961 Ink stand and cover

962 Dessert, 'Clifton' shape, scalloped

963 Cup and saucer, Old Derby, 'Conyngham' shape, two handled fluted cup, with very deep saucer

964 Vase, classical, with pointed handles 1 ft 2½ in.

965 Vase, plain, footed 6 in.

966 Sweet dish, 'Warwick' shape, oval, scalloped with embossing

967 Fern pot, heavily embossed

968 Menu L and S

969 Fern pot, hexagonal shape, heavily embossed

970 Bell

971 Vase, with wide base, narrow neck, and embossed top 9¾ in.

972 Vase, tall, with plain foot, fluted base and shoulders, and two small handles

973 Biscuit box, 'York' shape

974 Muffineer 3¼ in.

975 Muffineer 4 in.

976 Salad plate, crescent

977 Plant pot, with frilled top 6¾ in.

978 Marmalade, 'York' shape, stand 6½ in. wide

979 Honey and stand, 'York' shape

980 Egg basket

981 Butter and stand, 'York' shape

982 Hors d'oeuvres dish L 7 in. S 5 in.

983 Broth and stand, 'York' shape, two handled cup with cover, stand 6½ in. across

984 Covered muffin, 'York' shape

985 Sardine and stand, 'York' shape

986 Square ashtray

987 Broth and stand, 'Surrey' shape, with cover

988 Broth and stand, 'Vernon' shape, with cover, see 703

989

990 Porridge muller, 'Midland' shape

991 Mocha and saucer, 'Alford' shape, twisted flute

992 Mocha and saucer, 'Norwich' shape, plain

993 Tray, triple, with handle

994 Cruet

Royal Crown Derby vase of eggshell body decorated with a broad band of trellis roses with Sèvres style musical instruments and trophies, the whole on a pale turquoise ground. Royal Warrant mark for Queen Victoria, shape 1001. 13½ in. 1895.
Courtesy David John Ceramics

995 Dessert plate, 'Jenkinson Edinburgh' shape, twisted flute border

996 Vase, with wide base, narrow neck and fluted top L *1 ft*. M *9¾ in*. S *8 in*.

997 Vase, with embossed shoulder, two small handles, fluted top *6½ in*.

998 Vase, low, wide based, embossed

999 Vase, classical, with square foot, embossed base and shoulder, with domed cover *9½ in*.

1000 Vase, campana shape, with square foot and two handles *10½ in*.

1001 Vase, classical, with heavily embossed handles *1 ft 1½ in*. with cover

1002 Vase, plain, with embossed neck and top *9¼ in*.

1003 Asparagus tray, oblong

1004 Similar to 1001 but without cover *1 ft*

1005 Vase, classical, footed, with embossed handles and small cover *7 in*.

1006 Vase, urn shape, with two handles *5⅜ in*.

1007 Vase, large, plain, with embossed neck and top

1008 Box, round, with cover

1009 Box, round, with gadroon edge and cover L M and S

1010 As 1009 but heart shape, three sizes

1011 Dinnerware, 'Malvern' shape

1012 Lamp body, ovoid shape *5⅝ in*.

1013 Lamp body, with square foot and hexagonal body

1015 Lamp body, ovoid shape, with square foot and embossed shoulder

1016 Vase, plain, with embossed neck and top, and two small handles L *7¼ in*. S *5¾ in*.

1017 Ewer *5¾ in*.

1018 Slop pail, 'Midland Hotel'

1019 Vase, classical, with fluted foot, shoulder, two small handles, and domed cover *6¾ in*.

1020 Ewer, with inverted flute shoulder *7 in*.

1021 Vase, urn shape, footed *7¾ in*.

1022 Similar to 1021, fluted *7¾ in*.

1023 Puff box, with cover

1024 Teapot, 'York' shape, L M and S

1025 Cucumber tray, oblong

1026 Vase, small, with fluted top *3⅛ in*.

1027 Hairpin box, with cover *4⅛ in*. long

1028 Vase, globe shape with stopper *6½ in*.

1029 Vase, globe shape with fluted body and stopper *6½ in*.

1030 Bell *3½ in*.

1031 Vase, plain *4¼ in*.

1032 Vase, globe shape, with fluted neck and two small handles *4 in*.

1033 Vase, with cover, fluted *4 in*.

1034 Vase, fluted *3½ in*.

1035 Ewer, small, with embossed base and neck *4 in*.

1036 Vase, small, plain, with two handles *3¼ in*.

1037 Vase, globe shape, with two handles *3¾ in*.

1038 Similar to 1035 *4⅛ in*.

1039 Similar to 1036 *3¾ in*.

1040 Vase, plain, with cover and two small handles *3¾ in*.

1041 Vase, plain, with embossed handles and neck *4½ in*.

1042 Ewer, small *3⅞ in*.

1043 Vase, on pedestal, with embossed shoulder and domed cover *4¼ in*.

Very fine two-handled urn known as the Baroda
Jar, modelled by H. Warrington Hogg. Cobalt blue
and pink ground with raised and re-raised gilding
by Leroy, signed. c.1900.
Royal Crown Derby Museum

1044 Vase, plain, with frilled top 4¼ in.
1045 Vase, with base and shoulder ribbed, and
      two small handles 4¼ in.
1046 Box, plain, oblong
1047 Unidentified
1048 Vase, classical, ovoid body, and frilled
      top with cover 8 in.
1049 Similar to above 7 in.
1050 Vase, plain, with frilled top L 6¼ in.
      S 4¾ in., patterns 6299 and 1128
1051 Vase, urn shape, with cover 5½ in.
1052 Vase, urn shape, with ribbed base, no
      handles
1053 Similar to above but plain 6¾ in.
1054 Cow bell 4 in.
1055 Unidentified
1056 Teaware, 'Chester' shape, plain cup and
      saucer
1057 Pen tray, 'Fife' shape, small
1058 Ink stand and cover
1059 Box, small, with cover
1060 Vase, classical, with embossed foot,
      handles, shoulder and top 1 ft
1061 Vase, classical, with ribbed foot, neck
      and top, and embossed handles
      1 ft 0½ in.
1062 Jugs, 'Swansea' shape, fluted, with
      decorative handle, nine sizes
1063 Fern pot, hexagonal shape, embossed
      L 4 in. S 3½ in.
1064 Cup, 'Dorset' shape, with cover and
      two handles
1065 Cup, 'Sefton' shape, with cover and
      two handles
1066 Vase, classical, footed, with inverted
      flute shoulder, two small handles and

      domed cover 9¼ in.
1067 Vase, classical, with elaborate handles,
      domed cover and knob 1 ft
1068 Tray, 'Carlisle' shape
1069 Vase, classical, with cover 10 in.
1070 Dessert plate, 'Repton' shape
      Dessert comports, 'Repton' shape, tall,
      oval and shell
1071 Dessert plate, 'Ryde' shape
      Dessert comports, 'Ryde' shape, tall,
      oval and shell
1072 Dessert plate, 'Ashby' shape
      Dessert comports, 'Ashby' shape, tall,
      oval and shell
1073 Dessert plate, 'Chatham' shape
      Dessert comports, 'Chatham' shape,
      tall, oval and shell
1074 Tray, triple, scalloped
1075 Cruet, pepper, mustard and salt
1076 Sweet, 'Rouen' shape, with handle
1077 Luncheon tray, leaf shape, with
      acanthus handle
1078 Muffineer, 'Severn' shape 4 in.
1079 Vase, classical, with ribbed foot,
      acanthus base, narrow neck with two
      handles and scalloped top 1 ft 1 in.
1080 Bouillon cup and saucer, 'Dorset'
      shape, no cover
1081 Vase, classical, similar to 1079
1082 Egg stand, similar to 1075
1083 Vase, classical, footed, ovoid body,
      ornate handles and domed cover
1084 Vase, with embossed foot, handles,
      neck and top L S 8¾ in.
1085 Cup and saucer, 'Magnum' shape, with
      two twisted handles

The new Kedleston vase commemorating the connection between the Scarsdale family (one of the earliest and most famous of William Duesbury's customers) and Royal Crown Derby, produced in a limited collector's edition of 125, each numbered and authenticated by the signatures of Lord Scarsdale and a director of Royal Crown Derby. Shape 1134.

1086 Vase, footed, ovoid body, with two handles and domed cover
1087 Menu
1088 Menu
1089 Similar to 1079 *1 ft 1 in.*
1090 Vase, ovoid shape, with ribbed neck and two small handles *8½ in.*
1091 Fish plate
1092 Cruet, small, pepper, mustard and salt
1093 Similar to 1090, with plain neck *8 in.*
1094 Sweets, 'Rockingham' shape, heavily embossed, six sizes
1095 Vase, ewer shape, L *8½ in.* S *7 in.*
1096 Vase, with dolphin foot supporting, and cover *6½ in.*
1097 Vase, classical, with small embossed foot, slender embossed neck, and two handles *1 ft 0½ in.*
1098 Vase, globe shape, with heavily embossed shoulders and neck incorporating handles *6¾ in.*
1099 Jardinière, low, *4½ in.* high, *7¾ in.* wide
1100 Vase, same body, foot and handle as 1066, but with low cover *8½ in*
1101 Vase, plain, with heavily embossed neck, shoulder and top *9⅝ in.*
1102 Ink and fast stand
1103 Jardinière, round *11½ in.* across
1104 Sugar, 'Swansea' shape, to 1062
1105 Vase, globe shape, with wide neck and two handles *6¾ in.*
1106 Ewer, with broad base *6 in.*
1107 Vase, plain, with wide shoulder, inverted flutes, two small handles, scalloped neck *7⅜ in.*
1108 Ewer, with embossed handle *11 in.*
1109 Vase, with wide base and narrow neck incorporating two small handles *7¼ in.*
1110 Comb tray, embossed, length *1 ft 0¾ in.*
1111 Hair tidy, globe shape, cover with hole in centre *4½ in.*
1112 Box, globe shape, with cover and knob *5 in.*
1113 Tea caddy, same cover as 940 *4¼ in.*
1114 Urn, with cover, footed, with two handles, height *5¾ in.*
1115 Vase, classical, with ribbed foot and base, and domed cover, no handles *8¾ in.*
1116 Toilet ware, 'Midland Hotel, and St Pancras'
1117 Jar, with embossed shoulder and domed cover with knob *4⅞ in.*
1118 Ramekin, 'Midland Hotel' round ribbed dish
1119 Sweets, 'Bow' shape, diamond shape, embossed, six sizes
1120 Chocolate cup and saucer, 'Berlin' shape L and S coffee cup and saucer
1121 Sweet dish, leaf shape, with handle
1122 Fern pot
1123 Flower basket, small *4 in.* long, *3¾ in.* high
1124 Dish, leaf shape, footed
1125 Vase, cornucopia shape
1126 Flower bowl, footed, fluted, with embossed handle
1127 Jar, with cover, patterns 6299 and 1128
1128 Vase, plain, with small foot, embossed neck, domed cover and knob, two small handles L *10⅞ in.* S *9 in.*
1129 Dinner and tea plates, 'Bedford' shape

1130 Vase, ovoid shape, with small foot, heavily embossed neck, shoulder and top *1ft 0¾ in.*
1131 Similar to 1030, but with three handles at the shoulder
1132 Inkwell, small, with cover and stand
1133 Urn, with ornate foot, handles and domed cover *8 in.*
1134 Vase, swan necked
** Breakfast plate, 'Bristol' shape, 12 October 1896 *8 in.*
1135 Urn, with ornate foot, handles, inverted flute neck, and small domed cover *8½ in.*
1136 Menu, with rustic stand
1137 Coffee cup and saucer, 'Edinburgh' shape, plain
1138 Teapot stand, plain, square, with four ball feet
1139 Photograph frame *10¼ in.*
1140 Vase, classical, with embossed base and shoulder, two small handles, and flat cover
1141 Luncheon tray, triple, scalloped and with leaf handle
1142 Plates, (altered) with plain flat rim, 14 December 1896
1143 Teapot stand, square, with scalloped edge and four ball feet
Gadroon plates, altered for Crown Earthenware *8 in.* and *10 in.*
1144 Jardiniere L *14¾in.* long, *8 in.* high, S *9½ in.* long, *5¼ in.* high
1145 Fern pot *4¼ in.*
1146 Flower tube *6¾ in.*
1147 Vase, round, wide necked L *7½ in.* M *6¾ in.* S *5¾ in.*
1148 Basket, footed, L *7 in.* S *6½ in.*
1149 Dish, covered, oval
1150 Vase, with cover, small embossed feet and shoulder
1151 Fern pot, plain, with fluted top L *6 in.* M *5 in.* S *4 in.*
1152 Dessert plate, 'Empress' shape, oval dish, basket, and triple luncheon tray
1153 Dessert comports, 'Grosvenor' shape, oval, shell and diamond
1154 Urn, with cover *8½ in.*
New block, 'Clarence' shape, 26 March 1897 *10 in.*
New block, 'Rouen' shape, 26 March 1897 *8 in.*
New block, 'Brighton' shape, 26 March 1897 *8 in.*
New block, 'Surrey' shape, 26 March 1897 *8 in.*
1155 Vase, with embossed foot and neck incorporating two handles *10 in.*
1156 Cake stand, 'Midland'
1157 Vase, globe shape, with ornate neck and two handles *6¼ in.*
1158 Ewer L *8½ in.* S *7½ in.*
1159 Ewer *8 in.*
1160 Bon-bon dish, round, with cover *4¼ in.*
1161 Cover only
1162 Vase, ovoid shape, with embossed shoulder, two small handles, and fluted top L *8¼ in.* S *7⅛ in.*
1163 Dish, diamond shape, fluted and embossed L *9½ in.* S *8½ in.*
1164 Mirror frame, with embossed foliage style rim *1 ft 6 in.*

Vase and cover, shape 1239, with turquoise and white jewelling, raised gilding and painting by Leroy, shape F 498. Height 5¾ in. 1906.
Courtesy Sotheby's Belgravia

1165 Vase, with leaf shaped foot, wide base, embossed, fluted top *1 ft 1 in.*

1166 Vase, with small foot, embossed shoulder and combined handles *7¼ in.*

1167 Ink 1102 without stand

1168 Dessertware, 'Clarence' shape, modelled for Phillips, tall comport, low oval, round, square and shell comports

1169 Urn, with cover, on pedestal, with inverted flute shoulder, embossed handles, and knob *9¼ in.*

1170 Urn, with cover, small foot, embossed base, handles and knob *7¾ in.*

1171 Ewer, with rococo foot, embossed neck and incorporated handle *11 in.*

1172 Ewer, with embossed foot and neck, and plain spout *7 in.*

1173 Urn, with cover, small ribbed foot, embossed body, ribbed neck and cover with two small handles *6¾ in.*

1174 Vase, globe shape, with embossed shoulder, neck and handles *7¼ in.*

1175 Vase, classical, with embossed shoulder, foot and cover, and two small handles *11 in.*

1176 Similar to 1175 *10 in.*

1177 Vase, with broad base, four small feet, two small handles and domed cover *6 in.*

1178 Bottle, round, with pointed stopper *4¼ in.*, patterns 6299 and 1128, originally thrown and turned, but cast from February 1915

1179 Biscuit box, with three handles, pattern 895

1180 Feeding cup, 'Vernon' shape, breakfast cup with spout

1181 Dessert, 'Radnor' shape, modelled for Mitchell

1182 Inkpot, with cover, as 1132, but without tray

1183 As 1169 *8¼ in.*

Pair of Royal Crown Derby vases decorated in blue and white by W.E.J. Dean, but not signed. Much of this style of work was done by 'Billy' Dean but not all; other examples are to be seen in the Royal Crown Derby Museum painted by Remnant and Marples. Pattern 7412. 1905.
Courtesy M.K. Nielsen Antiques

1184 Measurements of plain plates as approved 23 November 1897

1185 Urn, with cover, and same knob as 1175

1186 Dessert, 'Hertford' shape, round tall comport, oval and oblong low comports

1187 Dishes, plain, remodelled December 1897

1188 Dessert, 'Anglesey' shape, oval comport and *10 in.* plate, twisted flute and embossed border

1189 Teacup and saucer, 'Cardiff' shape, similar to 1188 but with plain handle

1190 Basket, small, oblong, with twisted handle L *5½ in.* long S *4⅜ in.* long

1191 Ewer, with ribbed foot, shoulder and neck *4½ in.*

1192 Vase, with foot and neck as 1191, and two small scroll handles and domed cover *4½ in.*

1193 Vase, similar to 1166 *4½ in.*

1194 Ewer, similar to 1134 L *7½ in.* S *6 in.*

1195 Urn, with cover, globe shape, with embossed foot and handles, and domed cover

1196 Urn, with cover, similar to 1183 but with plain handles *4½ in.* boat shape

1197 Urn, with cover, ovoid shape, embossed as 1196 L *6 in.* S *4½ in.*

1198 Vase, similar to 1165 L *6 in.* S *4½ in.*

1199 Vase, similar to 1155 *4½ in.*

1200 Vase, similar to 1005 *4½ in.*

1201 Ewer, plain shape *4½ in.*

1202 Vase, campana shape, small *4½ in.*

1203 Cup, 'Rutland' shape, on oval fluted stand

1204 Bowl, with cover, on embossed foot, with leaf handles and knob

1205 Pepper, mustard and salt, 'Dover' shape, salt is as mustard but without cover

1206 Cup, on plain foot, with two embossed handles *3¾ in.*

1207 Mug, with three embossed handles *5½ in.*

1208 Dejeuner set, 'Dover' shape, teapot, open sugar, cream, tray and covered sugar, all small

1209 Dejeuner tray, 'Brighton' shape, large and small, large and small teapots, large and small creams, large sugar box, small open sugar

1210 Dessert plate and heart shaped comport, plain, Maple & Co. Patterns

1211 Vase, classical, footed, ovoid body with heavily embossed handles and cover with knob in the form of a bud *1 ft 2 in.*

A vase and cover shape 1419, cobalt blue and white with raised and flat gilding, panels of flowers by C. Gresley, signed. Height 8½ in. 1905. Also a pair of similar vases shape 1463 (see page 129) with panels of flowers, unsigned. Height 7 in. 1904.
Courtesy of Sotheby's Belgravia

1212 Vase, tall, with cover, embossed foot and handles L 1 ft. S 9½ in.

1213 Jardinière, oval, fluted

1214 Flower pot, fluted 7 in.

1215 Fern pot, fluted L and S

1216 Fern pot, hexagonal shape, with fluted top L 4⅜ in. S 3⅞ in.

1217 Jardinière, shape as 1216, L 7½ in. across top S 6½ in. across top

1218 Biscuit box, oval, cover with loop handle

1219 Loving cup, with embossed foot and three handles 7½ in.

1220 Box, with cover, plain, with four feet, two handles, and handle on cover

1221 Tazza, with small foot 2⅝ in. high, plain dish with two small handles

1222 Ink stand, for one or two pots

1223 Vase, campana shape 5¾ in.

1224 Vase, plain, footed, with two small handles and fluted top L 7¾ in. S 6¼ in.

1225 Stilton cheese stand and cover

1226 Cup, with cover and two handles 5½ in.

1227 Urn, small, globe shape, with two handles and domed cover 5½ in.

1228 Jardinière, with four leaf embossed feet and frilled top, as 1218 but without cover

1229 Fern pot, shape as 1228 L 4¼ in. S 3¾ in.

1230 Urn, campana shape, plain, with domed cover 6¼ in.

1231 Vase, with heavily embossed foot, base and handles, neck and top 1 ft 2 in.

1232 Vase, small, with angular handles, four feet and wide top, patterns 6299 and 1128

1233 Vase, classical, plain, with small twisted handles and cover

1236 Fern pot, with three feet and fluted top 4 in.

1237 Box, plain, with cover 5½ in.

1238 Base, with gadroon foot and top and two handles L 7½ in. S 5¾ in.

1239 Vase, footed, ovoid shape, two handles and conical cover 5¾ in.

1240 Pot-pourri vase, round, with plain foot, handles and domed cover

1241 Urn, with cover, leaf embossed foot and base, angular handles and inverted flute neck 9½ in.

1242 Ewer, with embossed foot and handle 8¾ in.

1243 Sweet dish, fluted, with four feet and two small handles

1244 Urn, with cover, small foot, and two small handles at shoulder 6¼ in.

1245 Vase, plain, with handles 4½ in.

Plate 42. Royal Crown Derby vase and cover, shape 1250, painted with flowers by Albert Gregory, signed. The gilding is amazing and brilliantly burnished. 11½ in. 1902. *Mr. I.T.M. St. George Collection*

Plate 43. Royal Crown Derby vase and cover decorated by A.F. Wood, signed, pattern 5355, shape 1114. 5¾ in. c.1910. *Private Collection*

Pair of vases, missing covers, shape 1282. Cobalt blue groundlay with rich raised and flat gilding. Panels of musical trophies and flowers by Leroy, signed. Height 9in.
George Woods Collection

1246 Urn, with embossed foot, handles from embossed shoulder, cover with knob 6½ in.

1247 Vase, globe shape, footed, with small handles and domed cover with leaf and bud knob 8 in.

1248 Vase, with plain foot, two small handles below embossed base, wide pierced top, and domed cover with embossed knob 11 in.

1249 Vase, classical, with plain foot, embossed base, two handles and cover with knob 9½ in.

1250 Urn, with cover, ovoid shape, with heavily embossed foot, handles and top, and pierced knob on cover 11½ in.

1251 Vase, classical, with embossed base, foot and cover, and two handles L 1 ft 6 in. S 1 ft 1 in.

1252 Spill vase, plain, with four small feet 4¼ in.

1253 Similar to 1247 10½ in.

1254 Butter tub, round, with fast stand

1255 Loving cup, with three handles 6½ in.

1256 Jugs, 'Jersey' shape, nine sizes, sugars three sizes

Gadroon dish, shape 1270. Painting
by J.P. Wale, signed. 1915.
Private Collection

1257 Urn, plain, with cover 6¼ in.
1258 Loving cup, with embossed foot,
handles and edge 9½ in.
1259 Vase, campana shape 7½ in.
1260 Vase, with straight sides and small foot
1261 Vase, campana shape 4½ in.
1262 Urn, plain, with cover, pattern 1128
5½ in.
1263 Vase, classical, with embossed foot,
handles and cover L 1 ft. S 10 in.
1264 Tea, breakfast and small coffee cups,
'Grafton' shape; 'Vernon' shape saucers
and other pieces go with this shape
1265 Urn, on elaborate foot, with embossed
handles and cover 10 in.
1266 Mug, Old Derby, 'Bacchus' shape
3¼ in.
1267 Vase, with embossed foot, handles and
part of neck, and plain top 9¾ in.
1268 Dish, oval, footed, with one handle
4¼ in. high 8¼ in. long
1269 Vase, globe shape, with two small
handles, domed cover with knob
L 10⅜ in. S 8¼ in.
1270 Dinnerware, 'Royal' shape
1271 Dessert plate, 'Eldon' shape, and oval,
shell, square and tall comports
1272 Dessert plate, 'Silver' shape, and round,
hexagonal and tall comports
1273 Sweet dishes, 'Silver' shape, six sizes
1274 Teaware, 'Silver' shape
1275 Dinnerware, 'Silver' shape

1276 Cup, two handles, same foot as 1257
4½ in.
1277 Urn, with embossed foot, two small
handles and conical cover 9½ in.
1278 As 1277 but with low cover 6½ in.
1279 As 1277 but without cover
1280 Vase, campana shape, with plain foot
and body, ornate handles, domed
cover with leaf and flower embossed
knob L 9 in. S 6¾ in.
1281 Cup, with stand, two handles, four
small feet and embossed rim
1282 Vase, classical, foot similar to 1279,
ovoid body with handles from slender
neck, and small cover L 11 in. S 9 in.
1283 Urn, plain, with cover, footed,
embossed handles and knob 6¼ in.
1284 Urn, 'Silver' shape, with embossed
foot and handles 4½ in.
1285 Two covers, 'Chelsea Derby' shape,
modelled for Mr Harding, St James,
London
1286 Urn, with cover, plain foot and body,
twist embossed handles, and knob
1287 Vase, classical, shape similar to 1251 9 in.
1288 Vase, campana shape, plain, with two
handles 5½ in.
1289 Vase, foot as 1279, plain body,
embossed handles from neck, and
domed cover with knob 8¼ in.
1290 Dessert plate, Rosenthal Aronson &
Co., London

Plate 44. Royal Crown Derby plate of 'Gadroon' shape painted with a full floral centre by Albert Gregory, signed, pattern 7490. 8¾ in. 1904.
Mr. and Mrs. W.H. Mordecai Collection

Pair of vases and covers, shape 1328. Dover green ground with floral sprays painted by W.E. Mosley, signed. Height 9in. 1904.
Private Colleciton

1291　Vase, Grecian, plain, two handles 7¼ in.
1292　Coffee pot and milk jug, 'Edinburgh' shape, plain shape
1293　Urn, with embossed foot, handles and cover with knob
1294　Similar to 1267 *8 in.* high
1295　Vase, ovoid body, small foot, handles and plain neck
1296　Vase, classical, with plain foot and body, embossed handles, and small cover with knob L *1 ft 3 in.* M *1 ft* S *9½ in.*
1297　Similar to 1296 L *1 ft 2 in.* S *11 in.*
1298　Vase, footed, with plain body and two small handles, domed cover with knob 7½ in.
1299　Similar to 1281, but fluted
1300　Similar to 1297 L *9 in.* S *7½ in.*
1301　Urn, with cover, plain foot and body, handles and cover with knob 5½ in.
1302　Vase, with plain foot and body, narrow neck with stopper, and embossed handles L *10 in.* S *9 in.*
1303　Dessertware, 'Royal' shape, oval and tall comports
1304　Coffee cup and saucer, 'Royal' shape, embossed edge

1305　Pastille burner, with embossed foot, mask corners and embossed cover 5½ in.
1306　Vase, with embossed foot and base, narrow neck, two handles and embossed top L *8½ in.* S *7½ in.*
1307　Vase, with small foot, plain body and embossed decoration
1308　Vase, plain, with small foot, embossed handles and cover L *9 in.* S *7¾ in.*
1309　Urn, with cover, embossed foot and handles and knob 5¼ in.
1310　Urn, with cover, embossed foot, fluted body, embossed handles and narrow neck with cover *7 in.*
1311　Tray, small, pierced L *6 in.* S *4½ in.*
1312　Vase, ovoid shape, small foot, embossed handles and cover 10¼ in.
1313　Dinnerware, 'Sheffield' shape
1314　Dessert plate, 'Napier' shape, embossed border, and oval, round and tall comports
1315　Vase, plain, with small foot, embossed neck and shoulder L *10 in.* S *8¼ in.*
1316　Vase, globe shape, with slightly embossed foot, base and shoulder, two leaf handles and domed cover with knob 9½ in.

'Emperor' vase, shape 1405 without cover, cobalt blue ground with raised gold decoration and solid gold handles. Flower sprays by W.E. Mosley, signed. 1904.
Courtesy Sotheby's Belgravia

Vase and cover, shape 1424. Dover green groundlay with raised and flat gilding. Floral inset by C. Gresley, signed. Height 6in. 1904.
Private Collection

1317 Vase, plain, with two handles and embossed neck and cover $9\frac{3}{8}$ in.

1318 Vase, with four small feet, plain body, two small handles from flower embossed top L *9 in.* S *7 in.*

1319 Vase, slender necked, with two handles and small foot $9\frac{1}{2}$ in.

1320 Similar to 1318 L *1 ft 8 in.* S *1 ft 3½ in.*

1321 Vase, ovoid shape, with embossed handles from slender neck and fluted top L *1 ft 0½ in.* S *10¼ in.*

1322 Jugs, 'Yacht' shape, plain shape, two sizes

1323 Teacup and saucer, 'Midland Hotel', plain shape

1324 Similar to 1321 L *10¾ in.* M *9 in.* S *7¼ in.*

1325 Bottle shape, with stopper

1326 Urn, with cover, narrow embossed base, curved handles to shoulder, and knob on cover *5¾ in.*

1327 Vase, globe shape, embossed neck and handles, and domed cover with knob *9 in.*

1328 Vase, urn shape, with embossed foot and base, handles and cover with knob *9 in.*

1329 Plate, 'Cromer' shape, scalloped *10 in.* Tea, dinner and breakfast sets, 'Yacht' shape

1330 Loving cup, with handles, plain, footed *5 in.*

1331 Coffee pot and cream, 'Bolton' shape

1332 Vase, plain, globe shape, pattern 1128 *4 in.*

1333 Vase, plain, with wide base, patterns 6299 and 1128 *4 in.*

1334 Vase, with wide base, narrow neck and two small handles *4½ in.*

1335 Vase, with wide base and narrow neck, patterns 6299 and 1128 *4¼ in.*

1336 Vase, globe shape, narrow neck *3¾ in.*

1337 Vase, globe shape, footed, with cover, pattern 1128 *4½ in.*

1338 Vase, plain, with fluted top, patterns 6229 and 1128 *4½ in.*

1339 Vase, plain, with small foot and domed cover with knob *4⅜ in.*

1340 Vase, globe shape, with short fluted neck *3¼ in.*

1341 Jar, plain with cover, pattern 1128 *4 in.*

1342 Vase, globe shape, with narrow neck *3½ in.*

1343 Similar to 1342 *4 in.*

1344 Vase, round, with two handles, patterns 6299 and 1128 *3 in.*

1345 Vase, plain, footed and with domed cover, pattern 1128 *4¼ in.*

1346 Vase, oval, with cover and knob *4½ in.*

1347 Teacup, 'Darley' shape, plain, low

1348 Teacup, 'Wallace' shape

1349 Vase, plain, footed, with two handles and embossed top *9¼ in.*

1350 Loving cup, footed, with two handles *4¾ in.*

Pair of heart-shaped vases with covers, shape 1465, pale green groundlay with painted floral sprays signed A.F. Wood. Height 5¾ in. 1904.
Private Collection

1351 Vase, with small foot, wide base, narrow twisted neck, fluted top, and handles entwining neck *11 in.*

1352 Jar, ovoid shape, domed cover with knob, two small handles *8 in.*

1353 Similar to 1349 L *7¼ in.* S *6 in.*

1354 Dessert plate, 'Russell' shape, pierced

1355 Similar to 1352 *6 in.*

1356 Cup and saucer, 'Apsley' shape, same cup and saucer as 'Duchess' shape

1357 Vase, with embossed feet continuing to base, plain body, embossed neck and fluted top, and embossed twisted flute handles L *1 ft 8½ in.* S *1 ft 4 in.*

1358 Cup, footed, with two handles *6½ in.*

1359 Similar to 1358 *6 in.*

1360 Similar to 1357 *11 in.*

1361 Magnum cup, 'Dorset' shape; 'Chester' breakfast cup handle and special saucer go with this cup

1362 Urn, tall, with cover, embossed foot, scroll handles, and plain cover with embossed knob *7 in.*

1363 Vase, classical, footed, with plain handles and small cover *8½ in.*

1364 Teacup and saucer, 'Granby' shape, low

1365 Teacup, 'Manners' shape, as 1364 but tall

1366 Teacup and saucer, 'Beaufort' shape, low

1367 Teacup, 'Somerset' shape, as 1366 but tall

1368 Dessert plate, 'Audley' shape, modelled for Goode

1369 Vase, classical, ovoid body, plain foot, narrow neck, embossed handles from shoulder to body, and small domed cover with knob L *1 ft 2½ in.* S *1 ft 0½ in.*

1370 Similar to 1284 but plain *5½ in.*

1371 Vase, globe shape, with cover, foot as 1370, two small handles, and domed cover *5½ in.*

1372 Dessert plate, 'Reading' shape, and square, oval, shell and tall comports

1373 Morning set, 'Dover' shape, teapot, sugar, cream, cup and saucer and stand

1374 Broth set, 'Dover' shape, broth, pepper, salt, bars, and stand modelled to broth *7 in.*

1375 Card basket, oval, on four small feet L *10¼ in.* long M *9¼ in.* long S *8⅜ in* long

1376 Urn, large, with cover, similar to 1362 *1 ft 0½ in.* long, *11½ in.* high

1377 Cup, with two handles, and saucer, 'Montreal' shape

1378 Dish, oval, with four feet *4 in.* high, *7½ in.* long

1379 Salad bowl, round, fluted, with two handles *4 in.* high

1380 Salad server handle *4 in.* long

1381 Teapot *4⅞ in.*

1382 Teapot *4½ in.*

1383 Biscuit box, with handles and cover with knob *6¼ in.*

1384 Biscuit box, with three handles and cover with knob *5⅞ in.*

1385 Tea caddy, with cover *4½ in.*

1386 Tea caddy, globe shape, with cover *3½ in.*

1387 Preserve, with cover, spoon hole in cover, and stand

1388 Honey pot, with spoon hole in cover $4\frac{1}{2}$ in.

1389 Salt $1\frac{1}{2}$ in.

1390 Pepper, with handle $2\frac{1}{8}$ in.

1391 Mustard, with handle $1\frac{7}{8}$ in.

1392 Cream $1\frac{1}{2}$ in.

1393 Sugar, open, to cream 1392 $1\frac{3}{4}$ in.

1394 Jug, with cover L $1\frac{1}{2}$ pints $6\frac{5}{8}$ in. M 1 pint $5\frac{7}{8}$ in. S $\frac{1}{2}$ pint $4\frac{7}{8}$ in.

1395 Ramekin and stand, American

1396 Terrapin and stand, with handle and cover

1397 Dessert plate, 'Ely' shape, with shell, oval and tall comports, height $2\frac{1}{2}$ in., round comport modelled for Phillips July 1912

1398 Nappie dish, 'Cromer' shape, $1\frac{3}{8}$ in.

1399 Nappie dish, 'Brighton' shape, $1\frac{3}{8}$ in.

1400 Loving cup, on tall foot, with three handles $8\frac{1}{2}$ in.

1401 Peacock, Old Derby $6\frac{1}{2}$ in.

1402 Vase, classical, footed, with two plain handles and small cover

1403 Vase, with small embossed foot, elaborate embossing on handles and neck, and fluted top L 1 ft 11 in. S 1 ft $6\frac{1}{2}$ in.

1404 Mug, plain, with two handles L $7\frac{1}{4}$ in. M $5\frac{1}{2}$ in. S $4\frac{1}{2}$ in.

1405 'Emperor' vase, campana shape, with square foot, embossed handles, and cover with embossed finial 1 ft 9 in.

1406 Tea and breakfast ware, 'Anson' shape

1407 Sugar and cream, 'Anson' shape

1408 Vase, campana shape, with embossed foot and handles and top, no cover 8 in.

1409 Urn, with cover, embossing on foot, handles and top $9\frac{1}{2}$ in.

1410 Vase, on round pedestal, with two small handles and small domed cover $8\frac{1}{4}$ in.

1411 Urn, with embossed feet, handles and cover $6\frac{1}{4}$ in.

1412 Coffee pot, plain

1413 Tray, triple, leaf shape, with handle 8 in.

1414 Vase, round, on embossed pedestal, with two small handles and cover $8\frac{1}{2}$ in.

1415 Vase, globe shape, footed, with two handles and cover 5 in.

1416 Cup, footed, with one or two handles $4\frac{1}{4}$ in.

1417 Cup, with two handles, on pedestal 7 in.

1418 Coffee cup and saucer and 8 in. plate, Army and Navy order for the 47th Regiment

1419 Urn, with cover, on tall foot, with two embossed handles and embossed knob on cover $8\frac{1}{2}$ in.

1420 Vase, campana shape, plain foot, embossed handles, cover with knob L $10\frac{1}{4}$ in. S $8\frac{1}{2}$ in.

1421 Bird, on scroll base 5 in.

1422 Peacock, tall, on scroll base 9 in.

1423 Bird, in birdcage, with scroll base 7 in.

1424 Vase, globe shape, with four small feet, twisted handles, embossed, and embossed cover 6 in.

1425 Vase, ovoid shape, with embossed shoulders, narrow neck, and plain top L 10 in. S $8\frac{1}{2}$ in.

1426 Vase, ovoid shape, with embossed neck and plain top L 10 in. S $8\frac{1}{4}$ in.

1427 Vase, globe shape, with embossed neck L 9 in. S $7\frac{1}{2}$ in.

1428 Vase, plain, with embossed neck and fluted top L 10 in. S $7\frac{1}{2}$ in.

1429 Vase, ovoid shape, with embossed neck and plain top L $8\frac{1}{2}$ in. S 7 in.

1430 Similar to 1426 but with fluted top L 11 in. S $9\frac{1}{2}$ in.

1431 Sweets, 'Alton' shape, four sizes

1432 Vase, plain $4\frac{1}{2}$ in.

1433 Vase, plain $4\frac{1}{4}$ in.

1434 Vase, plain, globe shape, with frilled top 4 in.

1435 Vase, plain, with broad base and narrow neck $4\frac{1}{4}$ in.

1436 Vase, plain $4\frac{1}{4}$ in.

1437 Vase, plain, with fluted shoulder $4\frac{1}{2}$ in.

1438 Figure, *Flower Girl*, with scroll base

1439 Figure, *Fruit Girl*, on scroll base

1440 Figure, *Wood Gatherer*, on round base

1441 Figure, *Fruit Gatherer*, on round base

1442 Vase, hexagonal shape, with domed cover and lion knob L 1 ft $0\frac{1}{4}$ in. M 10 in. S $8\frac{1}{4}$ in.

1443 Vase, hexagonal shape, no cover, pattern 1128 L 8 in. M $6\frac{1}{2}$ in. S $5\frac{1}{4}$ in.

1444 Vase, plain, with cover and lion knob, pattern 1128 L $11\frac{1}{2}$ in. M $9\frac{1}{2}$ in. S 8 in. and 7 7/10 in.

1445 Vase, plain L 8 in. M $6\frac{1}{2}$ in. S $5\frac{1}{4}$ in.

1446 Lion only, as on covers 1442 and 1444 $2\frac{1}{8}$ in.

1447 Rose bowl, footed, on fluted base, pattern 1128, three sizes

1448 Tray, small, oval, footed

1449 Vase, plain, patterns 6299 and 1128 $3\frac{1}{8}$ in.

1450 Vase, globe shape, patterns 6299 and 1128 $2\frac{3}{4}$ in.

1451 Vase, bottle shape, patterns 6299 and 1128 $3\frac{1}{4}$ in.

1452 Similar to above, patterns 6299 and 1128 3 in.

1453 Similar to 1451, patterns 6299 and 1128 $3\frac{1}{8}$ in.

1454 Vase, small, with frilled top, patterns 6299 and 1128 $2\frac{3}{4}$ in.

1455 Toy cup, saucer, plate, sugar and cream, 'Greek' shape, B and B

1456 Figure, *Mandolin Player* 6 in.

1457 Figure, *Singing Boy* 6 in.

1458 Vase, ovoid shape, similar to 1424 L 9 in. S 7 in.

1459 Cup, on pedestal, with two handles 6 in.

1460 Cup, small, footed, on pedestal $3\frac{3}{4}$ in.

1461 Vase, with cover and two small handles, on pedestal 7 in.

1462 Similar to 1461 $8\frac{1}{4}$ in.

1463 Urn, oval, with cover, on pedestal 7 in.

1464 Vase, with cover, two small handles, embossed knob and cover, on pedestal L 1 ft 2 in. S $11\frac{1}{2}$ in.

1465 Vase, ovoid shape, with four small feet, two embossed handles and cover $5\frac{3}{4}$ in.

1466 Bowl, modelled for R. E. Daniell L 9 in. S 7 in.

1467 Vase, on embossed foot, with small cover and embossed knob, and two handles L 1 ft 2 in. S $11\frac{1}{2}$ in.

1468 Vase, ovoid shape, with small embossed foot, handles from narrow neck and fluted top 1 ft $3\frac{1}{2}$ in.

1469 Vase, plain, bottle shape, with two small handles and frilled top $7\frac{1}{4}$ in.

Royal Crown Derby vase and cover with pale green groundlay and natural flowers painted and **signed** by Albert Gregory, shape 1462. 8½ in. 1904.
Courtesy M.K. Nielsen Antiques

Talbot shaped plate, painted with a view of Chatsworth, signed C. Gresley. c.1920.
Private Collection

Group of toys: saucepan 2½ in., iron and stand 1¾ in., watering can 3 in. pattern 6299, shapes 1673, 1681, 1478. Vases 1½ in., pattern 1128, shapes 1497 and 1498. Dates 1910, 1911, 1913 and 1932.
Private Collection

1470 Vase, plain, footed, with embossed handles, neck and knob on cover 6 in.

1471 As 1467 1 ft 5½ in.

1472 Vase, on embossed foot, with handles and embossed knob on cover 7 in.

1473 Tea and breakfast cups, plain, 'Wigmore' shape, modelled for Daniell and Son

1474 Vase, campana shape, with two small handles and foot, patterns 6299 and 1128 3¾ in.

1475 Dessert plate and comports, 'Stanhope' shape

1476 Toy coal scuttle, helmet shape, pattern 6299 2¾ in.

1477 Coal bucket, pattern 6299 2½ in.

1478 Watering can, pattern 6299 3 in.

1479 Kettle, pattern 6299 2½ in.

1480 Cauldron, pattern 6299 2⅝ in.

1481 Dinnerware, 'Ely' shape

1482 Vase, footed, with cover and two small handles 5¼ in.

1483 Similar to 1482 6¾ in.

1484 Similar to 1482 7 in.

1485 Similar to 1482 6 in.

1486 Ewer, footed 5¾ in.

1487 Vase, footed, with conical cover 7 in.

1488 Pastille burner, same body, foot and knob as 1305, but with plain cover 5¼ in.

1489 Vase, round, with slight embossing, patterns 6299 and 1128 3 in.

1490 Ewer 2½ in. high, and basin 3⅛ in. wide

1491 Teapot 2⅛ in. high

1492 Vase, classical, embossed foot, with handles from neck to body and domed cover L 1 ft 5½ in. S 1 ft 0½ in.

1493 Ewer, as 1486 8¾ in. *high*

1494 Toy mug, pattern 6299 1½ in.

1495 Toy tea caddy, pattern 6299 1½ in. high

1496 Toy teapot, sugar box and cream, 'Dublin' shape

1497 Toy vase, globe shape, with thin neck, patterns 6299 and 1128 2⅜ in.

1498 Vase, globe shape, patterns 6299 and 1128 1½ in.

1499 Similar to 1498 but with wider neck, patterns 6299 and 1128 1½ in.

1500 Dinner plate, scalloped, modelled for Army and Navy Stores

1501 Vase, campana shape, with beading on foot and base, and top L 5 in. S 4 in.

1502 Spill vase, with four small feet and beading on body, patterns 6299 and 1128 2½ in.

1503 Urn, ovoid shape, with embossed foot, handles and tall conical cover

1504 Vase, classical, similar to 1493 8 in.

1505 Vase, similar to 1482 6½ in.

1506 Vase, similar to 1470 7¼ in.

1507 Service plate, 'Ely' shape, with scalloped edge

1508 Service plate, 'Marlborough' shape, with embossed border

1509 Jardinière, modelled for Jenner & Co., Edinburgh, moulds sent to Jenner's

1510 Bedroom set, 'Dover' shape, jug, candlestick, matchbox and tray

1511 Vase, campana shape, patterns 6299 and 1128 3 in.

1512 Vase, similar to 1511 but with beading, patterns 6299 and 1128 2¾ in.

1513 Unidentified

Watercolour by W.E. Mosley.
Private Collection

1514 Loving cup, footed, with two handles, patterns 6299 and 1128
1515 Teacup and saucer, 'Ferrers' shape
1516 Jug, 'Belmont' shape, with cover L $1\frac{1}{2}$ *pints* M *1 pint* S $\frac{1}{2}$ *pint*
1517 Honey pot, 'Belmont' shape, with spoon hole in cover, and stand $5\frac{1}{4}$ *in.*
1518 Vase, similar to 1504 $10\frac{1}{4}$ *in.*
1519 Urn, round, with small embossed foot, handles and cover with knob
1520 Vase, campana shape, patterns 6299 and 1128 L *5 in.* S $4\frac{1}{8}$ *in.*
1521 Vase, hexagonal shape, on three round feet, pattern 6299 L $4\frac{5}{8}$ *in.* S $3\frac{1}{2}$ *in.*
1522 Vase, hexagonal shape, with round frilled top, and tripod foot, patterns 6299 and 1128 $3\frac{3}{4}$ *in.*
1523 Similar to 1519, but plain and without cover, patterns 6299 and 1128 $4\frac{1}{8}$ *in.*
1524 Vase, round, with frilled top and three small feet, patterns 6299 and 1128
1525 Vase, campana shape, with small foot, wide top and two small handles $2\frac{7}{8}$ *in.*
1526 Vase, with flat base, waisted with fluted edge, patterns 6299 and 1128 $3\frac{3}{4}$ *in.*
1527 Dinner- and teaware, 'Dover' shape
1528 Vase, globe shape, on three supports from square base, patterns 6299 and 1128 $4\frac{1}{8}$ *in.*
1529 Cup and saucer, 'Walmer' shape, as 'Dover' but with low cup
1530 Vase, classical, with embossed foot, handles and neck, and frilled top L $12\frac{3}{4}$ *in.* S $10\frac{1}{8}$ *in.*
1531 Vase, similar to 1518 L *1 ft* $1\frac{1}{4}$ *in.* S $10\frac{1}{2}$ *in.*
1532
1533 Vase, with heavily embossed foot, handles and narrow neck, and frilled top $11\frac{1}{2}$ *in.*
1534 Teapots, 'Belmont' shape, round, five sizes
1535 Ink well and cover, round $2\frac{3}{8}$ *in.*
1536 Plate, 'Lowestoft' shape, modelled for Army and Navy Stores
1537 Comports, 'Bow' shape, round and shell, see 947
1538 Card baskets, $2\frac{3}{4}$ *in.* high $11\frac{1}{2}$ *in.* long, see 1375 for other sizes
1539 Vase, classical, with plain foot, embossed base, shoulder and handles, and small cover with knob $9\frac{1}{4}$ *in.*
1540 Cup and saucer, new 'Globe' shape, similar to old but with well in saucer
1541 Dinnerware, 'Stanhope' shape, see 1475 for dessertware
1542 Coffee cup and saucer, 'Stanhope' shape, waisted cup with embossed edge
1535 Vase, classical, with octagonal foot, embossed base, neck and handles, small embossed cover with knob L *1 ft* $3\frac{3}{4}$ *in.* S $11\frac{1}{4}$ *in.*
1544 Vase, with round embossed foot, wide neck narrowing to small cover with knob, and scroll embossed handles L *1 ft* $2\frac{1}{2}$ *in.* S $10\frac{3}{4}$ *in.*
1545 Vase, round, with scallop edge, resting on scroll supports from embossed base $6\frac{1}{8}$ *in.*
1546 Fern pot, round or oval with inverted flutes $3\frac{3}{4}$ *in.*
1547 Vase, round, with two small handles and wide neck L *6 in.* S $4\frac{5}{8}$ *in.*
1548 Vase, hexagonal shape, with small foot, two small handles, narrow neck with wider frilled edge
1549 Vase, round, with frilled top $4\frac{1}{2}$ *in.*
1550 Jar, with cover, rounded hexagonal shape, patterns 6290 and 1128 L $8\frac{1}{2}$ *in.* S $6\frac{7}{8}$ *in.*
1551 Vase, with small round foot, embossed handles and cover *6 in.*
1552 Vase, with round foot and domed cover, and two embossed handles L $7\frac{3}{4}$ *in.* S $6\frac{1}{4}$ *in.*

'Brighton' dessert plate from the special productions (see card no. 9, plate 54) with raised and flat gold edge. Central figure subjects by Taillandier. 1894. It is interesting to note that this is probably one of the first pieces painted by the artist, although not signed, on his arrival from Coalport. *Private Collection*

1553 Vase, on four scroll feet with foliate embossing, patterns 6299 and 1128 L 6⅝ in. S 5⅛ in.

1554 Vase, plain, with pointed base and three supports to foot 5⅝ in.

1555 Fern pot, with four scroll feet and leaf shaped handles 3⅞ in.

1556 Jardinière, with embossed feet and scroll handles L 1 ft 2 in. S 11½ in.

1557 Figure, *Buy a broom*, 6 in.

1558 Creams, 'Belmont' shape, hexagonal shape, waisted, four sizes

1559 Vase, with narrow base, wider shoulder and frilled top 1 ft

1560 Vase, with hexagonal foot, oriental style handles and cover 1 ft 1½ in.

1561 Vase, with hexagonal foot and wide frilled top 1 ft 0½ in.

1562 Vase, 'Warwick' shape style, footed, with twisted ribbed handles, and cover with pineapple knob 1 ft 0½ in.

1563 Jar, narrow at the base and neck, with wide shoulder, embossed neck and cover 1 ft 4½ in.

1564 Soup plate, special 7 in., modelled for Burley

1565 Box, round, with cover, patterns 6299 and 1128 2¼ in.

1566 Tea and breakfast sets, 'Wilton' shape, plain with plain handle

1567 Comports, 'Bourbon' shape, tall, oval, square and shell

1568 Vase, with embossed foot, handles, neck and conical cover 10¼ in.

1569 Trinket set, 'Craven' shape, comb tray, powder box, pomade box, matchbox, pin tray, ring stand, candlestick and pen tray

1570 Trinket set, 'Dulcie' shape, number of pieces as 1569

1571 Fern pot, with four scroll feet and frilled top L 4½ in. S 4 in.

Service plate, one of a limited edition of twenty-four presented to Derby County Football Club by the Mayor and Corporation of Derby to commemorate their winning the F.A. cup Final in 1946. *Royal Crown Derby Museum*

1572 Jardinière, shape as 1571 *6 in.* long 2¾ *in.* high

1573 Inkwell, with four dolphins, one at each corner, and another as knob on cover *3½ in.*

1574 Plates, with embossed border with four medallions, *10 in.*, *9 in.*, *8 in.* and *6 in.*

1575 Dish, oval, with embossed handles and edge, on four scroll supports from octagonal base *5¼ in.* high

1576 Dish, small, round, with fluted top and three supports with claw feet *4 in.* high

1577 Vase, with round base, four supports to body, embossed handles and fluted top *6½ in.*

1578 Vase, globe shape, on embossed pillar and with beaded cover and knob *8¾ in.*

1579 Vase, campana shape, with three supports to triangular base, and cover with foliate knob *6½ in.*

1580 Vase, shape as 1579, with frilled top but no cover *5¾ in.*

1581 Dish, boar shape, on pedestal *5¼ in.*

1582 Vase, round, with cover, and four scroll feet and knob *3½ in.*

1583 Vase, with cover, on four small feet, pattern 6299 *4½ in.*

1584 Vase, round, with cover, four scroll feet and knob *3½ in.*

1585 Box, plain, round, with cover, foliate feet and knob $3\frac{1}{2}$ *in.*
1586 Urn, with cover, on pedestal 5 *in.*
1587 Box, hexagonal shape, with cover, small base, wide top and embossed knob, patterns 6299 and 1128 4 *in.*
1588 Tea and breakfast cup, 'Percy' shape, plain, low, with plain handle
1589 Tea and breakfast cup, 'Lennox' shape, tall, with straight sides and plain handle
1590 Candlestick, with four dolphins on base 10 *in.*
1591 Vase, hexagonal shape, with narrow neck and fluted top L 10 *in.* S $6\frac{1}{2}$ *in.*
1592 Vase, with cover, hexagonal, no foot L $9\frac{1}{2}$ *in.* S 8 *in.*
1593 Vase, with cover, hexagonal shape, footed L $10\frac{1}{2}$ *in*, S $8\frac{1}{4}$ *in.*
1594 Vase, with small round foot, and embossed scroll handles from shoulder, and plain top 7 *in.*
1595 Vase, plain, footed, with wide top $5\frac{1}{2}$ *in.*
1596 Vase, similar to 1595 $7\frac{1}{4}$ *in.*
1597 Vase, shape as 1502, patterns 6299 and 1128 $6\frac{1}{2}$ *in.*
1598 Urn, with cover, boat shape, with square embossed foot, handles and edge of conical cover 1 *ft* 2 *in.*
1599 Urn, with cover, shape as 1598 1 *ft* $6\frac{1}{4}$ *in.*
1600 Card basket, oval, plain, with two small handles
1601 Ink stand, with two covered inkwells, shape as 1535
1602 Pot-pourri, globe shape, with pierced cover, patterns 6299 and 1128 $3\frac{7}{8}$ *in.*
1603 Pieces, plain, modelled, plates, soups, salad plates, bakers, oval dishes, gravy boats, fish dishes, round chop dishes, fruit saucers
1604 Vase, shape similar to 1543 L 1 *ft* 3 *in.* S $11\frac{1}{4}$ *in.*
1605 Cake stand, fluted, modelled for Clarnico
1606 Magnum cup and saucer, 'Carlton' shape, plain
1607 Plate, 10 *in.*, 'Egginton' shape, modelled for Soane & Smith
1608 Vase, similar to 1484 L 1 *ft* 6 *in.* S 1 *ft* $0\frac{1}{2}$ *in.*
1609 Coffee can and saucer, 'Stirling' shape, straight sides with plain handle
1610 Dejeuner tray, 'Belmont' shape, scalloped edge with embossed handles
1611 Plaque, round, made for Army and Navy Stores, $10\frac{3}{8}$ *in.* wide $1\frac{3}{4}$ *in.* deep
1612 Dessert plate, scalloped, modelled for Goode & Co.
1613 Plates and comports, 'Lowestoft' shape, tall and low
1614 Teacup, 'Elgin' shape, low, with handle curving above rim
1615 Vase, angular, hexagonal shape L $4\frac{7}{8}$ *in.* S $4\frac{3}{8}$ *in.*
1616 Vase, square, plain 6 *in.*
1617 Vase, square, footed 6 *in.*
1618 Vase, hexagonal bottle shape L 1 *ft* $3\frac{1}{2}$ *in.* M 1 *ft* $1\frac{1}{2}$ *in.* S $11\frac{3}{4}$ *in.*
1619 Jar, small, square 4 *in.*
1620 Jar, small, hexagonal shape L $7\frac{3}{4}$ *in.* M $6\frac{1}{2}$ *in.* S $5\frac{1}{2}$ *in.*
1621 Pot-pourri, hexagonal shape similar to 1602, patterns 6299 and 1128 $4\frac{3}{4}$ *in.*
1622 Vase, rounded hexagonal shape L $6\frac{1}{8}$ *in.* S 5 *in.*
1623 Vase, square, with concave neck $5\frac{3}{4}$ *in.*
1624 Vase, square, with convex base $7\frac{1}{2}$ *in.*
1625 Lining, for Gowans Kent & Co.
1626 Fern pot, with two small scroll handles $6\frac{1}{4}$ *in.*
1627 Vase, round L 6 *in.* M $5\frac{1}{4}$ *in.* S $4\frac{1}{2}$ *in.*
1628 Vase, round, shallow, with fluted top, pattern 6299 $4\frac{1}{4}$ *in.*
1629 Vase, round, with wide fluted top, pattern 6299 $4\frac{1}{2}$ *in.*
1630 Toast rack, five bars
1631 Powder bowl, with embossed knob and four small feet $4\frac{1}{2}$ *in.*
1632 Vase, classical, with two handles and cover L $10\frac{3}{4}$ *in.* S $8\frac{3}{4}$ *in.*
1633 Dessert plate, 'Talbot' shape, with acorn motif border, square, oval, round and tall comports
1634 Teacup and saucer, remodelled 'Bradford' shape, with twisted flute base and plain border
1635 Dessert plate, 'Lovat' shape, coupe shape with scalloped edge
1636 Vase with cover $9\frac{1}{2}$ *in.*, abandoned in favour of 1643 S
1637 Urn, with cover, footed, with two foliate handles and knob on cover $6\frac{3}{4}$ *in.*
1638 Vase, with cover $7\frac{3}{4}$ *in.*, abandoned in favour of 1643 S
1639 Vase, with cover 7 *in.*, abandoned in favour of 1644 S
1640 Vase, with foliate scroll foot, two handles from shoulder to top cover with embossed knob $9\frac{1}{2}$ *in.*
1641 Fern pot, with scroll embossed base and fluted edge $4\frac{1}{2}$ *in.*
1642 Vase, shape as 1642 6 *in.*
1643 Vase, globe shape, on embossed foot, with foliate handles and knob on cover L $9\frac{1}{2}$ *in.* S $7\frac{3}{4}$ *in.*
1644 Urn, with cover, embossed foot, foliate handles and knob on cover L $9\frac{1}{2}$ *in.* S $7\frac{3}{4}$ *in.*
1645 Vase, footed, with embossed handles from wide shoulder to narrow neck, domed cover with foliate knob 9 *in.*
1646 Vase, campana shape, with ringed foot, leaf embossed base and top, scroll handles, and domed cover with knob $9\frac{1}{2}$ *in.*
1647 Vase, with embossed foot, handles and knob on cover, plain body 1 *ft* $1\frac{1}{2}$ *in.*
1648 Vase, large, round, heavily embossed with twisted ribbed handles $8\frac{1}{4}$ *in.*
1649 Vase, plain, goblet shape L $5\frac{1}{4}$ *in.* S $4\frac{3}{8}$ *in.*
1650 Loving cup, plain, footed, with two handles $5\frac{1}{4}$ *in.*
1651 Vase, campana shape, with plain foot and two small handles $6\frac{3}{8}$ *in.*
1652 Vase, similar to 1651 but with larger scroll handles $4\frac{1}{2}$ *in.*
1653 Ink stand, square, heavily embossed, modelled for General Navy $7\frac{1}{4}$ *in.*
1654 Casket, shape similar to 1653, and cover with heavily embossed knob $8\frac{1}{4}$ *in.* high, foot $11\frac{1}{4}$ *in.*, top 9 *in.*
1655 Soup, 'Savoy' shape, plain, round, height $1\frac{3}{8}$ *in.*, top $7\frac{1}{2}$ *in.*, foot $5\frac{1}{8}$ *in.*
1656 Powder bowl, similar to 1631 but with larger knob

Royal Crown Derby vase and cover decorated with pattern 6299, shape 1646. 1912.
David Holborough Collection

1657 Urn, with cover, two small handles and embossed knob on cover 6¼ in.

1658 Vase, with small foot, two embossed handles from shoulder to edge 7¼ in.

1659 Bowl, on claw feet with lion head masques L and S

1660 Vase, with embossed foot, neck, handles and conical cover 1 ft 2½ in.

1661 Vase, globe shape, on round embossed foot, with two scroll handles from narrow neck, and knob on domed cover 10 in.

1662 Jar, with cover, four claw feet, two lion head masques, and domed cover L 10 in. S 7½ in.

1663 Vase, with foliate foot, ovoid body and frilled edge 6¾ in.

1664 Vase, shape as 1663 4¾ in.

1665 Dinnerware, 'Selby' shape, plain

1666 Dessert set, 'Romney' shape, rounded octagonal shape plate with reeded border, oval, square and tall comports

1667 Tray, triple, 'Romney' shape

1668 Sweets, 'Romney' shape, round, three sizes

1669 Sweets, 'Romney' shape, oblong, three sizes

1670 Tray, four scallop shape, 7 in. long, 5½ in. wide

Small covered urn, shape 1657, cobalt blue ground with raised gilt panel containing floral decoration by G. Jessop. Height 6in. 1919. *Private Collection*

1671 Dish, round, with small foot and two small handles 4 in. high 6 in. across top
1672 Toy milk churn 2½ in.
1673 Toy saucepan 2 in.
1674 Toy fish kettle 1¾ in.
1675 Toy coffee pot 3 in.
1676 Tray, oval 3 in. long
1677 Tray, oblong 3 in. long
1678 Toy basket, scalloped 1½ in.
1679 Toy basket, oblong 1¾ in. long
1680 Toy tray, triple, 2½ in. long
1681 Toy iron and stand 1¾ in.
1682 Plates 10 in., 8 in., 7 in. and 5 in., and small coffee cup and saucer, with four embossed medallions on border, modelled for Tiffany & Co.
1683 Tray, oval scalloped, modelled for Stonier, Liverpool 8½ in. long
1684 Teacup and saucer, 'Ripon' shape, low, plain
1685 Card baskets, 'Talbot' shape, square and oval L M and S
1686 Salad bowl, round, with small foot
1687 Salad bowl, round, with small foot and embossed edge of foot and top
1688 Toy teapot, sugar box and cream, 'Greek' shape

1689 Mug, with one embossed handle L 4½ in. M 3¾ in. S 3 in.
1690 B and B, old, square, remodelled April 1912
1691 Vase, with embossed foot and neck, handles and knob on domed cover 10 in.
1692 Unidentified, but modelled for Wiley & Co.
1693 Can and saucer, 'Dawney' shape, plain
1694 Dinner- and teaware, 'Talbot' shape, oak leaf embossed edge
1695 Dinnerware, 'March' shape, as 'Ely' shape but foot and cover edges plain
1696 Dinnerware, 'Herga' shape, as 'Selby'
1697 Vase, embossed foot, with two small handles and edge L 9 in. S 7 in.
1698 Vase, campana shape, footed, with foliate embossed handles and edge L 8½ in. S 7 in.
1699 Vase, with heavily embossed foot, handles, shoulder and top 10½ in.
1700 Vase, inverted pear shape, on embossed foot, with twisted foliate handles L 9½ in. S 7¼ in.

'Talbot' card basket, shape 1685.
Landscape by J.P. Wale, signed.
1914.
Private Collection

Royal Crown Derby pair of unusual
shaped vases painted, but not
signed, by Albert Gregory. Incised
shape 1705. 6¾ in. 1916.
*Mr. and Mrs. W.L.C. Prosser
Collection*

Royal Crown Derby pair of vases
painted and signed by Albert
Gregory. Shape 1719 incised. 6in.
Mr. and Mrs. W.L.C. Prosser
Collection

1701 Vase, similar to 'Warwick' shape
6½ in.
1702 Jar, globe shape, with cover, patterns
6299 and 1128 5 in.
1703 Vase, slender bottle shape with
embossed neck L 7¾ in. S 6¼ in.
1704 Vase, bottle shape with narrow neck
and wide fluted top, patterns 6299 and
1128 7¼ in.
1705 Vase, with wide top and four foliate
embossed feet L 6¾ in. S 5¼ in.
1706 Jar, hexagonal shape, with cover,
patterns 6299 and 1128 7 in.
1707 Vase, hexagonal shape, with cover, and
two small handles and knob, patterns
S only 6299 L 8 in. S 6⅞ in.
1708 Vase, shape as 1706, patterns 6299 and
1128 6 in.
1709 Vase, globe shape, with narrow neck,
patterns 6299 and 1128 5½ in.
1710 Cream jug, with 'Montreal' shape
handle
1711 Vase, footed, with embossed handles
incorporated in neck 4⅝ in.
1712 Vase, footed, with wide embossed top
4 in.
1713 Vase, globe shape, footed 3½ in.
1714 Vase, similar to 1697, but without
handles 4⅛ in.
1715 Loving cup, with two handles 3¾ in.
1716 Vase, as 1714 3⅞ in.

1717 Vase, plain, slender, with two
handles
1718 Vase, footed, with two handles at
shoulder, and wide top
1719 Vase, similar to 1718 6 in.
1720 Vase, round, footed, with embossed
shoulder and top 4½ in.
1721 Vase, ovoid shape, with embossed foot
and neck 5¾ in.
1722 Vase, round, heavily embossed, footed,
with two handles 5½ in.
1723 Vase, footed, with foliate embossed
base, handles, narrow neck and top
6¾ in.
1724 Vase, with cover, footed, foliate
embossed base, ribbed domed cover
with conical knob 6 in.
1725 Vase, with cover, footed, similar to
1724 6¼ in.
1726 Vase, ovoid shape, with embossed foot
and base, and pierced neck 4¾ in.
1727 Vase, with small foot, plain body with
beaded shoulder and scroll edge 4½ in.
1728 Vase, shaped as loving cup with
embossed handles rising from the edge
5 in.
1729 Vase, globe shape, footed, with curved
foliate handles and pierced top 4 in.
1730 Vase, footed, with plain body and scroll
handles at wide top 6¾ in.

Plate 45. Royal Crown Derby
covered campana shaped vase,
painted and signed by Albert
Gregory, with flowers on both sides.
Shape 1250. 11½ in. 1902.
Mr. and Mrs. Peter Budd Collection

Plate 46. Royal Crown Derby
loving cup and stand, shape 1281,
pattern 7204, painted with flowers
by Cuthbert Gresley and signed.
5½ in. 1903.
Mr. and Mrs. W.H. Mordecai
Collection

Royal Crown Derby vase and cover, solid gold masque handles, cobalt blue ground, with floral panel by Albert Gregory. Signed. Height 13in. 1920.
Collection of Edward Knapper (deceased)

1731 Vase, embossed on foot and shoulder, with ribbed domed cover 6¼ *in.*

1732 Vase, shape as 1726 but without foot, patterns 6299 and 1128 4¼ *in.*

1733 Vase, bottle shape, embossed at edge, patterns 6299 and 1128 4½ *in.*

1734 Vase, plain, with small foot and wide top, patterns 6299 and 1128 3½ *in.*

1735 Vase, globe shape, patterns 6299 and 1128 3½ *in.*

1736 Vase, with four small foliate feet and fluted edge, patterns 6299 and 1128 3¾ *in.*

1737 Vase, with small foot and wide pierced neck, patterns 6299 and 1128 3⅜ *in.*

1738 Ice pail and liner, with two handles on base and twisted leaf handle on cover 10½ *in.*

1739 Pot-pourri jar, globe shape, patterns 6299 and 1128 3½ *in.*

1740 Vase, round, with four embossed corners at shoulder, patterns 6299 and 1128 3½ *in.*

1741 Pot-pourri jar, globe shape, with domed cover and knob, patterns 6299 and 1128 L 5 *in.* S 4 *in.*

1742 Pot-pourri jar, same body as 1386 3½ *in.*

1743 Bon-bon box, round, with flat cover, patterns 6299 and 1128 2⅝ *in.*

1744 Bon-bon box, oval, with flat cover, patterns 6299 and 1128 2½ *in.*

1745 Sweetmeat box, round, with cover and knob, patterns 6299 and 1128 3 *in.*

1746 Bowls, octagonal shape, patterns 6299 and 1128 5 *in.*, 6 *in.*, 7½ *in.*, 9 *in.*, 1 *ft*

1747 Sardine box, rectangular, with embossed knob on cover

1748 Teacup and saucer, 'Wirksworth' shape, tall cup with embossed edge and scroll edge, saucer matching

Yellow-ground cup and saucer, reproduction of a Nottingham Road pattern, with Dovedale landscape by Edwin Trowell. 1884.

1749 Teapots, 'Severn' shape, rounded hexagonal shape, two sizes, coffee pots two sizes, biscuit box, honey pot, dejeuner tray, hot milk jug
1750 Teaware, 'Thames' shape, tall teacup, with scalloped edge and plain handle, matching saucer
1751 Teaware, 'Walton' shape, shape as 1750 but with low teacup
1752 Box, rounded octagonal shape, with flat cover
1753 Box, oval octagonal shape, with flat cover
1754 Cigarette box, oblong octagonal shape
1755 Vase, with square foot, beaded base and shoulder, two scroll handles, plain wide top, patterns 6299 and 1128 L *6 in.* S 4⅞ *in.*
1756 Vase, with beaded foot and top, two small handles, scalloped edge, patterns 6299 and 1128 L 5¾ *in.* S 4⅝ *in.*
1757 Vase, shape similar to 1755 but without handles, patterns 6299 and 1128 L *5 in.* S 4⅛ *in.*
1758 Spill vase, with foliate embossed edging, patterns 6299 and 1128 L 5⅝ *in.* S 4½ *in.*
1759 Spill vase, beaded, with plain top, patterns 6299 and 1128 L 5¾ *in.* S 4½ *in.*
1760 Vase, with square foot, reeded base, two small handles at shoulder, and plain top
1761 Vase, inverted pear shape, on square foot, with cover and knob, patterns 6299 and 1128 6½ *in.*
1762 Vase, with plain round foot, two small handles and wide top, patterns 6299 and 1128 5¾ *in.*
1763 Vase, campana shape, without handles, with beading on foot and edge, patterns 6299 and 1128 L *5 in.* S 4¼ *in.*
1764 Cigarette box, round, with flat cover 3½ *in.*
1765 Cigarette box, octagonal shape, with flat cover 3½ *in.*
1766 Sugar caster, hexagonal shape *6 in.*
1767 Pepper caster, shape as 1766 3⅜ *in.*
1768 Tea caddy, shape as 1766 5¾ *in.*
1769 Drinking horn, 466 remodelled and numbered, October 1916 3½ *in.*
1770 Powder bowl, round, footed, with cover and knob 4¾ *in.*
1771 Vase, rounded hexagonal shape with scalloped top, patterns 6299 and 1128 2½ *in.*
1772 Vase, plain, patterns 6299 and 1128 2½ *in.*
1773 Vase, plain, with four small feet, patterns 6299 and 1128 2½ *in.*
1774 Vase, plain, with beading at base and edge, patterns 6299 and 1128 2½ *in.*
1775 Vase, hexagonal shape with beaded edge, patterns 6299 and 1128 2½ *in.*
1776 Vase, round, with beaded base and edge, patterns 6299 and 1128 2½ *in.*
1777 Fern pot, shape as 1774 L 4½ *in.* M 3¾ *in.* S 3⅛ *in.*
1778 Biscuit box, square, and cover with knob *6 in.*
1779 Butter, square, and stand
1780 Cheese cover, oblong, and stand
1781 Trinket box, round, and cover L *2 in.* M 1⅝ *in.* S 1¼ *in.*
1782 Trinket box, oval, and cover L *2 in.* M 1½ *in.* S 1¼ *in.*
1783 Jar, plain, with embossed cover L 2½ *in.* S 2⅛ *in.*
1784 Trinket box, with embossed cover L 1½ *in.* S 1¼ *in.*
1785 Bowl, round, with two small handles 3½ *in.* high
1786 Bowl, round, without handles L 2½ *in.* high x *5 in.* S *2 in.* x *4 in.*
1787 Bowl, shallow, with four small feet and two handles *2 in.* high 8¾ *in.* wide
1788 Box, with cover, round, with two handles *4 in.*
1789 Dish, square, with cover 3½ *in.*
1790 Vase, footed, with globe shape body, two handles and wide embossed neck 4¼ *in.*
1791 Dish, oval, shallow, footed *3 in.*

Coffee cups and saucer, primrose ground with panels of English water birds, painted by J. McLaughlin in natural colours. 1972/3.

1792	Vase, unusual triple shape, with three claw feet *5 in.*	1806	Inkwell, rounded *3¼ in.*
1793	Box, hexagonal shape, with cover, footed, and with two handles	1807	Inkwell, square, with four foliate embossed feet and cover *3½ in.*
1794	Vase, hexagonal shape, with wide pierced shoulders *3¼ in.*	1808	Pen tray, oval, plain
1795	Box, with cover, foliate embossed feet and knob *6¾ in.*	1809	Pen tray, shape as 1808
		1810	Powder bowl, *3⅛ in.* high, *7 in.* wide
1796	Sauce tureen, with embossed handles and knob on cover, and plain stand *5½ in.*	1811	Box, round, flat, with cover
		1812	Trays, octagonal shape, four sizes
		1813	Box, oblong, four foliate feet
1797	Sauce tureen, with small handles, embossed knob on cover, and plain stand *4½ in.*	1814	Boxes, small, round, with serrated edge, two sizes
		1815	Sweets, 'Talbot' shape, round, on foliate feet, three sizes
1798	Sauce tureen, and stand *5½ in.*	1816	Honey and stand, 'Old' plain shape
1799	Dish, shallow, diamond shape with handle, unsuitable, never produced	1817	Marmalade and stand, 'Old' plain shape
1800	Tray, small, oblong	1818	Powder box, with beading on cover
1801	Tray, small, square	1819	Box, flat, round, with beading on cover *7 in.* wide *1½ in.* high
1802	Tray, small, oval	
1803	Tray, small, square	1820	Box, oblong, with four foliate feet and beaded cover
1804	Teacup and saucer, 'Greek' shape, made for casting, straight sides with a foot	1821	Comport, fluted, footed L *4½ in.* high, *1 ft 0¼ in.* diameter
1805	Teacup and saucer, 'Doric' shape, as 1804 with incurving sides	1822	Slab, round, flat *7 in.* diameter
		1823	Slab, flat *6 in. x 8 in.*

Royal Crown Derby cup and saucer painted with garden flowers and signed by Cuthbert Gresley. 1937.
M.K. Nielsen Collection

1824 Cover dish, 'New Ely' shape, soup tureen and stand, sauce, salad bowl and plate, differs from the 'Selby' shape only in the scalloped edge

1825 Vase, globe shape, patterns 6299 and 1128 L *3⅛ in.* S *2½ in.*

1826 Vase, plain, patterns 6299 and 1128 L *4 in.* S *3¼ in.*

1827 Vase, inverted pear shape, patterns 6299 and 1129 L *4 in.* S *3¼ in.*

1828 Vase, globe shape, with narrow neck, patterns 6299 and 1128 L *4 in.* S *3¼ in.*

1829 Vase, octagonal shape, on pointed corners L *4 in.* S *3⅜ in.*

1830 Vase, square, with small foot, patterns 6299 and 1128 L *4 in.* S *3¼ in.*

1831 Vase, classical shape, embossed on foot, shoulder and top *7½ in.*

1832 Vase, shape similar to 1831 but with embossed handles from shoulder *9¼ in.*

1833 Vase, with embossed foot, shoulder and curving foliate handles *7¾ in.*

1834 Vase, with embossed foot, foliate handles from wide shoulder, embossed neck and top L *8½ in.* S *6¾ in.*

1835 Box, round, as 1819 *5½ in.* wide, *1 in.* high

1836 Vase, with plain foot, embossed shoulder and top, and two small handles *9½ in.*

1837 Vase, with four foliate corners on foot, masque handles, embossed neck and domed cover *1 ft*

1838 Vase, with round embossed foot, foliate handles, domed cover with knob *1 ft*

1839 Vase, globe shape, with embossed foot and base, and two plain handles *7¾ in.*

1840 Vase, ovoid shape with embossed foot, base, neck and top L *8½ in.* S *7 in.*

1841 Loving cup, on slender stem, with two handles *5½ in.*

1842 Jar, with cover, plain L *7½ in.* M *6½ in.* S *5½ in.*

1843 Ewer, *The Neptune*, plain, with masque lip L *6 in.* M *5½ in.* S *4½ in.*

1844 Loving cup, campana shape, with two foliate scroll handles *4½ in.*

1845 Lampshades, plain *5½ in.* and *10 in.*

1846 Vase, globe shape, with masque handles *9½ in.*

Very rare match case, cobalt blue ground with raised jewelling. Floral panel initialled A.G. (for Albert Gregory). Factory mark. Shape 1890. 2½ in. c.1905.
John Twitchett Collection

1847 Loving cup, plain, with two handles 2½ in.
1848 Dish, round, with cover and stand
1849 Vase, plain, ovoid shape, footed L 8¼ in. M 7 in. S 6 in.
1850 Vase, hexagonal shape, slight embossing on shoulder, and plain edge L 6¾ in. S 5¾ in.
1851 Biscuit box, 'Beaufort' shape, see 1366
1852 Vase, with four foliate feet, two handles, and scalloped edge L 7⅛ in. S 5½ in.
1853 Vase, campana shape, with two plain handles and foliate edge L 6½ in. S 5½ in.
1854 Vase, with unusual inverted scallop foot 6¼ in.
1855 Vase, plain, with small foot 5⅝ in.
1856 Vase, globe shape, with small foot and two plain handles 6½ in.
1857 Vase, plain, with scalloped edge 4½ in.
1858 Vase, globe shape, with narrow neck 5 in.
1859 Vase, unusual shape 4⅜ in.
1860 Vase, inverted flute shape 4¼ in.
1861 Vase, globe shape, with embossed edge 3⅞ in.
1862 Vase, globe shape, with four small feet and plain top 3⅝ in.
1863 Sweet dish, low, round
1864 Fern pot, hexagonal shape
1865 Bowl, with unusual pierced foot 3¼ in.
1866 Bowl, with fluted edge 3½ in.
1867 Jewel box, or condiment dish, triple 3 in.
1868 Ewer and basin, with twisted handle, and domed stopper with knob 5½ in.
1869 Teacup and saucer, 'Curzon' shape, fluted, as supplied to Cassidy, Montreal
1870 Vase, campana shape, with two small handles 8½ in.

1871 Cream jug, 'Sefton' shape
1872 Jardinière, with four small feet and scalloped top 4 in. high 6½ in. wide
1873 Jardinière, round, with beaded rim 3½ in. high 8 in. wide
1874 Dish, scalloped, with two scroll handles 3¼ in.
1875 Bowl, without foot, with three holes pierced at top for electric light, as 1746
1876 Sweets, 'Beverley' shape, fluted, with plain edge, oval six sizes, round six sizes
1877 Sweets, 'Cairn' shape, similar to 1876, oval six sizes, round six sizes
1878 Lampshade, fluted 3½ in.
1879 Match holder, stand and domed cover S 2¼ in.
1880 Sandwich tray, oblong
1881 Fruit bowl, 'Langham' shape, plain 9¼ in. x 3⅛ in. saucer to match 6⅛ in. x 1⅞ in.
1882 Salad bowl, 'Radstock' shape, square, 9 in. x 9 in. x 3½ in.
1883 Egg cup, 'Sydney' shape 2 in.
1884 Marmalade, 'Dundee' shape, with cover, fluted, with 1764 cover cut for spoon hole
1885 Sandwich set, oblong tray, six square plates
1886 Fruit set, square, bowl and six saucer dishes
1887 Slab, either oblong or upright, with 968 large support at back 8 in. x 6 in.
1888 Box, square, with cover, large 4½ in. S 3½ in. to top of knob
1889 Hair tidy, square, with cover 3¼ in.
1890 Matchbox, height 2½ in.
1891 Dinner plate, 'Portman' shape, as plain shape but with wider rim 10 in.

Royal Crown Derby vase and cover of unusual shape, painted and signed by Cuthbert Gresley.
Height 9½ in. 1915.
Courtesy John Ceramics

1892 Dinner plate, 'Ellsmere' shape, as 'Ely' shape but with wider rim *10 in.*

1893 Dinner plate, 'Clarendon' shape, as 'Royal Gadroon' shape but with wider rim *10 in.*

1894 Dinner plate, 'Strathmore' shape, as 'Silver' shape but with wider rim *10 in.*

1895 Teacup and saucer, 'Classic' shape, as 'Greek' shape but with 'Royal Gadroon' embossing

1896 Pin tray, oblong, plain

1897 Candlestick 6½ in.

1898 Dinner plate, 'Clive' shape, as 'Clarence' shape but wider rim

1899 Dinner plate, 'Sussex' shape, as 'Brighton' shape but wider rim

1900 Dinner plate, 'Tavistock' shape, as 'Talbot' shape but wider rim

1901 Coffee cup and saucer, 'Mostyn' shape, as 'Balmoral' but with 'Royal Gadroon' embossing

1902 Coffee cup and saucer, 'Royal Gadroon' shape, as 'Edinburgh' but with gadroon embossing

1903 Milk goblet, with cover, plain shape

1904 Milk goblet, 'Regent' shape, with cover, fluted base

1905 Bread and butter, square, small

1906 Teapot, 'Classic' shape, sugar box and cream, 'Royal Gadroon' shape

1907 Teacup and saucer, 'Cowley' shape, with looped handle, gadroon inside cup and on edge of saucer

1908 Coffee cup and saucer, 'Calder' shape

1909 Dinner plate, 'Octagon' shape

Plate painted with clematis by C.M. Pell, signed. c.1968.
John Twitchett Collection

1910 Teacup and saucer, 'Octagon' shape,
  after-dinner coffee and saucer, tall
1911 Teacup and saucer, 'Octagon' shape,
  low
1912 Teacup on tray
1913 Dish, round, 'Talbot' shape, embossed
  foot and edge, with double foliate
  handles
1914 Teacup and saucer, 'Erskine' shape, as
  'Beaufort' shape but without embossing

1915 Coffee pot, cream and sugar, 'Octagon'
  shape
1916 Cheese box, round, with cover
1917 Cigarette holder, 'New Claire' shape
1918 Cigarette holder, 'Claire' shape
1919 Dessert dish, oblong, with plain foot,
  gadroon inside edge, and foliate handles
1920 Cigarette box, oblong, plain
1921 Bowl, round, plain, footed
1922 Nut dish, with central looped handle

Royal Crown Derby vase and cover decorated with pink roses and buds in panels formed with raised gilt vine borders on cobalt blue ground and signed by Darlington. Height 10¼ in. 1921.
Courtesy David John Ceramics

1923 Jam pot, with cover and strawberry knob 3½ in.

1924 Jam pot, individual 2⅝ in.

1925 Bowl, plain, footed 3⅛ in. high 1 ft. 0⅞ in. diameter

1926 Tray, similar to 407 but with cigarette rests

1927 Jam and marmalade sets, two pots on tray, with spoons

1928 Mug, plain 5 in.

1929 Toy ware, 'Greek' shape, teacup and saucer, plate and bread and butter

1930 Toy ware, 'Chelsea' shape, teacup and saucer, teapot, sugar box and cream, coffee pot, coffee cup and saucer, plate, bread and butter, kettle and caddy

1931 Toy cup and saucer, 'Balmoral' shape

1932 Toy cup and saucer, 'Airlie' shape

1933 Tazza, as 1221 but without handle

1934 Vase, as 1844 but with 'Eagle' shape handles

1935 Mug, with horn handle 5 in., also made with two handles

1936 Trays, as 1800 but three larger sizes

1937 Trays, as 1802 but three larger sizes

1938 Trays, as 1803 but three larger sizes

1939 Cigarette holder, plain, with cover 4 in.

1940 Box, round, with cover, shape as 1810 with knob added

1941 Cigarette box, plain, square, with cover

1942 Goblet, gadroon embossing on foot 4¾ in.

1943 Cigarette box, as 1920 but gadroon edge on cover

1944 Cigarette holder, 'Mostyn' shape, on fast stand

1945 Sweets, 'Bedford' shape, round, three sizes

1946 Loving cup, with scroll handles 6¼ in.

1947 Powder box, round, with cover 5 in.

1948 Vase, as 1755, but without handle

1949 Vase, as 1756 but without handle

1950 Sweets, 'Duchess' shape, with pierced handles and foot, six sizes

1951 Vase, decorated for Tiffany 1941, pattern 2451 10½ in.

1952 Vase, campana shape, decorated for Tiffany 1941, pattern 2451 10½ in.

1953 Vase, octagonal shape, embossed 'Chinese Birds' shape 7 in.

1954 Vase, as 1252 but without foot 3¼ in.

1955 Vase, plain, as supplied to Plummer 9½ in.

Ornate covered chalice, decorated with mythological figures and band of formal motif in raised gold on white. This piece carries the cypher mark for 1940 and the Royal Warrant for His Majesty the King, and was made as a replica of the chalice referred to in Chapter 3.
Royal Crown Derby Museum

Plate and teacup and saucer (10 in.), 'Surrey' shape, 'Derby Posies', originally introduced c.1930 and in current production.
Courtesy Royal Crown Derby

1956	Tray, 'Vine' shape, embossed	**1972**	Tray, original 913 but no embossing
1957	Tray, leaf shape 4½ in. diameter	**1973**	Tray, original 1957 but no veins
1958	Tray, shape as 1957 but with stem handle	**1974**	Tray, original Rockingham but no embossing
1959	Tray, rectangular, embossed 'Chinese Birds' shape	**1975**	Celery jar, large, shape as 1777
1960	Tray, 'Rouen' shape, embossed 'Chinese Birds' shape	**1976**	Vase, plain, no foot or cover 8 in.
		1977	Vase, plain, gourd shape 7½ in.
1961	Tray, leaf shape, embossed 'Chinese Birds' shape	**1978**	Vase, plain, waisted, with two small handles 7¾ in.
1962	Tray, 'Silver' No. 1 shape, embossed 'Chinese Birds' shape	**1979**	Vase, plain, waisted, with band round the middle 7½ in.
1963	Tray, oblong, embossed 'Pershore' shape (fruit and flowers)	**1980**	Vase, globe shaped base, with slender neck and embossing on either side 7½ in.
1964	Box, oblong, embossed 'Pershore' shape, with cover	**1981**	Trinket tray, oval, with embossed edge 1 ft 0½ in. long 9 in. diameter
1965	Dish, 'Melton' shape, jollied, with cover	**1982**	Candlestick, double, embossed as 1981 5 in. long 4 in. diameter
1966	**	**1983**	Trinket box, as above 3 in. long 2½ in. diameter
1967	Tea- and dinnerware, 'Vine' shape, embossed	
1968	Tea- and dinnerware, 'Burford' shape, embossed	**1984**	Cigarette lighter, with cover 3¼ in. high 2¾ in. diameter
1969	Tea- and dinnerware, 'Kendal' shape, embossed	**1985**	Cigarette jar, plain, with cover 4 in. high 3 in. diameter
1970	Teacup and saucer, 'Chinese Birds' shape, dessert plate, embossed	**1986**	Ashtray, plain, round
		1987	Lighter base, Colibri
1971	Dessert plates, 'Pershore' shape, embossed	

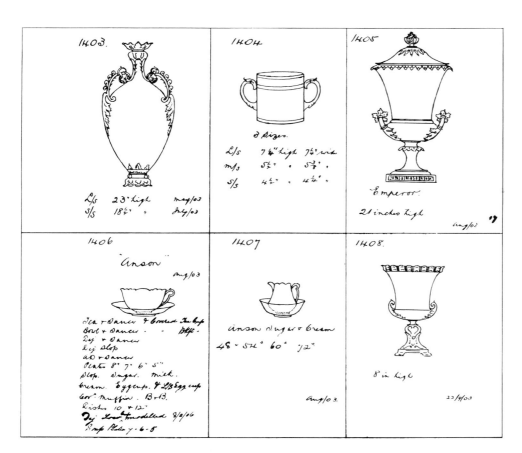

Line drawings from the shape books.

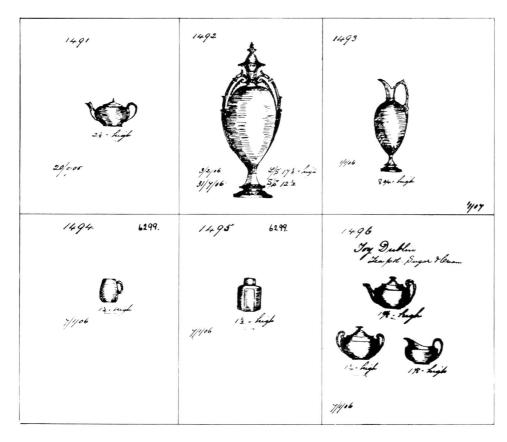

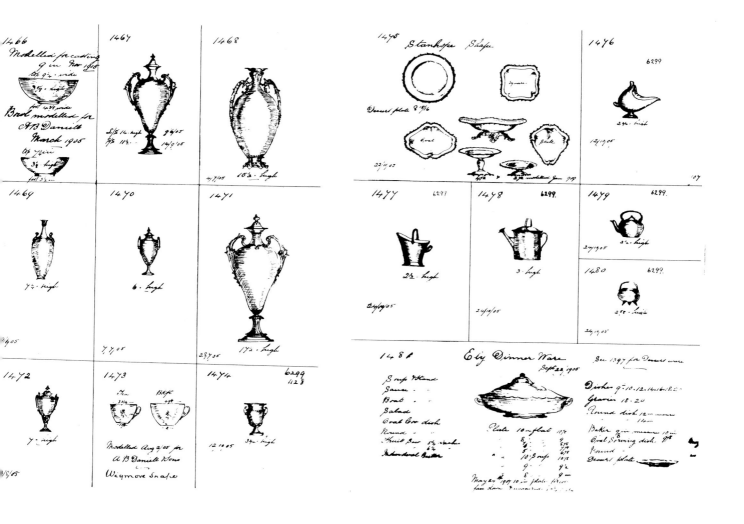

11 THE PATTERN BOOKS

Before a study of the named patterns from the Osmaston Road books is undertaken it should be pointed out that only the authenticated artist named patterns are listed in this book. The work of the anonymous painters (see p. 245) is not included. Further to this, in Brayshaw Gilhespy's account of the Osmaston Road factory many patterns are unfortunately wrongly attributed: see Gilhespy *Royal Crown Derby China* p. 71, pattern book 22, where patterns are stated to be by Birbeck and dated 1909, when in fact he did not join the company until 1931.

Painters' christian names are not consistently given in the factory's Pattern Books, but full identification is usually easily made by reference to the Biographies and the Index. Unless precluded by style, date or signature, we must assume that patterns by Rouse are by James Rouse sen.

A summary of the Pattern Books is given on p. 196.

PATTERN BOOK 1 August 1878

257 Teaware, painted fly and grass by *Corden*

280 Teaware, painted flowers by *Radford*

287 Plate, humming birds and spray on coloured ground by *Deakin*

296 Plate, bird by *Deakin* and flowers by *Radford*

303 Plate, large flower painted by *Deakin*

398 Plate, flower centre by *Radford*

488 Plate, flower sprays, gold and silver leaves by *Radford* or *Flowerdew*

505 Plate, ivory ground, birds and flowers by *Wale*

541 Plate, 'Octagon' shape, raised leaves and painted birds by *Wale*

571 'New Kensington' shape can, birds and flowers by *Wale*

572 Plate, painted flowers and flies by *Deakin*

592 Plate, 'Octagon' shape with 'Bamboo' edge, painted bird centre by *Wale*

596 Dessert plate, flowers by *Radford*

597 Teaware, gold bird, flowers and leaves, silver stem by *Hartshorn*

598 Teaware, painted birds, gold leaves by *Hartshorn*

600 Plate, flower sprays on border by *Radford*

601 Plate, flower sprays on border by *Radford*

602 Teaware, flowered border by *Radford*

603 As 598

604 Dessert plate, pierced, painted lily centre by *Brownsword*

613 Coffee and saucer, gold and silver birds by *Lambert*

618 Plate with acid border, painted bird and foliage centre by *Wale*

619 Plate, Japanese flower spray by *Marsh*

620 Plate with print border and Japanese flower spray by *Marsh*

621 Plate, wild flowers on coloured ground by *Marsh*

622 Plate, plants on coloured ground by *Marsh*

623 Plate, painted sprays on border and humming bird centre by *Deakin*

625 Plate, 'Octagon' shape with bamboo border, spray of blackberry by *Gadsby*

632 Plate, bird centre by *Deakin*

638 Plate, light and dark gold and silver sprays by *Lambert*

651 Plate, foxglove in raised gold on coloured ground by *Marsh*

652 Plate, autumnal border with gold leaves by *Lambert*

653 Plate, pierced border, painted birds and flowers by *Flowerdew*

655 Teaware, painted flowers by *Marsh*

657 Plate, birds and flowers by *Wright*

660 Plate, raised flowers by *Marsh*

665 Plate, birds and foliage by *Deakin*

677 Plate, new pierced, humming birds and flowers by *Deakin*

694 As 677

695 Plate, pierced border, painted with flowers by *Deakin*

696 Plate, pierced border, painted with flowers by *Radford*

706 Plate, pierced border, painted birds by *Deakin*

712 'Harrington', can and stand, old Nottingham Road pattern

713 Plate, painted roses in centre by *Deakin*

715 Plate, butterflies on border, small bird and spray centre by *Deakin*

716 Plate, painted orchid centre by *Deakin*

717 Plate, new pierced border, flower centre by *Marsh*

718 Plate, new pierced border, foxglove and other flowers by *Marsh*

719 Plate, painted plants by *Marsh*

720 Plate, painted plants by *Marsh*

721 Plate, central group of roses painted by *Deakin*

722 Plate, painted bird centre by *Deakin*

723 Plate, painted flower sprays by *Deakin*

724 Plate, painted bird and flowers by *Radford*

725 Plate, new pierced border, painting by *Wale*

726 Plate, large flower centre by *Deakin*

727 Plate, large flower centre by *Deakin*

728 Plate, bird and small spray painted by *Deakin*

729 Plate, large rose painted by *Deakin*

730 Plate, painted flowers and flies by *Wale*

733 Plate, flower sprays by *Gadsby*

734 Plate, birds and flowers by *Wale*

736 Plate, birds and flowers by *Wale*

737 Plate, bird and nest by *Corden*

738 Plate, flies and flowers by *Marsh*

750 Plate, flowers and central painting by *Deakin*

751 Plate, painted flowers by *Peach*

752 Plate, birds and flowers cut up with gold by *Wale*

764 Plate, coloured borders, landscapes and sea views by *Bradley*

767 Plate, acid border, flowers on white by *Bier*

772 Plate, 'Octagon' dessert, flowers by *Lambert*

786 Plate, shellfish and raised gold on coloured grounds by *Hartshorn*

787 Plate, painted birds on coloured grounds, by *Deakin*

790 Plate, flowers by *Deakin*

791 Plate, painted birds, fish and dog by *Hartshorn*

792 Plate, painted birds and flowers by *Gadsby*

Dessert plate with bamboo edge. Bird and flower painting by J.P. Wale. Pattern 541. c.1880.
Private Collection

794 Dessert plate, painted fish and seaweed by *Wale*
795 Plate, pierced border, painted birds and flowers by *Gadsby*
802 Plate, roses by *Deakin*
803 Plate, roses by *Deakin*
811 Plate, raised gold, turquoise and white enamel spots by *Lambert*
813 Plate, roses by *Deakin*
83C Plate, acid border, painted flowers and background by *Bier*
833 Dessert plate, flowers and leaves by *Peach*
841 Teaware, oak leaves and acorns by *Gadsby*
852 New dessert plate, flower spray by *Peach*
853 New dessert plate, flower spray by *Deakin*
854 Plate, roses by *Deakin*
855 'Bamboo' shape dessert plate, butterfly and leaves by *Wale*
856 'Bamboo' shape dessert plate, butterfly and leaves by *Wale*

859 Plate, flowers and butterflies by *Brownsword*
863 Plate, roses by *Deakin*
864 Plate, roses by *Deakin*
865 Plate, flowers by *Peach*
866 Plate, flower border on marone ground, children in centre by *Brownsword*
867 Plate, gold trellis and painted flowers on turquoise ground by *Radford*
875 Plate, celadon ground border with flower centre by *Bier*
878 Plate, acid border with painted roses on slight background colour by *Radford*
879 Dessert plate, with seaview by *Corden*
880 Dessert plate, centre painted by *Deakin*
881 Dessert plate, central painting of a dog by *Keene*
885 Teaware, painted flies and flowers by *Wale*

PATTERN BOOK 2

886 Coffee and saucer, painted flowers by *Deakin*
887 Coffee and saucer, painted flowers, silver and gold leaves by *Wale*
888 Teaware, painted flowers, birds and leaves by *Gadsby*
889 Coffee and saucer, painted roses by *Deakin*
890 Dessert plate, butterflies and flowers by *Deakin*

891 Dessert plate, similar to pattern 890
895 Dessert plate, peacock amongst flowers by *Wale*
897 Dessert plate, painted 'Chelsea Birds' by *Wale*
902 Dessert plate, Derby blue birds, painted flowers with gold and silver leaves by *Wale*

Campana vase, shape 1698.
Cobalt blue and white stripe with
gilding, central panel inscribed
'The Packhorse Inn, Ullswater'
and signed W.E.J. Dean. Height
7in. 1913.
Private Collection

903 Dessert plate, painted roses on white
ground, gold and silver leaves by
Radford
905 Vase 221, *Wale* painting
906 Vase 64, *Wale* painting
907 Vase 291, *Wale* painting
908 Dessert plate, birds, flowers and flies by
Wale
909 Dessert plate, birds painted by *Wale*
914 Dessert plate, 'Bamboo' shape, flowers
by *Gadsby*
916 Teaware, 'Chelsea Birds' painted by
Wale
917 Coffee and saucer, 'Chelsea Birds'
by *Wale*
930 Teaware, flowers with gold and silver
leaves by *Wale*
932 Teaware, flowers and flies by *Gadsby*
933 Teaware, painted flowers by *Wale*
934 Plate, roses by *Radford*
940 Sèvres dessert plate, fishes and
seaweed by *Wale*
947 Dessert plate, coloured spray and
landscape by *Statham*

948 Sèvres dessert plate, fish by *Wale*
952 Dessert plate, flowers and butterfly by
Wale
954 Dessert plate, cobalt ground, raised
gold by *Lambert*, cupid centre by *Platts*
955 Dessert plate, turquoise ground, gold
bird and white enamel foliage by
Lambert
956 Dessert plate, printed cupid, gilding by
Lambert
957 Dessert plate, printed cupid, gilding by
Lambert
959 Dessert plate, celadon ground, birds,
spray and flowers by *Wright*
962 Dessert plate, celadon ground, game
birds by *Deakin*
963 Dessert plate, salmon ground, fishes
and seaweed by *Deakin*
968 Dessert plate, floral centre by *Bier*
976 Coffee and saucer, pale pink inside,
gold and enamel bird and bamboo by
Lambert
977 Coffee and saucer, ivory ground,
decoration as 976

Plaque painted by D. Hague 'George Washington, President of the United States of America'.
Presented to Mr. Julius Garfinckel of Washington in 1956.

Rare pastille burner, shape 1305, pattern 1128, 5¼ in. 19
These were made in large quantities at the Nottingham R
China Works and to a lesser degree at King Street, but t.
the first to be recorded at Osmaston Road.
Paul and Sally Holborough Collection

Derby Crown plate ivory groundlay decorated with cut up
and platinum by John Porter Wale. Pattern 989. 9in. 1887
The pattern book states 'Sèvres dessert plate, flowers and
butterflies by Wale'. Retailer's mark for Osler Oxford Stre
London.
Roy Beeston Collection

978 Sèvres dessert plate, painted fishes by *Deakin*

980 Sèvres dessert plate, painted fishes by *Deakin*

983 Sèvres dessert plate, painted fishes by *Deakin*

987 'Devon' dessert plate, birds and butterflies by *Wale*

988 'Regal' dessert plate, cobalt ground, birds and flies by *Lambert*

989 Sèvres dessert plate, flowers and butterfly by *Wale*

997 'Devonshire' dessert plate, 'Chelsea Birds' by *Wale*

998 'Devonshire' dessert plate, marone ground, painted flowers, printed and filled in figures of children by *Brownsword*

1001 Sèvres dessert plate, celadon ground, painted fish by *Deakin*

1004 Teaware, celadon ground, flowers and butterflies by *Radford*

1005 Teaware, celadon ground, flowers by *Radford*

1006 Teaware, blue ground, painted flowers by *Radford* and *Brownsword*

1007 Sèvres dessert plate, painted fish and flowers by *Deakin*

1008 'Regal' dessert plate, salmon ground, fish and bird centre painted in *Hartshorn's* room

1011 'Devon' plate, acid border, birds and flowers by *Brownsword* and *Wale*

1012 'Devon' plate, celadon ground, birds, shell and seaweed in natural colours by *Deakin*

1013 Sèvres dessert plate, peacock and flowers by *Wale*

1014 Dessert plate, peacock blue ground, spray roses in raised gold by *Wale*

1015 Dessert plate, peacock blue ground, water lilies and grasses in raised gold, traced in black and red by *Lambert*

1016 Dessert plate, peacock blue ground, birds and leaves in raised gold by *Wale*

1019 As 136 with centres by *Deakin*

1024 'Regal' dessert plate, salmon ground, printed, coloured by *Firth*

1025 'Regal' dessert plate, golden fawn ground, printed, coloured by *Firth*

1033 Plate, yellow ground, printed flowers, fruit and flies coloured by *Lambert*

1034 Plate, salmon ground, centre as 1033

1045 Coffee and saucer, birds and flowers by *Wale*

1054 Plate, ivory ground, painted wreaths with sweet peas by *Corden*

1055 Plate, dark chrome green ground, painted shells by *Corden*

1057 'Devon' dessert plate, painted bird and spray centre by *Corden*

1084 Sèvres dessert plate, birds and flowers by *Wale*

1085 'Regal' dessert plate, bird and leaves by *Wale*

1106 Plate, etched landscape by *E L*

1111 Plate, 'Trotter' shape, water green ground panels, groups of flowers in centre, sprays in panel by *Rouse Sen*

1119 Plate, border by *Lambert*, centre by *Deakin*

1135 Sèvres dessert plate, seaweed and fishes by *Wale*

1136 Sèvres dessert plate, seaweed and fishes by *Wale*

1144 'Devon' plate, birds and flies by *Wale*

1150 'Regal' plate, plant centre by *Gadsby*

1155 'Devon' plate, orchid centre by *Storer*

1165 Sèvres plate, fishes and seaweed, landscape in panel by *Deakin*

1166 Sèvres plate, game birds by *Deakin*

1167 Sèvres plate, shells by *Deakin*

1168 Sèvres plate, landscape centre, border of shells by *Deakin*

1169 Sèvres plate, fish and seascape by *Wale*

1170 Sèvres plate, game and landscape by *Wale*

1171 Sèvres plate, fish and shells by *Deakin*

1172 'Devon' plate, orchid centre by *Brownsword*

1173 Sèvres plate, fish, seaweed and shells by *Deakin*

1174 'Devon' plate, raised gold birds, enamelled flowers by *Wale*

1175 Sèvres plate, rose du barri ground, birds and sprays by *Wale*

1176 Sèvres plate, alpine flowers by *Peach*

1177 Sèvres plate, shells and seaweed by *Wale*

1178 Sèvres plate, ivory ground, gold, silver and bronze leaves, cut with colour and an enamel bird by *Wale*

1179 Sèvres plate, humming bird, raised gold and coloured leaves by *Deakin*

1181 Sèvres plate, painted seascape and seaweed by *Wale*

1182 'Devon' plate, acid border, gold and coloured leaves by *Wale*

1183 Sèvres plate, painted fish by *Deakin*

1184 Sèvres plate, landscape centre by *Statham*

1185 Sèvres plate, cupid centre by *Platts*

1186 Sèvres plate, landscape centre by *Statham*

1189 'Gadroon' plate, flowers and fruit centre by *Rouse Sen*

1192 Coffee and saucer, egg-shell tinted body, enamelled birds by *Lambert*

1193 'Gadroon' plate, orchid centre by *Deakin*

1195 Plate, Derby blue border, flowers and fruit centre by *Deakin*

1196 Plate, Derby blue border, three groups of flowers by *Brownsword*

1197 'Regal' plate, flowers and flies by *Wale*

1199 Sèvres plate, fishes and landscape by *Deakin*

1200 Sèvres plate, orchid, flowers and landscape by *Brownsword*

1203 'Devon' plate, flower spray, bird and butterfly by *Wale*

1204 Similar to 1203

1205 Sèvres plate, game birds by *Deakin*

1208 Sèvres plate, bird and flowers by *Deakin*

1209 'Devon' plate, fishes and seaweed by *Deakin*

1210 'Regal' plate, birds and sprays by *Wale*

1212 Teaware, flowers and birds by *Wale*

1213 Sèvres plate, passion flowers by *Wale*

1214 Sèvres plate, canary ground, flower spray and butterfly by *Wale*

1215 'Duchess' coffee and saucer, egg-shell, coloured ground, bird and flowers by *Wale*

1218 Sèvres plate, celadon ground, painted leaves by *Gadsby*

1219 Sèvres plate, flowers and butterflies by *Brownsword*

Plate 47. Royal Crown Derby vase and cover decorated and signed by Albert Gregory. The raised gilding and elaborate decoration on this vase owes much to the inspiration of Leroy. 10½ in. 1909. *Private Collection*

'Argyll' dessert plate, not pierced.
Gold and white border, flower
centre by A. Gregory.
Date unknown.
Private Collection

1221 'Regal' plate, alpine plants by *Peach*
1222 'Regal' plate, flowers and butterflies by
Deakin
1233 'Regal' plate, rose du barri border,
flowers and grasses by *Deakin*
1234 'Devon' plate, orchid centre by *Deakin*
1236 'Regal' plate, gold and silver sprays by
Wright
1243 Sèvres plate, turquoise ground, raised
gold fish and seaweed by *Deakin*
1249 'Bute' coffee and saucer, sprays by
Wright
1250 Similar to 1249
1252 'Regal' plate, landscape and flowers by
Wright and *Brownsword*
1262 Sèvres plate, fish and landscape,
raised gold fishing tackle by *Deakin*
1263 Coffee and saucer, flowers and flies by
Wright

1264 Coffee and saucer, birds and flowers by
Wright
1265 Coffee and saucer, leaves and stems by
Wright
1266 Coffee and saucer, flowers and leaves by
Wright
1267 'Greek' s/s cup and saucer, gold birds
and leaves by *Wright*
1268 'Greek' s/s cup and saucer, flowers by
Wright
1275 Sèvres plate, flowers and butterflies
by *Peach*
1276 Sèvres plate, flowers by *Wale*
1282 Sèvres plate, rose du barri ground,
raised and re-raised gold and bronze
leaves by *Lambert*
1283 Sèvres plate, spray and bird by *Wale*
1284 Plate, pierced edge, painted flowers by
Brownsword

Plate 48. One of a pair of Royal Crown Derby campana shaped vases of exhibition quality, the gilding receiving the most elaborate treatment, the fine painting by Albert Gregory on both sides of the vases, signed. 10½ in. 1920.
Private Collection

Right:
Plate 49. Royal Crown Derby campana shaped vase, one of a pair, decorated in the 'Imari' style pattern 1128, shape 1699. 6½ in. 1920.
David Holborough Collection

Right:
Plate 50. Royal Crown Derby ice-pail, cover and liner decorated with two panels of birds in landscape reserved on cobalt blue ground and with raised and chased gilding, painted and signed by George Darlington. 10½ in. 1914. Although other pails have been seen in early photographs, at the time of writing (1988), this is the only known one.
Mr. and Mrs. W.L.C. Prosser Collection

Place setting showing the pattern 'Pinxton Roses', in current production.
Courtesy Royal Crown Derby

PATTERN BOOK 3

1292 Dessert plate, gold leaves by *Lambert*
1293 Dessert plate, gold leaves by *Lambert*
1294 Dessert plate, gold leaves by *Lambert*
1297 Dessert plate, pierced, flowers and butterflies by *Brownsword*
1300 'Devonshire' dessert plate, birds by *Wale*
1301 Pierced dessert plate, spray and flowers by *Wright*
1324 Dessert plate, silver and gold flowers by *Deakin*
1325 Dessert plate, silver and gold flowers by *Deakin*
1326 Dessert plate, silver and gold flowers by *Deakin*
1329 'Regal' dessert plate, wild rose and butterfly by *Wale*
1334 'Regal' dessert plate, fruit and corn by *Deakin*
1337 Old Derby teaware pattern by *Piper*
1363 Pierced dessert plate, cupid centre by *Platts*
1367 'Regal' dessert plate, flower centre by *Gadsby*
1378 Dessert plate, painted sprays by *Corden*
1379 Plate, three groups of flowers by *Brownsword*
1401 Sèvres dessert plate, dog-roses by *Brownsword*
1402 Sèvres dessert plate, dog-roses by *Brownsword*
1405 Danish dessert plate, flower spray by *T G*
1408 Sèvres plate, leaves and flower spray by *Wright*
1409 Danish pierced plate, spray by *Deakin*
1410 Danish pierced plate, spray by *Deakin*
1411 'Bute' teaware, flowers by *Brownsword*
1413 'Tankard' teaware, sprays and butterflies by *Peach*
1415 Danish half pierced plate, flower centre by *Rouse Sen*

1416 Danish half pierced plate, flowers and flies by *Rouse Sen*
1417 'Devon' dessert plate, acid border, flower groups in panels and centre by *Rouse Sen*
1418 'Regal' dessert plate, toadstool, mouse and grasses by *Smith*
1418 Danish dessert plate, half pierced, flowers by *Deakin*
1420 'Regal' dessert plate, flowers by *Rouse Sen*
1421 Danish dessert plate, pierced, flowers by *Deakin*
1423 'Devon' plate, flower wreaths by *Rouse Sen*
1424 'Regal' dessert plate, ivory ground, gold and silver spray cut up with red and green by *Corden*
1426 'Devon' dessert plate, acid border, raised gold, flower spray by *Deakin*
1427 Danish dessert plate, half pierced, flowers by *Deakin*
1428 Danish dessert plate, half pierced, flowers by *Rouse*, raised gold by *Wale*
1429 Danish dessert plate, not pierced, silver and gold stems by *Wright* and *Corden*
1430 Dinner plate, rose du barri and fawn ground, turquoise raised jewelling by *Piper*
1431 'Regal' dessert plate as 1430
1433 'Regal' dessert plate, raised gold spray with white enamel flowers, flower spray in centre by *Corden*
1433 'Regal' dessert plate, flowers by *G Smith*
1438 'Regal' dessert plate, ivory and celadon ground, gold and silver spray by *Corden*
1439 Sèvres dessert plate, painted birds and raised gold leaves by *Wale*
1440 'Victoria' dessert plate, full pierced, flowers and gold leaves by *Peach*

Royal Crown Derby 'Queen's Gadroon' plate decorated with a view of 'Wolfscote Dale Derbyshire'. Inscribed and signed on verso by Michael Crawley 1973. 9½ in. Fifty sets of twelve scenes in Derbyshire were planned but only some thirty sets were completed.
Courtesy David John Ceramics

1441 Sèvres dessert plate, butterflies and flowers by *Wale*

1442 Teacup and saucer, flower sprays, gold and silver leaves by *Wale*

1443 Teacup and saucer, ivory ground, chocolate band, raised enamel spots, small spray by *Wright*

1444 Teacup and saucer, flower sprays by *Brownsword*

1445 'Regal' dessert plate, flower centre by *Peach*

1446 'Regal' dessert plate, flowers by *G Smith*

1447 Teacup and saucer, 'Queen Anne', flowers and flies by *Gadsby*

1448 Teacup and saucer, 'Tankard', flowers by *Peach*

1450 Teacup and saucer, 'Queen Anne', leaf sprays, gold and silver by *G Smith*

1453 Teacup and saucer, 'Queen Anne', leaf sprays, gold and silver by *G Smith*

1454 Teacup and saucer, 'Tankard', leaf sprays, gold and silver by *G Smith*

1456 Teacup and saucer, 'Tankard', flowers by *Corden*

1457 Teacup and saucer, 'Globe', ivory ground, chocolate ground with flower sprays by *Peach*

1460 Danish dessert plate, not pierced, flowers by *Gadsby*

1461 Sèvres dessert plate, Derbyshire landscape by *Statham*

1462 Teacup and saucer, ivory ground, chocolate band, flowers by *Brownsword*

1463 Sèvres dessert plate, birds and flowers by *Wale*

1470 Danish dessert plate, pierced, flowers and butterfly by *Wale*

1472 'Regal' dessert plate, full centre painting landscape with figure and animals by *Rouse*

1473 'Regal' dessert plate, butterfly and flowers by *Wale*

1474 Sèvres dessert plate, gold and silver fruit and flowers by *Deakin*

1475 'Regal' dessert plate, gold and silver spray cut up with red and green by *Corden*

1476 'Devonshire' dessert plate, orchid centre by *Deakin*

1477 'Regal' dessert plate, flowers, leaves and butterfly by *Deakin*

1478 'Regal' dessert plate, flowers, leaves and butterfly by *Deakin*

1479 'Devonshire' dessert plate, alpine flowers by *Peach*

1481 'Regal' dessert plate, flowers by *Gadsby*

1482 'Regal' dessert plate, flowers by *Gadsby*

1483 'Regal' dessert plate, flowers by *Gadsby*

1484 Vase, shape 121 painted by *Holtzendorf*

1486 Vase, shape 345 painted by *Lunn*

1496 Sèvres dessert plate, alpine flowers by *Wale*

1497 Sèvres dessert plate, alpine flowers by *Wale*

1498 'Regal' dessert plate, alpine flowers by *Wale*

1499 Sèvres dessert plate, alpine flowers by *Wale*

1500 Sèvres dessert plate, flies and flowers by *Wale*

1501 Sèvres dessert plate, flies and flowers by *Wale*

1502 Vase, shape 264 *Lunn*'s design

1503 'Devonshire' dessert plate, ivory ground, painted flowers by *Wale*

Plaque painted with an adaptation of Reynolds' 'Lady Hamilton' by R. Hague, signed. 1951.
Courtesy M.K. Nielsen Antiques

A Royal Crown Derby Freedom
Casket is presented to a
distinguished person or an
Alderman who is made an honorary
Freeman of the County Borough of
Derby. The Freedom Scroll is
placed inside upon presentation.
The conferment of Honorary
Freedoms began in 1904, when the
Marquess Curzon of Kedleston was
admitted a Freeman.
Royal Crown Derby Museum

1504 'Regal' dessert plate, ivory ground,
flowers, gold and silver leaves by *Wale*
1505 'Royal' dessert plate, flowers on enamel,
raised and re-raised gold leaves by
Corden
1506 'Regal' dessert plate, flowers by *Wale*
1507 'Regal' dessert plate, flowers by *Wale*
1521 Sèvres dessert plate, flowers and
butterflies by *Corden*
1522 'Devon' plate, full centre landscape
'Scotch lakes' by *Rouse*
1524 Danish Dessert plate, not pierced,
flowers by *Wale*
1525 'Devonshire' dessert plate, flowers,
raised gold bird by *Wale*

1526 'Queen Anne' cup and saucer, raised
gold and enamel flowers by *Wale*
1527 Danish dessert plate, not pierced, raised
gold and enamel flowers by *Wale*
1529 'Devon' dessert plate, spray in gold,
silver, bronze and colour by *Wright*
1535 'Devon' dessert plate, spray in gold and
bronze by *Wale*
1538 'Devon' dessert plate, flower sprays by
Wale
1539 'Devon' dessert plate, game bird centre
by *Deakin*

PATTERN BOOK 4

1552 Centre by *Deakin*
1553 Fish by *Deakin*
1554 Sèvres shape plate, painted by *Deakin*
1555 Sèvres shape plate, painted bird and
gold and silver sprays by *Corden*
1557 Dessert plate, landscape by *J Rouse*
1560 Dessert plate, painted by *Wale*
1561 Dessert plate, fish by *Wale*
1563 Dessert plate, centre by *Gadsby*
1564 Dessert plate, centre by *Gadsby*
1565 Dessert plate, fish by *Deakin*
1566 Dessert plate, fish by *Wale*

1567 Dessert plate, game birds by *Deakin*
1568 Dessert plate, ferns by *Lambert*
1569 'Globe' tea and saucer, Old Derby
groups by *Brownsword*
1570 Plate as above
1575 Vase 344 painted by *Piper*
1576 Sèvres dessert, game birds by *Wale*
1577 Sèvres dessert, alpine flowers by *Peach*
1578 'Devon' dessert, fish and shells by *Wale*
1579 Sèvres dessert, bronze birds with gold
tree by *Wale*
1580 'Devon' dessert, flowers by *Brownsword*

Pair of vases with covers, cobalt blue and white, gold handles and gadroon edge, oval insets of flowers. 1901.
Dr. Whitehead Collection

Trio of inkstands and covers, shape
1102. Height 8¼ in. Patterns 1126,
6299 and 2444.
Courtesy of Sotheby's Belgravia

1734 'Regal' dessert, flowers by *Lambert*
1735 'Regal' dessert, leaves by *Lambert*
1736 Danish dessert, flowers by *Wale*
1739 Pot pourri jar with pierced cover
1741 'Victoria' pierced dessert, flowers by
Brownsword
1742 Pot pourri jar with pierced cover
1743 Pot pourri jar with pierced cover by
Brownsword
1744 Sèvres dessert, flowers by *Wale*
1745 Danish dessert, flowers by *Brownsword*
1748 Teaware, gold and enamel flowers by
Wale
1749 'Victoria' dessert, pierced, flowers by
Wale
1750 'Regal' dessert, flowers by *Brownsword*
1752 As 1736
1753 'Regal' dessert, fruit by *Deakin*
1754 'Victoria' dessert, pierced, flowers by
Deakin
1756 'Victoria' dessert, pierced, fruit by
Brownsword
1757 'Victoria' dessert, pierced, painting of
child by *Rouse*
1758 'Victoria' dessert, pierced, flowers by
Deakin, later by *Brownsword*
1759 As 1758
1768 'Regal' dessert, flowers by *Wale*
1776 'Victoria' dessert, not pierced, flowers
by *Deakin*, later by *Brownsword*
1780 'Regal' dessert, centre cupid painted
by *Platts*
1783 'Victoria' dessert, not pierced, flowers
by *Deakin*, later by *Brownsword*
1790 'Victoria' dessert, not pierced, flowers
by *Deakin*
1791 'Victoria' dessert, not pierced, birds by
Wale

1793 'Victoria' dessert, not pierced, fish by
Wale
1794 'Regal' dessert plate, fish by *Deakin*,
later by *Brownsword*
1796 'Regal' dessert plate, fish by *Brownsword*
1797 'Regal' dessert plate, fish by *Wale*
1798 Dessert plate, centre in golds and
bronzes by *Wale*
1800 Dessert plate, flowers and fruit by
Brownsword
1801 Dessert plate, bird and mistletoe by
Wale
1802 'Regal' dessert, flowers by *Brownsword*
1803 'Regal' dessert, landscape centre by
Smith
1809 Dessert plate, by *Deakin*
1810 'Regal' dessert, flowers and flies by
Wale
1811 'Regal' dessert, flowers by *Deakin*
1816 'Victoria' dessert, not pierced, raised
flowers in gold and enamel by *Wale*
1817 'Victoria' dessert, not pierced, flowers by
Deakin
1819 Dessert, painted by G *Smith*
1822 'Regal' dessert plate, fish by *Wale*
1825 Sèvres dessert plate, flowers, enamel
raised and flat gold by *Wale*
1830 'Victoria' pierced, cupids painted by
Platts
1835 'Devonshire' dessert, flowers by
Deakin, acid border
1837 'Regal' dessert plate, orchids by
Deakin, acid border
1843 Sèvres dessert, flowers and flies by *Wale*
1844 'Regal' dessert, fish by *Peach*, acid
border
1848 'Regal' dessert, game birds by *Deakin*
1849 Plate, bronze and gold flowers by *Wale*

'Antoinette' in current production showing the 18th century influence of the earlier factory.
Courtesy Royal Crown Derby

1854 Dessert plate, bronze and gold poppies by *Wale*
1859 Teaware, bronze flowers by *Wale*
1867 'Devonshire' dessert, enamel flowers, gold and bronze leaves by *Wale*
1869 'Regal' dessert, flowers, bronze and gold by *Wale*
1871 'Regal' dessert, game birds by *Deakin*
1880 Fluted dessert, flowers gold and bronze by *Wale*
1881 Fluted dessert, gold flowers by *Wright*
1883 Dessert plate, butterfly and flowers by *Peach*, acid border
1884 'Regal' dessert plate, landscape by *Peach*
1900 Fluted dessert plate, blue, red and bronze flowers by *Corden*

1901 'Cambridge' dessert, landscape by *Trowell*
1917 Teaware, yellow ground, landscape on cup by *Trowell*
1918 Plate, landscape by *Statham*, later by *Brownsword* and *Trowell*
1920 Dinner and teaware, landscapes by *Trowell*
1921 Teaware, flowers by *Trowell*
1923 Teaware, small flower swags by *Trowell*
1926 Fluted dessert, flowers by *Brownsword*
1927 Fluted dessert, flowers by *Brownsword*
1928 Fluted dessert, flowers by *Wale*
1930 'Victoria' dessert, not pierced, cherubs painted by *Platts*
1931 Fluted dessert, flowers by *Wale*

PATTERN BOOK 5

1947 'Regal' dessert plate, flowers by *Brownsword*
1948 Fluted dessert plate, flowers by *Wale*
1956 Fluted dessert plate, flowers and bird in raised colour by *Wale*
1960 Teaware, flowers by *Wale*
1964 Fluted plate, flowers in enamel, bird in modelled raised colour by *Wale*

1965 'Victoria' dessert plate, not pierced, flowers by *Wale*
1977 Sèvres dessert plate, butterflies and flowers by *Brownsword*
1988 Fluted dessert plate, seascape by *Wale*
1996 Coffee cup, saucer and plate, flat gold cut up with raised colour and red by *Wright*

'Mikado' teapot, tea bowl and cream jug. The drawings of this pattern were said to have been inspired by drawings on rice paper obtained from the Far East.
Courtesy Royal Crown Derby

1997 Coffee cup and saucer, raised and flat gold, white enamel spots by *Brownsword*

2011 'Cambridge' dessert plate, raised and flat gold, cut up with red by *Brownsword*

2016 'Cambridge' dessert plate, flower centre by *Brownsword*

2018 'Regal' dessert plate, flat gold and raised and chased gold flowers by *Brownsword*

2022 'Cambridge' dessert plate, light and dark bisque blue flowers by *Wright*

2027 'Victoria' dessert plate, not pierced, festoons of raised gold flowers, centre flat gold cut up with red by *Brownsword*

2028 'Cambridge' dessert plate, flower sprays by *Brownsword* and later by *Deakin*

2030 'Bute' coffee cup and saucer, raised and flat gold by *Brownsword*

2033 'Cambridge' dessert plate, flowers and leaf sprays by *Wale*

2052 Teaware, raised gold honeysuckle by *Wale*

2053 Coffee cup and saucer, egg-shell, peacock feathers painted by *Wright*

2058 'Devonshire' dessert plate, bisque blue and ivory, raised gold border with flat gold centre by *Brownsword*

2060 'Cambridge' dessert plate, flower sprays by *Brownsword*

2077 Teaware, flower sprays by *Brownsword*

2079 Coffee cup and saucer, egg-shell, flower and leaf sprays by *Wale*

2083 'Cavendish' dessert plate, light and dark ivory ground, flat gold in enamels by *Wale*

2086 'Bute' coffee cup and saucer, white with flat gold and enamels by *Wale*

2089 Sèvres dessert plate, flowers by *Wale*

2092 'Cambridge' dessert plate, seascape by *Wale*

2100 Coffee and saucer, egg-shell, sprays in gold and enamel by *Wale*

2101 Coffee and saucer, egg-shell, sprays in flat gold and enamel by *Wale*

2112 Chocolate cup and saucer with cover, head cameo and flowers by *Trowell*

2118 'Duchess' coffee and saucer, egg-shell, rose du barri and fawn grounds, flat gold and enamels by *Wale*

2125 Coffee and saucer, egg-shell, raised gold with white enamel spots by *Brownsword*

2130 'Regal' dessert plate, game birds by *Deakin*

2131 'Regal' dessert plate, marine subjects by *Deakin*

2137 'Bute' coffee cup and saucer, egg-shell, bisque blue with raised gold sprays by *Brownsword*

2144 'Regal' dessert plate, bisque blue and ivory ground with raised gold flowers and leaves by *Brownsword*

2185 'Gadroon' dessert plate, centre by *Corden*

2186 Coffee and saucer, egg-shell, slightly raised festoons in light and dark gold, chased by *Brownsword*

2187 'Bute' coffee and saucer, light and dark gold sprays cut up with enamels by *Brownsword*

'Royal Gadroon' dessert plate, cobalt blue border with solid gold and raised enamel edge, full floral centre by A. Gregory, signed. 1904.
Royal Crown Derby Museum

2193 'Gadroon' dessert plate, centre by *Corden*

2196 'Cambridge' dessert plate, centre by *Corden*

2200 'Cambridge' dessert plate, turckini centre in flat gold cut up with colour by *Wale*

2213 'Devonshire' dessert plate, light and dark ivory ground, raised fruit in light and dark gold by *Corden*

2214 'Cambridge' dessert plate, flowers and sprays in raised and chased gold by *Brownsword*

2215 'Cambridge' dessert plate, raised fruit by *Brownsword*

2218 'Cambridge' dessert plate, turckini flowers in enamels, gossamer in white gold by *Wale*

2219 'Devonshire' dessert plate, raised fruit by *Brownsword*, figures by *Platts*

2242 'Cavendish' dessert plate, ivory ground, flowers in light and dark gold cut up with enamel by *Wright* and later *Wale*

2248 'Tankard' teacup and saucer, bronze fishes cut up with gold by *Wale*

2256 'Oxford' teacup and saucer, ivory ground with gold and enamels by *Wale*

2259 'Duchess' coffee cup and saucer, egg-shell, white with raised gold landscape, chased by *Deakin*

2274 'Gadroon' dinner plate, painted flowers by *Brownsword*

2277 'Cambridge' dessert plate, ivory ground, gold flower sprays by *Deakin* and later *Brownsword*

'Green Derby Panel' on 'Ely/Chelsea' pattern A1237, a traditional design in gold with leaves and flowers in light and dark green. (See Chapter 7.)
Courtesy Royal Crown Derby

Plate 51. Royal Crown Derby pair of vases of unusual shape decorated with panels of birds and signed by George Darlington. Incised shape 1578. 9in. 1918.
Mr. and Mrs. W.L.C. Prosser Collection

Plate 52. Royal Crown Derby vase and cover decorated and signed by George Darlington, pattern 9145, shape 1411. 6¼ in. 1917.
Courtesy David John Ceramics

'Brocade' on 'Queen's Gadroon' shape, pattern A1286, knapweeds and thistles in raised gold on white,
1972. This example showing the addition of jubilee crest, 1977.
Courtesy Royal Crown Derby

2292 As 2259 but pink groundlay inside cup
and outside saucer
2299 'Cambridge' dessert plate, veronese
green band, coloured seaweed centre
by *Wale*
2306 'Cambridge' dessert plate, flowers in
ivory by *Corden*
2318 'Gadroon' dessert plate, light and dark
bisque blue with gold flower sprays
by *Corden*
2319 'Devonshire' dessert plate, bisque blue
and ivory with raised gold spray by
Deakin and later by *Brownsword*
2321 'Cambridge' dessert plate, celadon and
ivory ground, centre light and dark
gold cut up with enamel by *Wright*
and later *Brownsword*
2322 'Gadroon' dessert plate, bisque blue
ground, centre raised gold flowers by
Corden
2324 'Duchess' coffee and saucer, rose du
barri, marone and ivory ground,
gilding and white enamel spots by
Brownsword

2331 'Cambridge' dessert plate, ivory ground,
coloured sprays by *Brownsword*
2332 'Cambridge' dessert plate, ivory band,
flower centre by *Wale*
2333 'Cambridge' dessert plate, ivory ground,
flower centre by *Wale*
2355 'Vernon' teacup and saucer, raised gold
fruit border by *Brownsword*
2365 'Gadroon' 8 in. plate, ivory ground,
painted seaweed by *Wale*
2368 'Cambridge' dessert plate, raised centre,
enamel flowers, light and dark gold and
bronze by *Lambert*
2369 Similar to 2368, also by *Lambert*
2370 'Cambridge' dessert plate, cameo in
centre by *Lambert*
2372 'Gadroon' dessert plate, light and dark
ivory with raised and chased sprays by
Brownsword
2376 'Cambridge' dessert plate, raised figures
in centre by *Wright*
2380 Coffee and saucer, one head (cameo) on
cup by *Lambert*

Brian and June Branscombe at the launching of the new 'Queen's Gadroon' shape at Kedleston Hall in July 1972.

'Caliph' — garland of jade, turquoise and white flowers and leaves on white bone china, pattern A1287, on Derby's new 'Queen's Gadroon' shape designed by Brian Branscombe Des.R.C.A., and June Branscombe Des.R.C.A.
Courtesy Royal Crown Derby

PATTERN BOOK 6

2381 Plate *10 in.*, marone and ivory ground, fruit raised and chased by *Wright*

2382 'Victoria' dessert plate, pierced, flowers by *Brownsword*

2384 'Gadroon' dessert plate, raised flowers (gold) in centre by *Corden*

2408 'Cambridge' dessert plate, centre by *Trowell*

2411 'Cambridge' dessert plate, centre in bronze and gold by *Lambert* and later by *Clark*

2429 'Bute' coffee cup and saucer, egg-shell, yellow ground with green band rose du barri inside cup, cameo medallions by *Wright*

2448 'Harrington' can and saucer, Derby blue, white enamel spots by *Lambert*

2449 'Vernon' can and saucer, painted flowers by *Wale*

2450 Derby twist flute tea and saucer, painted flowers by *Wale*

2455 'Cambridge' dessert plate, Derby blue bands, cameo by *Lambert*

2459 'Cambridge' dessert plate, flowers and fruit painted by *Deakin*

2460 'Cambridge' dessert plate, flowers by *Deakin*

2479 Sèvres dessert plate, two-shaded ivory ground, sprays in flat gold (light and dark) cut up with red and green by *Townsend*

2480 'Cambridge' dessert plate (egg-shell), bisque blue border with raised gold, raised figures in centre by *Townsend*

2483 'Gadroon' dessert plate, flowers by *Deakin*

2490 'Gadroon' dessert plate, light and dark ivory, raised spray by *Brownsword*

2500 'Gadroon' dessert plate, light and dark ivory, raised and chased centre by *Corden*

2542 'Gadroon' dessert plate, flower centre by *Deakin*

2543 'Gadroon' dessert plate, flower centre by *Deakin*

2546 'Cambridge' dessert plate, thistle centre by *Brownsword*

2547 'Cambridge' dessert plate, ivory ground, flowers by *Wale*

2548 'Victoria' dessert, not pierced, flowers by *Wale*

2552 'Cavendish' dessert, flowers by *Wale*

2559 'Cambridge' dessert plate, fruit by *Wale*

2561 'Cambridge' dessert plate, flowers by *Wale*

2566 'Cambridge' dessert plate, flowers by *Wale*

2577 'Victoria' dessert, not pierced, raised and enamel centre by *Wale*

2584 'Cambridge' dessert plate, landscape centre by *Trowell*

2585 'Cambridge' dessert plate, landscape centre by *Trowell*

Pair of Royal Crown Derby candlesticks, pattern 2451. Height 6½ in. 1915.
David Holborough Collection

2586 As 2585 by *Trowell*
2587 'Gadroon' dessert plate by *Corden*
2590 'Cambridge' dessert plate, centre in raised gold and colour by *Wale*
2592 'Cambridge' dessert plate, flower centre by *Wale*
2594 'Cavendish' dessert plate, centre in raised colour and dry colour by *Corden*
2597 'Cambridge' dessert plate, centre in flat gold and colour by *Brownsword*
2598 'Cambridge' dessert plate, flower centre by *Wale*
2599 'Harrow' dessert plate, raised and chased centre by *Wale*
2602 'Harrow' dessert plate, landscape centre by *Trowell*
2604 'Cambridge' dessert plate, flowers by *Wale*
2605 'Cambridge' dessert plate, flowers by *Corden*
2609 'Cambridge' dessert plate, landscape centre by *Trowell*
2610 'Vernon' teacup and saucer, sprays in raised colour and flat gold cut up with brown and chased by *Gregory*
2612 'Harrow' dessert plate, raised and chased centre, enamel flowers by *Wale*
2614 'Carlton' teacup and saucer, flowers painted by *Corden*

2621 'Harrow' dessert plate, raised and flat gold, cut up with brown and chased by *Greatorex*
2630 'Harrow' dessert plate, raised colour and enamel flowers by *Wale*
2642 'Harrow' dessert plate, white centre and panel flowers painted by *Wale*
2659 Derby twist teacup and saucer, acorn wreath, burnished gold by *Wale*
2660 Derby twist teacup and saucer, painted roses by *Wale*
2665 'Cambridge' dessert, landscape centre by *Gregory*
2666 'Harrow' dessert, landscape centre by *Gregory*
2667 'Harrow' dessert, landscape centre by *Gregory*
2681 'Cambridge' dessert, ivory ground, landscape in sepia by *Gregory*
2702 'Lichfield' dessert, landscape centre by *Trowell*
2703 'Carlton' teacup and saucer, flat gold, cut up with red, green and purple by *Greatorex*
2739 'Harrow' dessert, orchid centre by *Wale*
2740 'Harrow' dessert, flower centre by *Wale*
2741 'Harrow' dessert, flower centre by *Wale*

Sucrier and cream jug, 'Chelsea' shape decorated with 'Olde Avesbury', pattern A73.
Courtesy Royal Crown Derby

'Queen Anne' shape breakfast cup and saucer with 'Red Aves', pattern A74, a printed variation of the 'Olde Avesbury' design.

'Mandarin' on 'Dublin' shape, a pattern of oriental blossoms in blue and gold with touches of green and maroon.
Courtesy Royal Crown Derby

2742 'Harrow' dessert, flower centre by *Corden*
2744 'Harrow' dessert, flower centre by *Trowell*
2745 'Cambridge' dessert, flower centre by *Corden*
2746 'Harrow' dessert, flower centre by *Corden*
2749 'Harrow' dessert, flower centre by *Wale*

2750 'Harrow' dessert, flower centre by *Wale*
2809 'Harrow' dessert, turquoise band and painted flowers by *Clark*
2813 'Durham' dessert, raised and chased centre by *Townsend*
2829 'Harrow' dessert plate, landscape centre by *Trowell*
2871 'Surrey' teacup and saucer, orchids by *Wale*

PATTERN BOOK 7

2890 'Harrow' dessert plate, ivory centre, landscape centre by *Trowell*

2891 'Harrow' dessert plate, landscape centre by *Trowell*

2894 'Rugby' dessert plate, flower centre by *Wale*

2905 'Harrow' dessert plate, flower centre by *Wale*

2912 'Gadroon' dessert plate, flower centre by *Wale*

2945 'Rugby' dessert plate, ivory and marone ground, raised gold, painted flowers by *Wale*

2946 'Rugby' dessert plate, raised and chased centre by *Brownsword*

2947 'Rugby' dessert plate, raised and chased centre by *Brownsword*

2959 'Rugby' dessert plate, flowers painted by *Wale*

2976 'Portland' dessert, flowers by *Wale*

2978 'Surrey' plates, flowers by *Wale*

2991 'Rugby' dessert plate, painted flower centre by *Wood*

2995 'Portland' dessert plate, painted fruit by *Wood*

2999 'Harrow' dessert plate, painted flowers by *Wood*

3001 'Lichfield' dessert, painted fruit and flowers by *Wood*

3011 'Lichfield' dessert, painted flowers by *Wale*

3027 'Portland' dessert, painted flowers by *Wood*

3055 'Harrow' dessert plate, painted flowers by *Wood*

3065 'Rugby' dessert plate, painted flowers by *Wale*

3076 'Stafford' dessert plate, painted flowers and birds by *Peach*

3077 'Lichfield' dessert plate, painted flowers and birds by *Peach*

3078 'Surrey' teacup and saucer, ivory and turquoise, painted birds by *Peach*

3079 'Gadroon' dinner plate, painted flowers by *Clark*

3080 'Stafford' dessert plate, painted begonias by *Wale*

3081 'Gadroon' dinner plate, white with painted roses by *Peach*

3082 As 3081 but with gold leaves painted by *Peach*

3087 'Portland' dessert plate, flowers by *Wood*

3103 'Portland' dessert plate, view in Dove-

dale by *Trowell*

3104 'Lichfield' dessert plate, raised centre, two golds, chased landscape by *Brownsword*

3106 'Portland' dessert, painted begonias traced on gold by *Wale*

3107 'Gadroon' dessert plate, painted flowers, raised and chased gilding by *Peach*

3122 'Stafford' dessert plate, flowers by *Peach*

3168 Vase 669, painted flowers, raised and chased gilding by *Williams*

3172 'Rugby' dessert plate, flower centre by *Williams*

3176 'Portland' dessert plate, centre raised and chased gilding by *Wood*

3177 'Rugby' dessert plate, centre flowers by *Williams*

3181 'Portland' dessert plate, centre flowers by *Williams*

3184 'Clarence' dessert plate, panels and centre raised and chased by *Wood*

3186 'Stafford' dessert plate, centre flowers by *Williams*

3203 'Clarence' dessert plate, flowers by *Wale*

3204 'Clarence' dessert plate, ivory ground, flower sprays by *Wale*

3205 'Clarence' dessert plate, ecru ground, flower border by *Clark*

3206 'Clarence' dessert plate, ecru ground, flower border by *Wale*

3207 'Clarence' dessert plate, ivory ground, two sprays painted by *Clark*

3208 'Clarence' dessert, ivory ground, painted centre by *Williams*

3211 'Clarence' dessert plate, ivory ground, wreaths of flowers and gold sprays by *Wood*

3213 'Rugby' dessert plate, flowers and gilding by *Clark*

3234 'Rugby' dessert plate, roses by *Wood*

3254 'Clarence' dessert plate, painted birds and flowers by *Peach*

3258 'Gadroon' dessert plate, warm ivory ground, raised animals and birds on border (See *Rouse*)

3259 'Clarence' dessert plate, flowers and leaves painted under glaze by *Wale*

3282 'Clarence' dessert plate, two gold cut up with red and green, centre raised and chased by *Wood*

3285 'Portland' dessert plate, flowers by *Clark*

'Royal' shaped Royal Crown Derby plate decorated with 'Imari' style pattern 3563. 8½ in. 1890. *David John Ceramics*

PATTERN BOOK 8

3300 'Gadroon' *8 in.* plate, centre flowers by *Williams*

3321 'Harrow' dessert plate, centre, fruit by *Wood*

3330 'Essex' teaware, white, raised and chased, two golds by *Wood*

3331 Similar to 3330

3340 'Lichfield' dessert plate, fruit and birds in two golds, raised and chased, by *Brownsword*

3341 'Stafford' dessert plate, landscape with raised and chased gold by *Brownsword*

3342 'Paris' teaware, flower sprays by *Peach*

3349 'Clarence' dessert plate, raised and chased birds and gold leaves by *Peach*

3353 'Clarence' dessert plate, rose du barri ground, tinted and gilt flowers by *Williams*

3378 'Gadroon' dessert plate, ground laid border, with raised and chased gold, three panels of birds and flowers by *Peach*

3385 'Stafford' dessert plate, bisque blue, enamel birds, leaves and flies, raised and chased gold festoons by *Leroy*

3398 'Clarence' dessert plate, landscape by *Clark*

3425 'Harrow' dessert plate, landscape by *Clark*

3427 'Rouen' dessert plate, rose du barri ground, white centre with vignette landscape by *Clark*

3428 'Rouen' dessert plate, amber band and turquoise embossments, flower centre by *Wale*

3429 'Clarence' dessert plate, flowers by *Wale*

3489 'Duchess' coffee and saucer, egg-shell, raised and chased sprays by *Bednall*

3490 'Rouen' dessert plate, landscape centre by *Clark*

3498 'Lichfield' dessert plate, solid gold centre, modelled gold classical subjects, richly chased figures and birds by *Brownsword*

3499 Dessert plate, two colour gold, richly raised cupids and leaves by *Brownsword*

3523 'Rouen' dessert plate, raised and chased sprays by *Bednall*

3531 'Clarence' teaware, painted sprays by *Wale*

3532 'Paris' teaware, painted sprays by *Wale*

3543 'Stafford' dessert plate, painted birds by *Brownsword*

3544 'Stafford' dessert plate, raised and chased fish, painted fisherman by *Brownsword*

3547 'Rouen' dessert plate, raised and chased sprays and birds by *Wale*

3548 'Rouen' dessert plate, raised and chased sprays by *Bednall*

3582 'Clarence' dessert plate, landscape, raised, two golds chased by *Clark*

3585 'Rouen' dessert plate, landscape by *Clark*

3592 'Gadroon' dessert plate, painted Sèvres birds by *Clark*

3602 'Rouen' dessert plate, Veronese green with painted flowers by *Williams*

3648 Dessert plate, richly raised and chased birds and fish by *Brownsword*

3649 Dessert plate, richly raised and chased gold classical figures by *Brownsword*

3660 'Portland' dessert plate, painted fish by *Williams*

PATTERN BOOK 9 May 16th 1892

3676 'Argyll' dessert plate, not pierced, flower centre by *Wale*

3680 'Rouen' dessert plate, ivory ground, fish centre by *Wale*

3681 'Rouen' dessert plate, rose du barri ground, fish centre by *Wale*

3682 'Clarence' 8 in. plate, print border, fish centre by *Wale*

3683 'Paris' 8 in. plate, fishes by *Wale*

3728 'Argyll' dessert plate, not pierced, full landscape centre by *Clark*

3773 'Argyll' dessert plate, not pierced, flowers and 'Chelsea Birds' by *Wale*

3780 'Argyll' dessert plate, not pierced, landscape centre by *Clark*

3807 'Hastings' dessert plate, seahorses by *Wale*

3808 'Brighton' dessert plate, flower centre by *Williams*

3822 'Hastings' dessert plate, print border, fish centre by *Wale*

3827 'Hastings' dessert plate, flowers by *Wale*

3830 'Brighton' dessert plate, game birds centre by *Clark*

3831 'Brighton' dessert plate, fish centre by *Clark*

3846 'Hastings' dessert plate, flowers by *Williams*

3864 'Hastings' dessert plate, fish by *Clark*

3870 'Crescent' teacup and saucer, painted roses by *Peach*

3871 'Crescent' teacup and saucer, painted flowers by *Peach*

3878 'Cope' teacup and saucer, shadow green ground, white enamel sprays outlined in raised colour by *Williams*

3881 'Cope' teacup and saucer, flowers by *Wale*

Plate 53. Royal Crown Derby vase and cover in several tones of gilding on a bright red ground, illustrating the craft of gilding. Shape 786 incised. Height 15in. 1893.
The Kathy Sewell Collection

Royal Crown Derby 'Berlin' or 'Empire' shape chocolate cup and saucer, shape 1120, pattern 3788. 1897.
David Holborough Collection

3884 'Hastings' dessert plate, flower sprays by *Wale*
3894 'Hastings' dessert plate, flower sprays by *Wale*
3895 'Hastings' dessert plate, tinted background and green edge, flower centre with raised and chased gilding by *Williams*
3945 'Hastings' dessert plate, fish centre by *Brownsword*
3972 'Rouen' dessert plate, fish centre by *Wale*
3975 'Brighton' dessert plate, fruit centre by *Brownsword*
4008 'Rouen' dessert plate, landscape centre by *Clark*
4009 'Rouen' dessert plate, landscape centre by *Clark*

4010 'Brighton' dessert plate, flower centre by *Williams*
4017 'Brighton' dessert plate, flower centre by *Williams*
4031 'Brighton' dessert plate, landscape by *Clark*
4032 'Brighton' dessert plate, flower centre by *Clark*
4040 'Brighton' dessert plate, fish centre by *Wale*
4066 'Brighton' dessert plate, landscape centre by *Clark*
4071 'Brighton' dessert plate, fish centre by *Wale*
4080 'Hastings' dessert plate, landscape by *Clark*
4081 'Hastings' dessert plate, pink landscape by *Clark*

PATTERN BOOK 10

4082 'Brighton' dessert plate, birds painted by *Wale*
4085 'Hastings' dessert plate, game bird centre by *Williams*
4096 'Warwick' dessert plate, landscape centre by *Clark*
4100 'Brighton' pierced plate, landscape centre by *Clark*
4114 'Warwick' dessert plate, flower centre by *Clark*
4115 'Exeter' dessert plate, game birds by *Williams*
4120 'Brighton' dessert plate, fish by *Williams*
4148 'Warwick' dessert plate, rose centre by *Wood*
4153 'Paris' *10 in.* plate, flowers by *Peach*
4162 'Warwick' dessert plate, flowers painted by *Williams*
4185 'Hastings' dessert plate, painted roses by *Gregory*
4186 'Clarence' *10 in.* plate, painted roses by *Gregory*
4187 'Sefton' teacup and saucer, painted roses by *Gregory*
4191 'Exeter' dessert plate, painted fishes by

Williams
4195 'Exeter' dessert plate, landscape in bisque blue by *Clark*
4202 'Dorset' teacup and saucer, painted roses by *Gregory*
4207 'Dorset' teacup and saucer, painted flowers by *Peach*
4208 'Dorset' teacup and saucer, painted flowers by *Peach*
4209 'Dorset' teacup and saucer, painted flowers by *Peach*
4210 'Dorset' teacup and saucer, painted flowers by *Peach*
4219 'Exeter' dessert plate, bisque blue landscape by *Clark*
4256 *10 in.* plate, bisque blue band, roses and oak wreath by *Gregory*
4372 'Brighton' dessert plate, painted roses by *Gregory*
4373 'Warwick' dessert plate, centre painted group (old Derby style) by *Gregory*
4389 'Brighton' dessert plate, painted roses by *Gregory*
4395 'Brighton' dessert plate, apple green border, flower centre by *Gregory*

PATTERN BOOK 11 Feb 15th 1895

4612 'Warwick' dessert plate, blue border with raised and chased gold, centre 'Conway Castle' painted by *Clark*

PATTERN BOOK 12 April 1st 1896

PATTERN BOOK 13 May 1897

5497 Vase painted by *Leroy*
5655 Vase painted by *Leroy*

5660 Vase painted by *Leroy*
5661 Vase painted by *Leroy*

Royal Crown Derby plate decorated with pattern 5193. Width 8½ in. 1897.
David Holborough Collection

Royal Crown Derby cabaret teapot and cover, pattern 6299, 'Queen Anne' shape. Height 3¾ in. 1890.
David Holborough Collection

Top left.
Plate 54. Royal Crown Derby figure of Anna Ahlers, the
actress, specially produced by Royal Crown Derby and
modelled by Tom Wilkinson, shape F 473, 10½ in. 1933.
David Holborough Collection

Above:
Plate 55. Royal Crown Derby figure of 'Mistress Ford' from
the 'Merry Wives of Windsor'. 8 in. 1930.
David Holborough Collection

Plate 56. Royal Crown Derby 'Chelsea' shape sugar box and
cover decorated wth a variation of 'Derby Posies', pattern
A 512. 4½ in. 1939.
Brian Quinn Collection

Royal Crown Derby covered pot,
pattern 6299, 4¾ in. 1909.
David Holborough Collection

PATTERN BOOK 14

5688	Vase painted by *Leroy*	**5779**	Vase painted by *Leroy*
5722	Vase painted by *Leroy*	**5780**	Vase painted by *Leroy*
5723	Vase painted by *Leroy*	**5786**	Vase painted by *Leroy*
5724	Vase painted by *Leroy*	**5797**	Vase painted by *Leroy*
5725	Vase painted by *Leroy*	**5811**	Vase painted by *Leroy*
5726	Vase painted by *Leroy*	**5812**	Vase painted by *Leroy*
5756	Vase painted by *Leroy*	**5813**	Vase painted by *Leroy*
5757	Vase painted by *Leroy*	**5821**	Vase painted by *Leroy*
5776	Vase painted by *Leroy*	**5823**	Vase painted by *Leroy*
5777	Vase painted by *Leroy*	**5824**	Vase painted by *Leroy*
5778	Vase painted by *Leroy*	**5825**	Vase painted by *Leroy*

End of Pattern Book 14. June 10th 1899

PATTERN BOOK 18 Feb 1903

7195	'Clarence' dessert plate, cobalt border, shipping centre by *Dean*	**7303**	'Reading' dessert plate, cobalt border, seascape centre by *Dean*
7197	Miniature vases, painted seascapes by *Dean*	**7305**	'Reading' dessert plate, amber border, seascape centre by *Dean*
7200	Vase, seascapes by *Dean*		

Royal Crown Derby artist Michael Crawley, with four of the six hand-painted plates featuring Derbyshire scenes which were presented to H.R.H. Princess Anne when she visited the Royal Crown Derby factory on November 27th 1974.
Courtesy Royal Crown Derby

PATTERN BOOK 19

7467 'Ely' *10 in.* plate, cobalt ground and rich painting by *C Gresley*

7489 'Ely' dessert plate, rich painted centre by *Gregory*

7490 'Royal Gadroon' plate, cobalt band, rich painted flower centre by *Gregory*

7491 'Clarence' dessert plate, rich painted flower centre by *Gregory*

7515 'Ely' *10 in.* plate, white, rich flower painting by *C Gresley*

7534 'Royal Gadroon' dessert plate, cobalt band, painted seascapes by *Dean*
Pattern Book 20. Commenced February 1906

7571 'Royal Gadroon' dessert plate, empire and apple green border, flower painted centre by *Gregory*

7575 'Argyll' dessert plate, painted by *Gregory*

7675 'Royal Gadroon' dessert plate, cobalt band, painted figure in centre by *Boullemier*

7729 'Stanhope' dessert plate, cobalt band, flower centre by *Gregory*

7732 Vases, marine views by *Dean* in colours, all over on plain shapes

PATTERN BOOK 20 Feb 1906

7775 'Stanhope' dessert plate, cobalt border, painted flowers by *Gregory*
Pattern Book 21. Commenced June 1907

7916 'Royal Gadroon' dessert plate, cobalt border, flowers by *Gregory*

PATTERN BOOK 21 June 1907

8237 'Royal Gadroon' *8 in.* plate, cobalt blue border with raised gold, richly painted flower centre by *Gregory*

Group of miniatures: coffee pot, height 3in. shape 1675 pattern 6299; teacup and saucer, height 1in. shape 1455 painted roses; teapot 1¾in., sugar box 1½in., cream 1in. shape 1496 pattern 2451. Dates 1905, 1913 and 1915. *Private Collection*

'Imperia' on the new 'Queen's Gadroon' shape A1289, turquoise blue and gold scroll design. *Courtesy Royal Crown Derby*

"Titanic" sails on first voyage from Southampton to
New York on Wednesday, April 10th, 1912.

The front cover of a leaflet
published by the Royal Crown
Derby Porcelain Company.

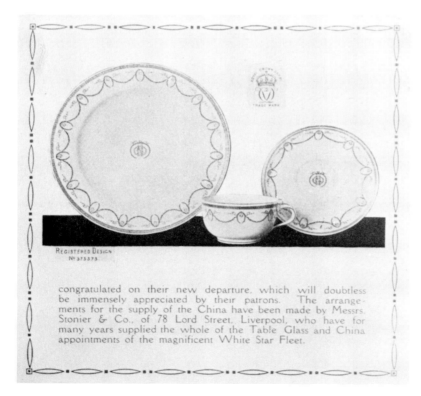

congratulated on their new departure, which will doubtless
be immensely appreciated by their patrons. The arrangements for the supply of the China have been made by Messrs.
Stonier & Co., of 78 Lord Street, Liverpool, who have for
many years supplied the whole of the Table Glass and China
appointments of the magnificent White Star Fleet.

Plate and cup and saucer from the
service commissioned for use on the
SS Titanic, with gold acid etched
border and chaplets and garlands in
delicate green. 1912.

'Vine' with cobalt blue border,
white and gold leaves and grapes,
solid gold handles, pattern A920.
Courtesy Royal Crown Derby

PATTERN BOOK 22 Feb 1909

8473 'Lowestoft' dessert plate, centre blue
and white seascape by *Dean*

8483 'Royal Gadroon' dessert plate, pink
border with insects and centre painting
of game birds by *C Gresley*

8484 'Stanhope' dessert plate, pink ground
with reserves of flowers and birds by
Mosley

8506 'Stanhope' dessert plate, cobalt band,
shipping in natural colours by *Dean*

8523 'Stanhope' dessert plate, centre painted
roses by *Harris*

8524 'Dorset' teaware and 'Apsley' coffees
decorated as 8484

8537 'Royal Gadroon' 8 in. plate, grey border,

game bird centre by *Harris*

8538 'Royal Gadroon' 8 in. plate, grey border,
fish centre by *C Gresley*

8539 Plain 8 in. plate, apple green border,
game bird centre by *Harris*

8540 'Ely' 8 in. plate, cobalt band, game bird
centre by *Harris*

8567 'Ely' 8 in. plate, cobalt band, painted
centres (castles) by *Mosley*

8568 'Stanhope' dessert plate, landscape
centre (various) by *C Gresley*

8765 'Talbot' dessert plate, flat, raised and
chased gold border, fish centre by
C Gresley

Pattern Book completed January 24th 1911

PATTERN BOOK 23 Jan 24th 1911

8864 'Royal Gadroon' dessert plate,
landscape centre by *Mosley*

8865 'Royal Gadroon' dessert plate,
landscape centre by *Mosley*

8925 'Empress' dessert plate, painted
landscapes by *Mosley*

8930 'Clarence' dessert plate, painted
landscapes by *Mosley*

8968 'Royal Gadroon' dessert plate, flower
centre by *Gregory*

8997 'Stanhope' dessert plate, painted fish by
C Gresley (done for G Rouard Paris)

9026 'Royal Gadroon' dessert plate, cobalt
band landscape centre by *Dean*

9098 'Empress' dessert plate, seascape centre
in colours by *Dean*

End of Pattern Book March 23rd 1914

Royal Crown Derby tableware decorated on 'Duesbury' shape with a new pattern 'Kedleston', A1313, introduced 1987.

PATTERN BOOK 25 July 1926

9633 'Brighton' dessert plate, cobalt border, landscape centre by C Gresley

9639 'Talbot' dessert plate, landscape centre by C Gresley

9640 'Talbot' dessert plate, landscape centre by C Gresley

9645 'Ely' dessert plate, flower group centre by C Gresley

9646 'Talbot' dessert plate, flower group centre by C Gresley

9647 'Talbot' dessert plate, 'Rockingham Posies' by C Gresley

9651 'Ely' dessert plate, roses by C Gresley

9656 'Royal Gadroon' dessert plate, flower centre by Gregory

9661 'Anson' teacup and saucer, seascape in rhodian blue by Dean

9662 Plain 10 in. plate, seascapes in three panels painted in rhodian blue by Dean

9671 Teacup and saucer, 'Royal Gadroon', seascapes painted in rhodian blue by Dean

9704 'Talbot' dessert plate, painted fish centre by C Gresley

9705 'Royal Gadroon' plate, painted fish or game centre by C Gresley

9706 'Royal Gadroon' plate, painted fish or game centre by C Gresley

9707 'Stanhope' dessert plate, painted fish or game centre by C Gresley

9708 'Talbot' dessert plate, painted fish or game centre by C Gresley

9712 'Stanhope' dessert plate, green border, painted fish or game by C Gresley

9713 'Stanhope' dessert plate, blue border, painted fish or game by C Gresley

9715 'Royal Gadroon' dessert plate, painted game or fish centre by C Gresley

9716 'Tavistock' 10 in. plate, flowers in centre by C Gresley

9720 'Talbot' 8 in. plate, Japan border as 9011, fish or game centre by C Gresley

9721 'Talbot' 8 in. plate, painted fish or game centre by C Gresley

9723 Vase decoration, ships by Dean in oven blue

9725 'Clarendon' 10 in. plate, painted seascape in colour by Dean

9749 'Portman' 10 in. plate, painted flower centre by Gregory

9751 'Ely' 10 in. plate, flower group in centre by Gregory

9753 'Audley' 10 in. plate, fruit and flower group by Gregory

9761

9784 'Royal' dessert plate, centre country scene by Dean

9795 'Sussex' 10 in. plate, centre country scene by Dean

9799 'Harrow' dessert plate, three small landscapes on rim and full landscape centre by Dean

9800 'Clarendon' 10 in. plate, cobalt band, English country scenes in natural colours by Dean

9801 As 9800

9802 'Tavistock' 10 in. plate, decoration as 9800

9822 'Chelsea' teacup and saucer, rhodian blue seascapes by Dean

9823 As 9822 but ships in natural colours

9842 'Clarence' dessert plate, landscape centre by Dean

9877

9908 Vases, various shapes, painted flowers by C Gresley

Royal Crown Derby wares decorated with 'Grenville' pattern A1303, on 'Surrey' shape. Introduced in 1986.
Courtesy Royal Crown Derby

9909 Vase, 1831 shape, cobalt ground, painted flowers by *Gregory*
9943 'Chelsea' sweet, painted landscape by *Dean*
9944 Tray, 1803 shape, seascape by *Dean*

9955 'Royal Gadroon' *8 in.* plate, cobalt blue ground, three panels and centre landscapes by *Dean*
9961 Covered boxes 1743, covers painted with landscapes by *Dean*

PATTERN BOOK A1

A34 'Portman' *10 in.* plate, green and ivory ground, flower centre by *Jessop*
A40 'Portman' *10 in.* plate, cobalt and ivory ground, flower centre by *Gregory*
A42 'Tavistock' *10 in.* plate, green and ivory ground, flower centre by *Jessop*
A44 'Clarendon' *10 in.* plate, six painted groups and centre by *Jessop*
A112 'Clarendon' *10 in.* plate, painted flowers by *C Gresley*
A123 'Chelsea' teacup and saucer, painted flowers by *C Gresley*
A130 'Talbot' *8 in.* plate, green ground, full centre, Scottish view by *Dean*
A141 Vase, shape 1258, ivory ground with three painted landscapes by *Dean*
A173 'Silver' *10 in.* plate, ivory ground with seascape centre by *Dean*
A185 Vase, ivory ground with painted landscapes by *Dean*
A235 'Brighton' *10 in.* plate, ivory ground with racing yachts in colour by *Dean*
A227 'Silver' *10 in.* plate, ivory ground, painted flower centre by *Gregory*

A299 'Stanhope' *10 in.* plate, ivory ground, painted ship centres by *Dean*
A300 'Stanhope' *10 in.* plate, flower centre by *C Gresley*
A301 'Royal Gadroon' *8 in.*, flowers in panels by *C Gresley*
A302 'Royal Gadroon' *8 in.*, green ground, with rose centre by *C Gresley*
A303 'Ely' *8 in.* plate, marone border, flower centre by *C Gresley*
A317 'Clarence' dessert plate, ivory border, rose centre by *C Gresley*
A322 Vase shape 1658, green ground painted flowers by *C Gresley*
A323 Vase, shape 1832, ivory ground, painted flowers by *C Gresley*
A324 'Ely' *10 in.* plate, rose centre by *C Gresley*
A331 'Clarence' dessert plate, landscape centre by *Dean*
A343 'Clarence' dessert plate, flower centre by *C Gresley*
A334 'Clarence' dessert plate, small flower centre by *C Gresley*

SUMMARY OF PATTERN BOOKS

Book No.	Pattern Numbers	Date (where known)	Book No.	Pattern Numbers	Date (where known)
1	1-885	August 1878	18	7081-7415	Feb. 1903-Jul. 1904
2	886-1285		19	7416-7760	Aug. 1904-Jan. 1906
3	1286-1548		20	7761-8082	Feb. 1906-Jun. 1907
4	1549-1942		21	8083-8433	Jun. 1907-Feb. 1909
5	1943-2439		22	8434-8777	Feb. 1909-Jan. 1911
6	2440-2888		23	8778-9166	Feb. 1911-Mar. 1914
7	2889-3299		24	9167-9621	Mar. 1914-
8	3300-3663		25	9622-9999/1	July 1926
9	3664-4081	May 1892	26	Prints off coppers	
10	4082-4508		27	Prints off coppers	
11	4509-4889	Feb. 1895	28	Prints off coppers	
12	4890-5295	Apr. 1896	29	Prints off coppers	
13	5296-5685	May 1897-Mar. 1898	A1	A1-A.389	
14	5686-6067	Apr.1898-Jun. 1899	A2	A.390-A.888	
15	6068-6397		A3	A.889-A.1213	
16	6398-6736	Sep. 1900-Dec. 1901	A4	A.1215-A.1318	Sept. 16 1959-present
17	6737-7080	Dec. 1901-Feb. 1903			(April 4 1988)

'Royal' shaped plate with outline printed hunting scene, coloured and signed by P. Maynard.
Originally similar subjects were painted by male artists includng Barlow and Browning whose names do
not appear in the biographies. Amongst the women enamellers who later painted them were: J. Doyle,
P. Webb, S. Scott, M. Townsend and C.M. Pell.
Courtesy Royal Crown Derby

H.M. Queen Elizabeth the Queen Mother signing the visitors' book on the occasion of her visit, June 1971.
Courtesy Royal Crown Derby

H.R.H. The Princess Anne being greeted by the Chairman of Royal Crown Derby Porcelain Co. Ltd., Derby, Mr. John Bellak, on the occasion of her visit to Osmaston Road, November 27th 1974.
Courtesy Royal Crown Derby

Walter Lowndes holding part of a tea service which was later presented to H.R.H. Princess Alexandra when she laid the foundation stone of the new Chichester Festival Theatre. On each piece a different Shakespearian scene is depicted. 1961.
Courtesy Royal Crown Derby

The Venezuelan Ambassador with two presentation plaques; one of the President and the other of the Arms of the Republic of Venezuela. Painted by Douglas Hague.

12 LEROY AND TAILLANDIER SPECIAL PRODUCTIONS

The records of the vase cards (cards on which the patterns and shapes of the vases were drawn in detail) are so incomplete that it has proved impossible to reproduce them; we can however, list some of the specially produced plates and vases, largely the work, both in design and execution, of Leroy, who was joined by the very talented artist P. Taillandier from the beginning of 1894 until 1895. All the Leroy special productions bore the prefix 'F', and are not found in the general pattern books (see plates 37a, b and c, p.83).

CARD 2

2 'Gadroon' dessert plate, central panel of flowers reserved in ornate gilt frame on turquoise ground, border white with festoons of flowers, turquoise and gold gadroon edging. *Leroy*
(*This record made March 3rd 1892, from plate sent to Phillips, the original being sent to Caudwell & Co. in 1891*)

6 'Gadroon' dessert plate, cobalt and turquoise ground with centre panel of exotic bird reserved in gold frame, border raised gold flowers and natural flowers. *Leroy July 23rd 1892*

CARD 3

5 'Gadroon' dessert plate, centre panel, flowers in gold reserve, border panels, flowers and raised gilding. *Leroy July 23rd 1892*

7 'Gadroon' dessert plate, centre panel, vase of flowers on table by a musical instrument, all reserved in ornate gilt frame, border panels, flowers and raised gilding. *Leroy July 23rd 1892*

CARD 4

8 'Argyll' pierced dessert plate, rose du barri ground, full centre birds, border panels, musical instruments and flowers. *Leroy April 1892*

9 'Argyll' pierced dessert plate, central panel of birds in gold reserve, rose du barri ground to shoulder, border panels of flowers and musical instruments. *Leroy May 1892*

CARD 5

11 'Argyll' dessert plate, not pierced, centre panel of flowers in gold reserve, heliotrope ground to shoulder, border panels of bird and flowers

12 'Argyll' dessert plate, pierced, the same as 8 but has green with raised chased flowers in all six panels. These flowers are raised and chased by *Leroy* but covered by *Brown*. Gilt exactly as 8

13 'Argyll' dessert plate, not pierced, Sèvres flowers on white. Flat gilt by *Barker*. *December 1892*

14 'Argyll' dessert plate, pierced, gilt as 9 by *Brown*, but finished in turquoise with group of flowers in centre, three trophies in large panels, three roses in small panels, white enamel spots on border. *December 1892*

CARD 6

15 'Gadroon' dinner plate, heliotrope border, white centre with flower group, three reserves of flowers with raised gilding on border. *December 1892*

16 'Gadroon' plate 8 in., similar to 2 except for centre, and that gilding on shoulder is on a ground colour. *January 1893*

17 'Brighton' plate 8 in., marone and ivory border with reserves of painted trophies and flowers, raised gilding. *March 1894*

18 'Brighton' plate 10 in., pink, marone and ivory ground border with raised gold and painted floral panels. *March 1894*

[From 19 to 46 missing]

CARD 7

47 'Brighton' dessert plate, pansy spray centre reserved in raised gold, rose du barri and celadon ground, with panels of musical instruments and roses, raised gold finish. *May 1894*

48 'Brighton' dessert plate, raised gilding at shoulder, rose festoons between two shades of blue groundlay and raised gilding to the rim. *May 1894*

49 'Brighton' dessert plate, flower spray centre within raised gold circle, celadon green ground to shoulder, border of celadon, pink and raised gold, with inset panels of flowers. *May 1894*

50 'Brighton' dessert plate, marone and pink ground with centre panel of flowers and border panels of roses and cornflowers. *May 1894*

Pierced 'Argyll' dessert plate from the special productions (card no. 11, plate no. 77). Woman's head in central raised gold reserve, pink ground to edge with panels of flowers and birds and raised gilding. Painting by P. Taillandier, signed. 1893. It is interesting to note that the cypher mark was not always changed immediately at the year end and this plate and that shown right were obviously painted by Taillandier shortly after his arrival at Osmaston Road early in 1894. Both plates bear the Royal Warrant, and mark over glaze in green.
Courtesy George Woods

CARD 8

51 'Brighton' dessert plate, border picked out in turquoise and ivory with raised gilding and festoons of painted flowers. *May 1894*

52 'Brighton' dessert plate, two shades of blue and ivory ground border, with panels of painted flowers between raised gold trophies. *June 1894*

CARD 9

54 'Brighton' dessert plate, narrow raised gold border, with enamel tracing

55 Similar to 54

56 'Argyll' pierced dessert plate, centre raised gold circle, celeste ground to rim, border panels of musical instruments and roses with raised and flat gold

57 'Argyll' dessert plate, not pierced, border only panels of flowers with raised gold surrounding

CARD 10

58 Vase 394 pink and green ground, with cameo of musical instruments and flowers, raised and flat gilding

59 Vase 394 pink and green ground, cameo, female head, reserved in raised gold

60 Vase, foot and neck dark blue green ground, body lighter green, panel possibly flowers reserved in ornate gilding

CARD 11

61 'Argyll' dessert plate, not pierced, ivory ground centre, celadon border with panels of flowers and raised gilding

62 'Coupe' shape dessert plate, ivory ground, painted centre by *Leroy*. Trophy of musical instruments with flowers

63 As 62, painted centre by *Leroy* flowers, clover and dandelion.

77 'Argyll' dessert plate, pierced. Woman's head in central raised gold reserve, pink and green ground to edge with panels of flowers and birds, raised and flat gold

78 'Argyll' dessert plate, not pierced. Woman's head on ivory ground reserved in ornate gilding, Dover green ground to shoulder, with panels of flowers and birds

CARD 12

64 Vase 394 light and dark green ground, front panel, heads painted and reserved in ornate gilt frame, flowers on the reverse side

65 Vase 686 marone and pink ground, painting and gilding similar to 64

66 Vase 1233 celadon and ivory ground, painted with cupids and flat and raised gilding

67 Vase 653 dark green and light green ground, panel of cupids reserved in raised gold

CARD 13

68 Vase 394 pale blue and ivory ground, painted with full length figures of children, raised gilding

69 Vase 972 dark and light green ground, painted with two cupids reserved in raised gilt frame

70 Vase 550 pink and green ground, ornate raised gilding with small panels of painted flowers

CARD 14

71 Vase 653 dark and light green ground, painted with children's heads reserved in raised frame

72 Vase 328 celadon and ivory ground, painted with single children full length

73 Vase 328 dark and light green ground, painted with children's heads reserved in raised gilt frame

'Argyll' dessert plate from the special productions (card no. 16, plate 79). Two children's heads in centre, pale blue ground border with panels of birds and musical instruments reserved in raised gilding. Painting by P. Taillandier, signed. 1893.
Private Collection

74 Vase 328 dark and light green ground, painted with cupids reserved in raised gilt frame

CARD 15

75 Vase 862 celadon, ivory and pink groundlaying, chased gold trophies, painted flower groups, rich raised gilding
76 Vase 394 ivory, marone, pink and celeste groundlaying, festoons of flowers and raised gilding

CARD 16

79 'Argyll' dessert plate, not pierced, two children's heads by *Taillandier* in centre panel, blue ground border with panels of musical instruments and birds reserved in raised gilding
80 'Gadroon' dessert plate, solid gold edge, figure subjects from Girardel in centre by *Taillandier*
81 'Argyll' dessert plate, pierced, cupid playing flute in centre by *Taillandier*, reserved in ornate gilt frame, celadon ground to edge with panels of flowers
82 'Gadroon' dessert plate, as 80 but rustic figures in centre by *Taillandier*

CARD 17

83 'Argyll' pierced dessert plate, ivory, light and dark green ground border with panels of roses; centre, mother and child after Bougereau by *Taillandier*

CARD 18

84 'Brighton' dessert plate, ivory with pink and blue ground, raised and chased flower panels with painted flowers. *March 7th 1895*
85 'Brighton' *10 in.* plate, ivory ground centre with pink and green border, and flower panels, raised and chased gilding. *March 7th 1895*
86 'Gadroon' *8 in.* plate, marone and ivory ground, decoration as 7
87 'Brighton' *10 in.* plate, ivory, marone and pink ground with border panels of roses and cornflowers

[88 to 106 missing]

CARD 27

107 Vase 1067 pink, ivory and celeste ground, festoons of painted flowers and raised gold sprays, small cameo head on front

108 Vase 328 ivory, celadon and blue ground, floral festoons and raised gilding

CARD 29

111 'Gadroon' 8 in. plate, basket and floral festoons, celeste and gold edge with white and red enamel spots
112 'Brighton' dessert plate, yellow, ivory and green ground with border panels of flowers
113 'Brighton' dessert plate, yellow, pink and green ground with border panels of flowers

CARD 30

114 'Gadroon' dessert plate, ivory ground with blue edge, border of floral festoons and raised gilding
117 'Argyll' dessert plate, not pierced, ivory and green with border panels of flowers

CARD 31

115 Vase 328 ivory, green and celeste ground, with panels of birds and fruit, festoons of flowers
118 Vase 328 green, ivory and celeste ground with roses and forget-me-nots

13 LIST OF FIGURES, ANIMALS AND BIRDS

Although sadly very incomplete, a list of figures, animals and birds is included, as in the case of the Special Productions. The reader is warned that both the Leroy special productions and the figures were numbered by Royal Crown Derby with the prefix 'F'.

The women enamellers were responsible for the colouring of the following items and many have signed their work. They will not be found amongst the biographies of the painters.

22	Love letter, a figure of a girl holding a letter
34	Girl with a turkey
	Boy with a goose
	Lady with a basket on head
	Man with a basket on head and holding a spade
	Man with a basket
	Mule and a monk, possibly 'Persuasion'
40	Boy seated and wearing a hat
41	Boy with a bat
52	Dr. Syntax
53	San Grada
54	Coquet
55	Coquette
56	Don Quixote
57	Sancho Panza
	Friar Tuck
	Robin Hood
63	Robinson Crusoe
64	Man Friday
69	Eros
70	Winged figure
73	Bacchus
74	Bacchus
83	Little Dorrit
85	Shepherd
86	Shepherdess
F14	Derby dwarfs
F82	Oliver Twist
	Elements
F303	Earth
F304	Air
F305	Fire
F306	Water
	Seasons
F308	Summer
F309	Autumn
F310	Winter
F311	Peacock (tall)
F312	Peacock (low)
F466	Spanish girl
F467	Spanish man
F468	Olga
F469	Margery
F470	Wings modelled by *M R Locke 1921*
F471	Hunting Girl } *pair*
F472	Huntsman
F473	Anna Ahlers modelled by *Tom Wilkinson*
F474	Gypsy girl
F476	Hawking modelled by *G Baker*

F477	Japanese girl (geisha)
F478	Fisherwife modelled by *M R Locke*
F480	Ski-ing girl modelled by *M R Locke 1933*
F482	Eve } *pair*
F483	Adam
F484	Lady reading a book. Modelled by *M R Locke 1927*
F485	Rustic lamp with a female figure on base
F486	Peter Pan modelled by *M R Locke*
F487	Jockey
F489	Donkey with Panniers s/s
F490	Donkey with Panniers l/s
F491	Fox
F492	Terrier (toy)
F493	Scotch terrier modelled by *Arnold Mikelson*
F494	Terrier
F495	Spaniel (lying down) modelled by *Arnold Mikelson*
F496	Greyhound
F497	Setter
F498	Pointer
F499	Foxhound modelled by *Arnold Mikelson*
F500	Kingfisher s/s
F502	Scottish terrier
F504	Spaniel (standing) modelled by *Arnold Mikelson*
F505	Alsatian (standing) modelled by *Arnold Mikelson*
F506	Alsatian (lying) modelled by *Arnold Mikelson*
F507	Rabbit l/s modelled by *Arnold Mikelson*
F508	Rabbit s/s on stand, modelled by *Arnold Mikelson*
F509	Lamb modelled by *Arnold Mikelson*
F510	Shire horse (running) modelled by *Arnold Mikelson*
F511	Horse on stand, modelled by *Arnold Mikelson*
F512	Foal (lying down) modelled by *Arnold Mikelson*
F513	Little eagle modelled by *Arnold Mikelson*
F514	Cockatoo modelled by *Arnold Mikelson*
F515	Ptarmigan modelled by *Arnold Mikelson*
F516	Bald eagle modelled by *Arnold Mikelson*
F517	Magpie modelled by *Arnold Mikelson*
F518	Macaw modelled by *Arnold Mikelson*
F519	Falcon modelled by *Arnold Mikelson*
F520	Jay modelled by *Arnold Mikelson*

Pair of Mansion House dwarfs, originally produced at Nottingham Road, then at King Street and currently at Osmaston Road. Shape F 14.
Courtesy Royal Crown Derby

Spanish Girl and Spanish Man, shapes F 466 and F 467. c.1930.
David Holborough Collection

Right:
Figure representing 'Autumn' from a set of seasons, first produced in the 18th century. c.1950.
Royal Crown Derby

Far right:
'Olga', shape F 468. c.1930.
F. Rasmusson Collection

'Foxhound', 'Hunting Girl' and 'The Huntsman', shapes F 499, F 471, F 472.
Courtesy Royal Crown Derby

'The Geisha', 'Ski-girl' and 'The Gipsy', shapes F 477, F 480 and F 474. c.1930.
Courtesy Royal Crown Derby

Group of animals.
Courtesy Royal Crown Derby

Royal Crown Derby 'Beefeater', lacking his pike, made specially for James Leather Ltd., later Leather & Snook, Piccadilly, London. Height 12in. 1950s.
David Holborough Collection

'The Fox' and 'The Greyhound', shapes F 491 and F 496. c.1930.
Courtesy Royal Crown Derby

Fox terrier and Aberdeen terrier, shapes F 494 and F 502. c.1954.
Courtesy Royal Crown Derby

The Barn Owl. Shape F525.
Courtesy Royal Crown Derby

F521 Green woodpecker modelled by *Arnold Mikelson*

F522 Cockerel modelled by *Arnold Mikelson*

F523 Pheasant modelled by *Arnold Mikelson*

F524 Pheasant (lamp) modelled by *Arnold Mikelson*

F525 Owl modelled by *Arnold Mikelson*

F528 Little shepherd (feeding time) modelled by *Arnold Mikelson*

F528a Terrier (puppy) modelled by *Arnold Mikelson*

F529 Blue tit and chicks modelled by *Arnold Mikelson*

F530 Australian kingfisher modelled by *Arnold Mikelson*

F531 Blue tit modelled by *Arnold Mikelson*

F532 Setter (on stand) modelled by *Arnold Mikelson*

F532a Setter s/s (on stand) modelled by *Arnold Mikelson*

F533 Mallards on base modelled by *Arnold Mikelson*

F534 Pekingese modelled by *Arnold Mikelson*

F535 Kingfisher modelled by *Arnold Mikelson*

F536 Goldfinch modelled by *Arnold Mikelson*

F537 Red-rumped swallow modelled by *Arnold Mikelson*

F538 Bullfinch modelled by *Arnold Mikelson*

F539 Long-tailed tit modelled by *Arnold Mikelson*

F540 Fairy wrens (Austr.) modelled by *Arnold Mikelson*

F541 Tern modelled by *Arnold Mikelson*

F542 Thrush chicks modelled by *Arnold Mikelson*

F543 Golden oriole modelled by *Arnold Mikelson*

F544 Bee-eater modelled by *Arnold Mikelson*

F545 Fan-tailed pigeon modelled by *Arnold Mikelson*

F546 Playtime modelled by *Arnold Mikelson*

F547 Hobby (kestrel) modelled by *Arnold Mikelson*

F548 Leapfrog modelled by *Arnold Mikelson*

F550 Green woodpecker modelled by *Arnold Mikelson*

F551 Owl s/s modelled by *Arnold Mikelson*

F552 Chelsea Bird (left) modelled by *Arnold Mikelson*

F552a Chelsea Bird (right) modelled by *Arnold Mikelson*

F553 Chelsea Bird (centre) modelled by *Arnold Mikelson*

F554 Macaw s/s modelled by *Arnold Mikelson*

F555 Budgerigars modelled by *Arnold Mikelson*

F556 Pheasant s/s modelled by *Arnold Mikelson*

F557 Cloncurry parrot

F558 Robin modelled by *Arnold Mikelson*

F559 Swan

F560 Redstart modelled by *Arnold Mikelson*

F561 Playtime girl

F562 Playtime boy

Owl (salt & pepper) modelled by *Arnold Mikelson*

Hornbill (salt & pepper) modelled by *Arnold Mikelson*

The Long Tailed Tit, shape F 539,
in current production.
Courtesy Royal Crown Derby

Plate 57. Bird study in watercolours by Donald Birbeck. c.1935.
Royal Crown Derby Archives

Royal Crown Derby group, shape F 548. 'Leapfrog', dating from
the 1950s. 6½in. high.
Courtesy David John Ceramics

Royal Crown Derby figure of 'Playtime', shape F 546, modelled by
Arnold Mikelson. 5¼in. c.1948.
Mrs. Joan Neat Collection

Pair of Royal Crown Derby figures
representing Adam and Eve, shape
F 483 and F 482. Height 5in. 1937.
Courtesy M.K. Nielsen Antiques

Golden Oriole, shape F 543. c.1958.

Plate 58. Bird study in watercolours by Donald Birbeck. c.1935.
Royal Crown Derby Archives

Plate 59. Bird study in watercolours by Donald Birbeck. c.1935.
Royal Crown Derby Archives

Group of P.R. figures modelled by Edward Drew. From left to right, 'Stepping Stones', 'Harvest Time', 'First Attempt', 'Joy', 'Romeo and Juliet'. c.1959. The prefix 'PR' was used for these figures because they were designed by Philip Robinson, son of H.T. Robinson, at that time both Managing Director and Art Director.
Courtesy Royal Crown Derby

PR 1 Flower seller (girl) modelled by *Edward Drew*

PR 2 Fruit seller (boy) modelled by *Edward Drew*

PR 3 Peace modelled by *Edward Drew*

PR 4 Joy modelled by *Edward Drew*

PR 5 April (Spring time) modelled by *Edward Drew*

PR 6 June (Harvest time) modelled by *Edward Drew*

PR 7 September (Stepping stones) modelled by *Edward Drew*

PR 8 December (First attempt) modelled by *Edward Drew*

PR 9 Shepherd modelled by *Edward Drew*

PR10 Shepherdess modelled by *Edward Drew*

PR11 Boy (Romeo) modelled by *Edward Drew*

PR12 Girl (Juliet) modelled by *Edward Drew*

PR13 Cat modelled by *Edward Drew*

PR14 Kitten A, modelled by *Edward Drew*

PR15 Kitten B, modelled by *Edward Drew*

PR16 Mouse modelled by *Edward Drew*

PR17 Mouse on cheese modelled by *Edward Drew*

PR18 Duck modelled by *Edward Drew*

PR19 Baby deer modelled by *Edward Drew*

PR20 Foal A, modelled by *Edward Drew*

PR21 Foal B, modelled by *Edward Drew*

PR22 Horse modelled by *Edward Drew*

PR23 Canadian goose modelled by *Edward Drew*

PR24 Boxer modelled by *Edward Drew*

PR25 Dachshund modelled by *Edward Drew*

PR26 Poodle s/s modelled by *Edward Drew*

PR27 Poodle l/s modelled by *Edward Drew*

PR28 Beagle modelled by *Edward Drew*

Royal Crown Derby animals from the Paperweight Collection designed by Brian Branscombe and modelled by Robert Jefferson. The cat is 6in. and the harvest mouse 2in. This series of animals, birds and fish has been received with much approval by collectors and lovers of fine china.
Courtesy Royal Crown Derby

PAPERWEIGHTS

P 1	Duck	**P 13**	Cat
P 2	Owl	**P 14**	Harvest Mouse
P 3	Quail	**P 15**	Pig
P 4	Penguin	**P 16**	Snail
P 5	Rabbit	**P 17**	Badger
P 6	Wren	**P 18**	Chipmunk
P 7	Fox	**P 19**	Golden Carp
P 8	Frog	**P 20**	Dolphin
P 9	Hedgehog	**P 21**	Crab
P 10	Pheasant	**P 22**	Dragon
P 11	Turtle	**P 23**	Koala Bear
P 12	Seal	**P 24**	Duckbilled Platypus

Plate 60. Watercolour painting of a red squirrel by Donald Birbeck. c.1935.

14 DESIGNERS, MODELLERS, PAINTERS AND GILDERS

ABLOTT, Richard. Born in Canada, son of an English soldier whose regiment was serving at Fort Garry, Manitoba. Their return to England was not long delayed and without the regiment being engaged in active service. Whilst writing Ablott's biography a letter was received from his great-granddaughter, Mrs. Olive Hendrickson who wrote that the family in Canada and South Africa have signed specimens of his work. He was said to have the ability to 'convey the effect of distance'. A good landscape painter, Richard Ablott was one of the last apprentices at the old Nottingham Road factory and was stated by Dr. Gilhespy to have worked at King Street. Haslem wrote that he had been employed by different manufacturers, chiefly in the Potteries and for a time at Coalport. In 1875 he was working for Messrs. Davenport. In the Derby Exhibition of 1870 there was a Coalport service painted with scenes by Ablott, for a Mr. Carter of Derby. Mrs. Hendrickson had in her possession a plaque measuring 9 in. x 11 in. executed in Coalport china. The subject is an urn of flowers with a lakeland background. It is signed in the lower left corner.

BAILEY, Annie. *King Street.* A native of Breadsall, she began working as a flower painter when J.J. Robinson was in control of the King Street works, c.1900. Often signed her work.

BAKER, G. *Osmaston Road.* Miss Baker was a figure modeller known certainly to have modelled 'Polo' and 'Hawking'. Believed to be working in the twenties and thirties.

BAKER, John. Mentioned in W.H. Brock's notebook, left in 1906.

BARKER, *Osmaston Road.* A gilder working with M. Leroy in 1892 on special plate productions (see card No. 5, plate 13).

BARNET, James. King Street. Haslem listed in his collection, no. 119 'pair of small bisque baskets, modelled flowers by James Barnet'. He was still working in 1876.

BARRATT, Robert. *Osmaston Road.* Apprenticed at Osmaston Road c.1900, and according to his daughter, attended Art School for some fifteen years. Like many of the painters he was fond of gardening and had given considerable thought to the landscaping of his garden. It is not surprising that he was a very good flower painter. W.E. Mosley (q.v.) seems to have been a very close friend and the two painters left England for Australia in 1932. It was whilst camping in the bush that Barratt caught typhoid and was in hospital for some seventeen weeks. Bill Mosley had to leave him when he returned to this country, but Barratt returned home as soon as he had fully recovered. In his youth he was a great lover of sport, sharing his enthusiasm with another close friend, Cuthbert Gresley (q.v.). He played football, was a keen swimmer, and so much loved tennis that he had his own well maintained court, where tennis parties seem to have been the order of the day. Unfortunately owing to the low wages in the industry his talents were lost. He joined the Inland Revenue. His friendship with Mosley and Gresley continued and on occasions Gresley would call in at the office and discuss problems

concerning his work. He followed in the Old Derby painters' tradition of painting in watercolours for pleasure and, presumably, to subsidise his earnings. He died before retirement age in 1940. His daughter bequeathed many interesting items from her father's collection to the Royal Crown Derby Museum and included amongst this generous gift was the rare scent bottle painted and signed by him illustrated on p. 108.

BECK, W. Mentioned in W.H. Brock's notebook, left 1900.

BEDNALL, Samuel. *Osmaston Road.* Gilder who did raised and chased sprays in the nineties. Patterns 3523 and 3548.

BENTLEY, H. Mentioned in W.H. Brock's notebook, 'gone to war' 1914.

BIER. *Osmaston Road.* Nothing is known about this painter although he was allocated floral patterns, and indeed his flowers, signed, often accompanied Landgraf's paintings on the reverse panels of vases. An imposing pair of Derby Crown Porcelain Company Moon Flasks indicate that he was of some importance as they are also signed by him, and show his high standards. Patterns 767, 875, 968.

BIRBECK, Donald. *Osmaston Road.* From a family of ceramic painters. He had trained at the Cauldon factory where he worked until 1931 when he joined his former employer H.T. Robinson at Osmaston Road. He had studied bird and animal life in America during his period at Cauldon and these subjects were made his very own. He designed many services with game, animal and floral subjects during his long stay at Derby. His watercolours always have a natural and alive look. He was also responsible for the football plaques made for the foreign teams visiting England. (See illustration p. 209, and plates 58-60, pp. 212, 213 and 216.)

BIRD, E. *Osmaston Road.* A female gilder in the early days. A pierced plate with very fine raised and chased gilding has been seen dated 1885, signed on the reverse. It was unusual for the women gilders or enamellers to do this kind of work which was reserved for the men! (See plate 27, p. 57.)

BLAND, H. Mentioned in W.H. Brock's notebook as painter.

BLOOD, W. Mentioned in W.H. Brock's notebook, leaving 1909.

BOULLEMIER, H. or **L.** *Osmaston Road.* In pattern book 19 dated about 1904, Pattern 7675 states 'Royal Gadroon Dessert plate, cobalt band, painted figures in centre by Boullemier'. Also at the Bemrose Sale, Elmhurst, Derby, Friday March 5th 1909, Lot No 1047 (under heading Derby China: Royal Factory) was a 'pair vases, Rose du Barry ground, richly gilt, on raised work; with panels painted by Boullemier' — 'Cupid's Peep-Show' and 'Cupid made captive'. None of these give an initial and thus we have to determine which of the famous ceramic decorator Antonin Boullemier's sons, Henri or Lucien, painted at Osmaston Road. Papers discovered recently indicate that Lucien Boullemier was the painter of pattern 7675, but that he worked as an outside decorator and that the wares were sent to him already ground-laid for him to paint with figures and to return to the factory for gilding and fixing. He was working at Shelton, Stoke-on-Trent, in 1905

BOURNE. *Osmaston Road.* Stated to have been an early modeller working with Warrington Hogg (q.v.), c.1880.

BRADLEY, Tom. *Osmaston Road.* Pattern 764 landscapes and sea views c.1878-80.

BRADSHAW, A. Derby Crown period painter mentioned in W.H. Brock's notebook.

BRADSHAW, W. Mentioned in W.H. Brock's notebook; subjects unknown.

BRANSCOMBE, George Brian. *Osmaston Road.* Born at the Glebe House, Widecombe-in-the-Moor, Devon, he was the son of a landscape painter. In 1947 he attended the Penzance College of Art, came briefly under the influence of Bernard Leach who first inspired his interest in pottery, and in 1949 was awarded special entry to the Royal College of Art. After National Service returned to South Kensington to the School of Ceramics under Professor R.W. Baker. Later joined Ridgway Potteries at Stoke-on-Trent. After the merger into Allied English Potteries he became chief designer of Royal Crown Derby (1964). Worked closely with Antonio Burrell on the development of silk screenprinting. Modelled 'Duesbury' and 'Queen's Gadroon' shape ranges, and the Prince of Wales Bell (see p. 78). In 1973 Branscombe was appointed Art Director of Royal Crown Derby, with certain responsiblities at Minton Ltd. He initiated the Connoisseur Collection to promote the talents of individual painters and gilders. Brian Branscombe died suddenly in 1988. (See illustrations pp. 177, 178 and 215.)

BRANSCOMBE, June Roberta. *Osmaston Road.* Born in Leicester, her early life was spent with parents attached to military establishments in Mauritius, Kenya and England. Attended Leicester College of Art and later Royal College of Art, where she studied industrial design. Des. R.C.A. In 1965 she joined Royal Crown Derby as a designer and married Brian Branscombe in 1970. She has been responsible for the design of 'Brocade', 'Caliph' and 'Imperia'; the Prince of Wales Dragon; special plates for H.M. Queen Elizabeth the Queen Mother; the Aldeburgh Festival Services; the Kedleston Vase; and the bird study coffee cans. She has also been responsible for the design of most of the special inscriptions, backstamps, monograms, cyphers and the certificates which accompany the limited editions produced at Osmaston Road during the last few years. (See illustrations pp. 177 and 178.)

BRASSINGTON, Samuel. *King Street.* Came to King Street in 1919 from Goss and worked for a short time as a figure modeller leaving in 1921. Born June 4th 1883 in Manchester and died February 6th 1951.

BRENNAN. Mentioned in W.H. Brock's notebook, left in 1906.

BROCK. W.H. Retired in 1922 after having been in charge of the women's department for over 40 years. He made it his business to record names and activities, which have been of great assistance to the writers.

BROOKS, A. Mentioned in W.H. Brock's notebook, leaving 1909.

BROUGHTON, Joseph. *King Street.* Aged eleven, he had been apprenticed at the old Nottingham Road factory as a gilder and Japan painter. He was working at King Street until 1875.

BROWN, Thomas. *Osmaston Road.* Worked as a gilder with Leroy on special plate productions.

BROWNSWORD, John Joseph. *Osmaston Road.* This fine painter has over 80 patterns numbered in the Osmaston Road books! His subjects include flowers, figures, fish, and fruit; he was an equally fine gilder. After leaving Derby he became Principal of the Hull School of Art. He designed the Ypres War Memorial for the dead of the European Great War 1914-18, a model of which was exhibited in Hull. He was a keen lecturer and gave many talks about the Royal Crown Derby factory, including a B.B.C. broadcast in 1930.

BUCKNALL, Frank. *King Street, Osmaston Road.* Painter who worked with Annie Bailey (q.v.) at King Street. Later stated to have been in charge of the Osmaston

Road pattern books. He died on August 1st 1915 aged only thirty-nine, and was buried in Breadsall churchyard. He formerly lived at New House, Breadsall. (See illustration p. 62.)

CHAPMAN. Mentioned by W.H. Brock; drowned skating in January 1904.

CHIVERS, Frederick H. *King Street, Osmaston Road.* It would appear that this very talented painter of fruit and flowers commenced his career at Worcester, later moving to Coalport where some of his finest work was executed. His time at King Street probably lasted only a few years, c.1930-35. When Royal Crown Derby took over in 1935 it had been previously thought that Chivers had left Derby, however some 'Stanhope' ten inch plates painted and signed by him have been recently discovered. They are dated 1939 and carry the full Osmaston Road mark and cypher. Clearly his work had deteriorated and by about 1940 he had left the china works and for a time he worked as a shop cleaner, earning a few shillings extra by painting small pictures for his employer. He died in 1965 aged 84.

CLARK, Ellis. *Osmaston Road.* Although landscapes were this painter's main subject, he also did 'Chelsea Birds'. He worked at Osmaston Road from about 1885-1901, and later became a teacher at the Derby Technical College.

COPE, Hiram. Mentioned in W.H. Brock's notebook as a modeller who called at Osmaston Road on March 16th, 1923. Present at Leroy's funeral.

CORDEN, Joseph. *Osmaston Road.* A Derby Crown Porcelain Company painter and gilder whose subjects included flowers in enamels and raised gilt decoration.

COTTON, Robert. Mentioned in W.H. Brock's notebook, left in 1906.

CRAWLEY, Michael. *Osmaston Road.* A very talented painter of landscapes. He was apprenticed at Osmaston Road under Albert Haddock (q.v.). In 1971 he was concerned with the head gilder, John McLaughlin (q.v.), in executing a series of dinner plates and a cream jug presented to Her Majesty Queen Elizabeth the Queen Mother on her visit to Osmaston Road. Crawley painted the cream jug with two scenes, the front panel depicting the Castle of Mey and the reverse a view of the Royal Lodge, Windsor. The plates by John McLaughlin and the cream jugs were impressed with Her Majesty's cypher and the shape was then named 'Queen's Gadroon'. A very keen watercolourist, Crawley has produced some fine Derbyshire views which seem to capture the greyness of the rural country. His paintings have been shown at several very successful exhibitions. He is also responsible for painting the sets of Limited Edition Derbyshire views. (See illustrations pp. 165, 190 and 232.)

DALE, John Joseph. *Osmaston Road.* 'Jack' Dale was born on February 12th 1864 and later served his apprenticeship at Osmaston Road. He was a fine gilder and after Leroy's arrival at the factory joined George Darlington (q.v.) in assisting in his studio. He assisted in the getting up of the Princess May of Teck's wedding service. J.J. Dale was also a singer and sang in a quartet, as a counter-tenor, with George Darlington, Burrows and Cheadle. He was a member of a concert party

Joseph Dale, gilder.

Edward Drew, modeller, working on a bullfighter, c.1959.
Courtesy Royal Crown Derby.

at one time and they included in their repertoire a black and white minstrel show. The make-up they used was charcoal and vaseline which required hot water to remove it; at one of their winter concerts, the water had frozen in the pipes and consequently they had to return to their respective homes as minstrels. This almost caused the future Mrs. Dale to break off the engagement! He was responsible for much of the raised paste and chased gilding of his time, but a disagreement about wages eventually caused him to leave. He took over as sub-postmaster of the Old Normanton Post Office from his father, who felt too old to learn telegraphy which had become necessary with the building of Normanton Barracks. On J.J. Dale's death in 1938 the business passed to his son, Mr. A. Dale, and has been in the family for over 100 years.

DARLINGTON, George William. *Osmaston Road.* Born in Stoke-on-Trent in 1872, and apprenticed at the Minton factory. Later he moved to Derby where his technique was greatly influenced by Leroy. Was responsible for much lovely flower painting and his individual roses in particular have a soft natural appearance. He was also a fine gilder. George Darlington was a kindly man, not given to temperament, a keen gardener and musician. He belonged to the Derby Opera Company, singing as a tenor. He also gave painting lessons, but dissuaded his own son from ceramic painting, although he always encouraged his love of music. Sadly Darlington died in 1927, aged only 55, while walking home after having gathered some roses for a pupil. (See illustration p. 100 and plates 51 and 52, pp. 174 and 175.)

DEAKIN, Henry H. *Osmaston Road.* The son of a pottery painter also named Henry. The writer has been informed by his granddaughter, Mrs. Dorothy Jones, of Market Drayton, Shropshire, that he worked at Osmaston Road with his sister Martha who was later to marry Charles Newbold Wright (q.v.) another painter and gilder. Henry Deakin jun. was to be allocated over one hundred patterns in the Osmaston Road books covering a wide range of subjects including flowers,

George William Darlington, painter.

William Dean, painter

birds, fish and farm animals during the Derby Crown Porcelain Company years. (See illustration p. 56.)

DEAN, William Edward James. *Osmaston Road.* The son of a Derby manufacturer, as a boy he and his two younger sisters lived in a large Georgian house on the Burton Road, about five hundred yards from Babington Lane. At the age of seven his knee was injured when a nursemaid was trying on a new pair of shoes and, in spite of the best medical treatment available at the time, he remained a cripple and walked with a crutch for the rest of his life. Known as 'Billy' to his friends, he was always active and jolly despite his disability. After leaving school, he was apprenticed as a painter at Osmaston Road. He was at Derby from the late 1890s until shortly before his death in 1950, and is buried at the Boundary Road Cemetery.

He is best remembered for his marine subjects, and so seriously did he study them that he made several trips on trawlers from Grimsby, taking photographs and sketching the activity around him. He is also remembered for his charming Derbyshire views such as Matlock's High Tor and like Cuthbert Gresley, for his views in Dovedale. A Mr. Milligan has in his possession twenty-five watercolours, some dated in the early 1890s, in which the standard of the floral painting is so high that one can only speculate on what might have been had not his marine and scenic painting been so highly prized by the Royal Crown Derby Company, that they only allowed him to concentrate on these subjects. Dean has become a cult figure in the world of collectors. (See illustrations pp. 110, 112, 119 and 156.)

DREW, Edward. *Osmaston Road.* Followed Arnold Mikelson as a modeller at Osmaston Road. He worked closely with Mr. Philip Robinson in the production of the series of PR figures. Born in 1914 and trained at the Longton School of Art. An exhibition of his work was held in Derby in January 1958. (See illustration p. 214.)

DUNN, J. Derby Crown painter mentioned by W.H. Brock, subjects unknown.

ELLIS. Probably a fictitious name appearing on productions of the 1930s-1950s. *See also* **Garnett, F.**

FEARN, Samuel. *King Street.* A potter at the old Nottingham Road factory and later a founder-partner in the King Street factory.

FIRTH, Edward E. *Osmaston Road.* A gilder in the Derby Crown Porcelain Company period. Given pattern nos. 1024 and 1025 to colour.

FLOWERDEW, *Osmaston Road.* Allocated patterns 488 with Radford and 653. On May 11th 1981 Christie's sold a fine pair of Derby Crown plaques, 16½ in. x 22½ in., signed 'C.E. Flowerdew' and dated 1882, for £750 (bid price). The plaques depicted river landscapes which included peasant figures and animals.

FROST, W. Mentioned in W.H. Brock's notebook, left 1899.

GADSBY, T. *Osmaston Road.* Derby Crown painter whose name appears in the named patterns for a variety of subjects including flowers.

GARNETT, F. This name and that of Ellis appear on productions between the 1930s and 1950s as a signature. It is added to partly hand-executed ware, and should not be confused with F. Garnett, mentioned in W.H. Brock's notebook, who left in 1899, or with Ellis whose name appears to be fictitious.

GERRARD, Florence. *Osmaston Road.* A remarkable woman who gave almost sixty years' service to the company, firstly as a gilder and later as an inspector of wares. Bright and cheerful, she was a great example to the younger generation. She told the writers that although she commenced working at 2s. 6d. per week, she was always proud of her association with Royal Crown Derby. Before her death in the early 1980s she was a very regular and welcome visitor to the Museum Open Days.

GREATOREX, B. *Osmaston Road.* Painter and gilder allocated patterns 2621 and 2703. Left in 1915.

GREENLAY, W. Mentioned in W.H. Brock's notebook, leaving October 1915.

GREGORY, Albert. *Osmaston Road.* Apprenticed at Minton and at Osmaston Road in the 1890s, he was probably the best natural flower painter ever to work at the factory. Especially famous for the 'Gregory' rose which is so often the dominant flower of his groups. He was a bachelor and later in life became almost a recluse. An interesting story told by his brother Arnold, a metallurgical chemist, related how Albert used to feed his fireplace with fuel. He bought a large pole, and being unable, or unwilling to cut it into logs, he made a hole in the back of the chimney and fed it through into the fire as it gradually burnt away! He had two brothers and three sisters and latterly would not allow the sisters to visit him if he could prevent them. From the foregoing account one would believe him to have been a singularly insular man, but this was not always the case. In fact he had left Osmaston Road and travelled to America; the date is not clear but a small notebook about the movements of workpeople at the factory states that he left the decorating department in April 1908. Fortunately for lovers of fine ceramic painting, he returned to Osmaston Road and continued to paint delightful services, vases and other wares, so much sought after today, until the 1940s. (See illustrations pp. 62, 88, 124, 130, 139, 140, 142, 146, 161, 172 and plates 42, 45, 47 and 48, pp. 121, 141 160 and 162.)

GRESLEY, Cuthbert. *Osmaston Road.* From a family of artists. His grandfather J.S. Gresley, his father, Frank, and his brother, Harold (q.v.) were all very talented watercolourists. It was not surprising that Cuthbert should follow the

Cuthbert Gresley, painter.

224

Albert Haddock gilding a pair of
Chelsea birds.

tradition, he, however, choosing ceramics as the vehicle for painting. Commenced working under John P. Wale (q.v.) in 1893; he became a very good landscape and flower painter, decorating many services, vases etc., and was involved in decorating the Duke of Bedford's yacht services in 1912. A pair of plaques by this artist, extremely finely painted with lakeland scenes are known to the writers. He had a business interest with Miss Francis, a colleague from Osmaston Road, in 'Traveller's Joy' a restaurant where good food and conversation were the order of the day. Many of his sporting mementoes were kept there. He was living in 1960, aged 84, but had died before 1964. (See illustrations pp. 58, 65, 103, 120, 127, 131, 145, 147 and 234, and plate 46, p. 141.)

GRESLEY, Harold. Cuthbert Gresley's brother (see above) mentioned in W.H. Brock's notebook; left in 1907 and became art master at Repton College.

HADDOCK, Albert. *King Street, Osmaston Road.* One of the finest twentieth-century gilders, apprenticed in 1902 under George Hemstock (q.v.). After his training he moved to Minton in 1912 but joined the army in 1914. He later worked for King Street and following the take-over, re-joined Royal Crown Derby where he worked on many very fine services including those for Middle Eastern rulers. In latter years he taught male apprentices, retiring at the age of 79. He died in 1971 at the age of 83. (See illustration p. 242.)

HAGUE, Douglas. Son of Reuben Hague (q.v.). Attended Hanley Art College in 1937 and was apprenticed as a ceramic designer with Thomas Hulme (transfer manufacturers). In 1951 he moved to Ben Capper (also transfer manufacturers). One of his portrait plaques is illustrated on p. 157.

Douglas Hague, painter.

Plate 61. Royal Crown Derby collection of 'Royal Cats' designed and modelled by Robert Jefferson. The first four members are Abyssinian, Siamese, Persian and Egyptian and depict Oriental princes each wearing the authentic headgear of the Royal Houses of these ancient kingdoms. 1987.
Courtesy Royal Crown Derby

HAGUE, Rebuen E. *Osmaston Road.* Apprenticed at Osmaston Road as a painter in 1893, aged thirteen. He moved to Stoke-on-Trent in 1906 to work as a freelance china painter. He painted a large number of tiles which were exported, and many were used in the palaces of eastern potentates. The subjects were very large and when they were built up represented life size mermaids and other mythological subjects. He later did ceramic design work for Thomas Hulme and the Universal Company. Earlier, concurrent with his apprenticeship, he attended the Derby College of Art. Like so many Derby painters, he was very fond of watercolour paintings and in particular landscapes. Later he again worked for Royal Crown Derby as a freelance, painting the portraits and reproductions of the Old Masters which have made him justly famous. Reuben Hague decided in 1946 to train his son Douglas (q.v.), already a ceramic designer, as a portrait painter. He died in 1969. (See illustration p. 166, and plate 1, p. 2.)

HANCOCK, Harry Sampson. *King Street.* Taught to paint by Sampson Hancock (see below), he busied himself with this side of the business, leaving his cousin,

Reuben Hague, painter.

226

Plate 62. Royal Crown Derby figures forming the 'Classic Collection'. Introduced in 1986, created by Jo Ledger, Design Director, and modelled by Robert Jefferson. Left to right Persephone, Penelope, Dionë and Athena.
Courtesy Royal Crown Derby

J.J. Robinson, to run the commercial affairs. He worked at the factory until his death, from cancer, in 1934, and has left much fine work, usually signed. The subjects were varied, but he was both a fine landscape and flower painter. (See illustrations pp. 18 and 22, and plates 4, 5 and 11, pp. 20, 24 and 36.)

HANCOCK, Sampson. *King Street.* Although not apprenticed at the old Nottingham Road factory, he was working there as a flower painter during the closing years. He is best known as a founder-partner of the King Street factory, of which he eventually became sole proprietor. As the illustration on p. 228 shows, he was a 'character'; we have been told stories of how he had, on occasions, to be fetched from his favourite hostelry by a grandchild to attend to some pressing matter. However, it must be stated that this enjoyment of life did not prevent him from being highly respected not only in the ceramic world but also in the town of Derby. He found time to impart his knowledge of the arts of potting, decorating etc. to his grandsons, Harry Sampson Hancock (q.v.) and James J. Robinson, both of whom lodged with their grandparents. He had been a very good flower

painter and his authenticated work is much sought after. He died in 1895 and was succeeded by James Robinson. (See illustrations pp. 12 and 23.)

HARDY. A vase signed by this painter passed through Sotheby's Belgravia, the subject being floral.

HARGREAVE, William. *King Street.* Bill Hargreave was a talented painter working at King Street in the 1930s. He painted birds, flowers and dogs.

HARRIS, Charles. *Osmaston Road.* Apprenticed at Osmaston Road in the 1890s. A painter of 'Chelsea Birds', which were mythological rather than natural, flowers, and also game birds. He is said to have worked in America after leaving Derby about 1911, and it is thought that he did not return to this country. (See illustrations pp. 65 and 97.)

HARTSHORN. *Osmaston Road.* This Derby Crown Porcelain Company painter is known only through the Osmaston Road pattern books. One pattern, 791, 'painted birds, fish and dog Mr. Hartshorn' gives us an indication of his subjects.

HELLETT, W. Derby Crown painter who is mentioned in W.H. Brock's notebook. Left in 1891.

HEMSTOCK, George. *King Street.* Head gilder at the time the Duke of York and Princess May were presented with a service to celebrate their marriage in 1893. He assisted Désiré Leroy (q.v.) in the production of the service, doing both gilding and burnishing. His daughter, **Kate,** was very talented and produced some very fine watercolour paintings and drawings. It is unfortunate that her talents had to be confined to the department of women gilders! (See illustration p. 242 and plate 27, p. 57.)

HENSON, John. *King Street.* A potter from the old Nottingham Road factory who was a founder-partner in the King Street factory.

HILL, James. *King Street.* A clever flower painter from the old Nottingham Road factory, who was a founder-partner in the King Street factory.

HOGG, Herbert Warrington. *Osmaston Road.* A fine modeller, who was responsible for creating the many new vase shapes in the first few years of the Osmaston Road factory's history. His talents were recognised by the acceptance of two busts for the 1893 Royal Academy Exhibition. It is also very likely that some of the fine early figure models were created by this modeller. So highly was he esteemed by the company that they paid for a cruise for him, so that he might recover from an ailment. An extract from the Minutes Book stated 'May 1886 Mr. Hogg is at present on a Mediterranean cruise paid for by the company'. (See illustration p. 115 and plate 17, p. 50.)

HOLTZENDORF, G. *Osmaston Road.* Count Holtzendorf was a Saxon nobleman about whom little is known. He was a figure and landscape painter during the Derby Crown Porcelain Company's period at Osmaston Road. He painted the landscapes in the centre of the 'Gladstone' service. His stay at the factory was from 1878 to about 1888. Pieces by this painter are extremely rare and much sought after by collectors. His work is usually signed with his initials, G.H. (See illustrations pp. 56, 74 and 102, and plate 23, p. 54.)

Thomas Hough, chemist.

HOPKINSON, Ida and May. Decoraters at the Royal Crown Derby China Works, and reported (1988) by Vicky Williams to be living in New York City, both aged over 90. Two brothers with this name, who worked at the Old Nottingham Road China Works. **William** was a figure maker who later worked with Sampson Hancock at King Street and the younger brother **Edward** jun was a painter and gilder. It has been noticeable that many names seem to continue in the china works for several generations.

HOUGH, Thomas. *Osmaston Road.* See Chapter 4, Parian.

INGRAM, W.R. *Osmaston Road.* The principal modeller at the commencement of operations at Osmaston Road, having as his chief apprentice H. Warrington Hogg (q.v.).

JACKSON, Charles. *Osmaston Road.* Painter apprenticed at Osmaston Road in 1904 and from whom we had some interesting details of Désiré Leroy (q.v.). He left the factory in March 1911 and worked in America, where he was still living, aged over eighty in 1974.

JACKSON, G. Mentioned in W.H. Brock's notebook, left 1899.

JEFFERSON, Robert. Studied at Liverpool College of Art, Burslem School of Art and the Royal College of Art, in the years immediately following the Second World War. Jefferson became chief designer at Poole Pottery in 1957, and design director of Purbeck pottery in 1970. He was retained by Royal Doulton as a designer/modeller in 1972. His first project for Royal Crown Derby was to design and model the 'Quail' teaset. Since then he has designed and modelled all the paperweight series, the 'Royal Cats', 'Dogs' and a series of figures.

JESSOP, George. *Osmaston Road, King Street.* Born 1882 and apprenticed at Osmaston Road as a painter about 1896. A very fine flower painter who left in

George Jessop, painter.

Désiré Leroy, painter and designer.

the First World War to work in a munitions factory in Coventry. Returned to Osmaston Road after the war and stayed until 1927 when he left to work at the L.M.S. Carriage and Waggon works as a sign-writer for three years. He moved to King Street where he worked until the 1935 take-over by Royal Crown Derby. He was a keen footballer. Married a gilder at Osmaston Road, Annie Saville. Died 1944 aged 62. (See illustrations pp. 111, 138 and 218.)

JONES, W. *King Street.* A plate was brought into the Royal Crown Derby Museum, painted with wildfowl and signed by this painter. It was probably painted during the first quarter of this century.

KEENE, A.J. *Osmaston Road.* Painter of the Derby Crown period. He was allocated pattern no. 881 dessert plate (central painting of a dog by A.J. Keene). He also painted large plaques in the manner of Landgraf (q.v.), but owing to a withered arm, he found difficulty in holding china and thus turned to watercolour painting. He found some success in this field and locally was held in high repute.

KNUTTON, T. Mentioned in W.H. Brock's notebook, leaving 1910.

LAMBERT, G. *Osmaston Road.* Perhaps the best gilder to have worked at Osmaston Road. He was responsible for much of the egg-shell gilding and is mentioned many times in the Osmaston Road patterns. (See plate 25, p. 55.)

LANDGRAF, G. *Osmaston Road.* One of the truly great painters, who was to have an influence upon James Platts and W.N. Statham (qq.v.) before his untimely death deprived the Works of his service. He returned to his native Bavaria and died at Bamberg aged forty-two in 1882.

The following letter from Landgraf is of great interest. The fact that he had previously been engaged by the Royal Manufactory in Berlin for over five years as their first artist indicates that he was not in England during the years 1872-78 before he took up his appointment at Osmaston Road in the summer of 1878. Previously he was thought to have come to Derby via an English manufactory.

Lützow Str 23. II
Berlin 26 March 1878

Dear Sir,

In reply of your last of the 24 Feb. I must tell you, that I have not yet closed with the Stockholm people but the director of the works shall be on a journey in Berlin next month or beginning of May where we shall arrange matters personally. Now you wrote me that your partner should like to see some specimens of my paintings, and in that respect he is quite right. But the circumstances are different to me. Being engaged at the R.M. I have very little time left for private occupation, which prevents me of doing something important which I esteem worth to be seen as a specimen of my style of painting. On the other hand you have seen some of my works personally at Berlin and I think the fact, that I am now engaged over 5 years at R.B.M. as their first artist, might suffice you regarding my works. However, if you mean by your partner Mr. Phillips at Derby, of whom you told me that he is superintending your works, I should like very much to have some correspondence with that gentleman, regarding his intentions of what style of work he wants to produce, and to exchange some ideas with him. My education as an artist is not onesided and I can put my hands to anything that should be wanted in the market.

Awaiting your further kind answer.

I remain Dear Sir most respectfully

G. Landgraf

Mr. William Litherland, Liverpool.

This painter executed some exceedingly fine portrait plaques which have always commanded great interest in the salerooms. A pair of Derby Crown vases were sold by Sotheby's New York, March 21st 1987, lot 6. They were 27½ in. high, with panels reserved upon robin's-egg blue ground. Two panels were of floral subjects by Bier and two were painted with maidens in classical style by Landgraf. (See illustrations pp. 46, 47 and 49, and plate 14, p. 48.)

LARCOMBE, W. *King Street.* Became proprietor of the King Street factory in 1916. Previously had been proprietor of a business repairing china, calling it the China Hospital. He lived at Morley and died on his way to Breadsall Church on Palm Sunday 1940 aged 68.

LATHER, Percy. Mentioned in W.H. Brock's notebook, left in 1906.

LEROY, Désiré. *Osmaston Road.* See chapters 9 and 12 and illustrations on pp. 70, 85, 98, 115, 118, 122 and plates 29-31, 33-37, and 38-40, pp. 60, 69, 82 and 109.)

LILLEY, H. Mentioned as painter in W.H. Brock's notebook, left 1893.

LOCKE, M.R. *Osmaston Road.* Miss Locke was a figure modeller in the twenties and thirties.

Left to right: Michael Crawley, John McLaughlin and Stefan Nowacki.

LOCKER, William. *King Street.* Had been chief clerk at the old Nottingham Road factory, and on its close in 1848 he led his five collegues in starting the King Street factory under the style of 'Locker and Co Late Bloor'. He was in control until his death in 1859.

LUNN, Richard. *Osmaston Road.* Was appointed Art Director on August 2nd 1882. Stated in Cassell's *Magazine of Art* in 1884 to have designed 'Venetian Vignettes' for raised gold dessert plates. He designed the pair of vases presented to Queen Victoria by the Ladies of Derby to mark her Jubilee in 1887 and, amongst other important designs, the 'Gladstone' Service. He was later accused of only being good at elaborate and very expensive articles. He left in 1889. (See plate 27, p. 57.)

McLAUGHLIN, John. *Osmaston Road.* Apprenticed at Osmaston Road under Albert Haddock (q.v.) in 1957, after having attended the Joseph Wright School of Art. Became head gilder in 1968 and in 1971 painted and gilded a series of dinner plates presented to Her Majesty Queen Elizabeth the Queen Mother. He was also responsible for painting, in the Connoisseur Collection, six coffee cans and stands in the 'Queen's Gadroon' shape, each being painted with a British wild bird subject, with a similar painting of the young and eggs on the reverse. The ground is yellow, upon which is raised gold decoration. These are limited to 50 sets. He is now a freelance painter. (See illustration above and p. 144.)

MACHIN, Arnold. *King Street.* Apprenticed at Minton and at King Street in 1930 as a painter, chiefly of flowers. He left before the take-over and turned his hand to sculpture, with such success that he is now a Royal Academician.

MARPLE, F. *Osmaston Road.* A very good flower painter at Osmaston Road from about 1900. Left in 1918 to work as a clerk at Rolls Royce.

MARSH. *Osmaston Road.* Painter and gilder mentioned in first pattern book.

232

MARSHALL, John. *King Street.* Worked as a potter. (See illustrations pp. 16 and 228.)

MEREDITH, W. Mentioned in W.H. Brock's notebook, left 1895.

MICKLEWRIGHT. Derby Crown painter who left in 1890; mentioned in W.H. Brock's notebook. Possibly the Copeland painter mentioned in Geoffrey Godden's *Victorian Porcelain.*

MIKELSON, Arnold. *Osmaston Road.* Born January 1922. Studied at the Riga College of Art, Riga, Latvia. In 1939 was awarded a gold medal. He came to Osmaston Road after the War and was responsible for modelling about sixty original subjects for the company, the majority of which were birds. It is not at all surprising that, with such talent, Arnold Mikelson has made a considerable name for himself in British Columbia, to which he emigrated. He has his own gallery, known as the 'Mind and Matter Gallery', where his sculpture in wood is created. Mr. Mikelson has always been influenced by birds, animals and fish as well as human behaviour. He once said of his work that it was 'somewhat stylised, simplified, symbolic but not abstract'. (See illustration p. 210.)

MINNS, F. Mentioned by W.H. Brock as having died 1898.

MORRIS, R.G. *Osmaston Road.* A modeller working with H. Warrington Hogg (q.v.) during the early Derby Crown period.

William Edwin Mosley, painter.

MOSLEY, William Edwin. *Osmaston Road, King Street.* Apprenticed at Osmaston Road about 1893 as a painter, chiefly of floral subjects. He left in April 1912 to work at King Street for James Robinson. During the depression of the early thirties he went with Robert Barratt to Australia but returned to work again at King Street until the take-over, when he again returned to Osmaston Road. Those who worked with him both at King Street and Osmaston Road described him as a very quiet, unassuming and gentle person. He loved his garden and often went out sketching in the Derbyshire Dales. He was very talented, and clever at painting miniatures of landscapes, portraits and birds. He painted a dessert dish with a view of Elford, the family home of Howard Paget, partner in the King Street works from 1917 to the merger with Royal Crown Derby. Mosley lived in Garden Street, Derby, until his death in 1954. He had painted many important productions, but possibly amongst his own favourites were the pair of traditional Derby dwarfs for Her Majesty Queen Elizabeth II and the christening mug for Prince Charles. (See illustrations pp. 90-94, 98, 125-6, 133 and 218.)

MOUNTFORD, John. *King Street.* Legend has it that John Mountford had returned to Derby to assist Sampson Hancock in the King Street Works. Mountford claimed to have discovered Parian body whilst working at the Copeland Works, trying to rediscover the recipe for the Old Derby Biscuit china.

NICHLINSON, Charles. *Osmaston Road.* Known to have been a gilder because he is listed with the head gilder George Hemstock (q.v.) on the verso of a photograph given to the Museum by a grandson of Mr. Hemstock. (See illustration p. 242.)

NOWACKI, Stefan Damian. *Osmaston Road.* Apprenticed at Osmaston Road this very fine and talented painter is no longer at the China Works but works as a small manufacturer in Derby. His talent was rewarded with an exhibition at the Barbican, London, which received media acclaim. Like Sampson Hancock in the past, Nowacki is able to combine decorating wares with running the day to day workings of a small china works. (See illustration p. 232.)

ONCAL, L. Mentioned in W.H. Brock's notebook.

OWEN, Alan. *Osmaston Road.* Modeller who had formerly been a student at Burslem Art School. In October 1962 there was a display of new pottery shapes at the Wolverhampton Art Gallery; the shapes were evolved by the Vice-Principal, Mr. Tom Arnold. Alan Owen modelled 'Astra' for production at Osmaston Road keeping strictly to Mr. Tom Arnold's design.

PACEY, Doris. *King Street.* Started working in 1918, mainly on Imari type patterns. She also decorated Toby jugs, thimbles and Mother Gamps.[14]

PATES, Alice. Listed as a decorator in the *Derby Porcelain International Society Newsletter,* No. 8.

PEACH, Joseph Arthur. *Osmaston Road.* Many patterns were allocated to this flower painter of the Derby Crown period. He is reported by Gilhespy to have gone to Australia, because of chest trouble, but obviously returned to Osmaston Road as he is recorded as leaving there for a second time in March 1895. He is sometimes recorded as Arthur Peach as well as Joseph Arthur.

PELL, Catherine Mary. *Osmaston Road.* Mary Pell worked at Osmaston Road on hunting scenes. She also painted a limited series of natural botanical plates which she signed. She worked at the factory from 1965 until 1970 and after leaving became well known for her watercolours and, in particular, for her lively hunting scenes. She has exhibited in London and is a Fellow of The Royal Society of Arts. (See illustrations pp. 148 and 197.)

PILSBURY, Richard. *Osmaston Road.* Born 1830; attended the Burslem School of Design, where he won twelve national medals. Later he worked many years for Minton. He could not have been engaged for long at Osmaston Road but there is a Derby Crown dish painted and signed by him (1888) in the Osmaston Road Museum, and in the Bemrose sale catalogue, lot 559, reads 'FINE VASE, painted in flowers by Pilsbury, Derby Royal Factory. The first piece bearing the Royal Arms; 17' (see illustration p.6). This piece would be dated 1890 to coincide with the new title Royal Crown Derby. It seems likely that he was at Osmaston Road between 1888 and 1892 when he must have left to take up his appointment as Art Director at Moore Brothers. M.L. Solon wrote of him in an obituary in the *Art Journal,* 1897, ('Pilsbury may be said to have witnessed the dawn of the new era

14 Article by Hilda Moore, *Derby Porcelain International Society Newsletter,* No. 8.

which was to change the face of Englsh decorative art and to have been one of those whose artistic work has materially assisted in bringing about the revolution in the public taste...he turned to nature, the only guide which never misleads, and by his untiring work in the greenhouses, his conscientious reproductions of the best models he found there, he gained the experience and the skill he wanted to emerge from the swamp of the old routine and bud out as a true and complete flower painter.'

PIPER, A. *Osmaston Road.* A gilder and painter in the Derby Crown period. He is mentioned for his raised jewelling on pattern no. 1430; pattern no. 1337 'Old Derby Teaware Patt.' by Mr. Piper.

PLATTS, James. *Osmaston Road.* A fine Derby Crown period painter responsible for painting figure subjects in enamels as well as gold. He was allocated many patterns, including miniature insets on egg-shell coffee cups. He is listed as dead in 1888. (See illustration p. 107 and plate 22, p. 51.)

PRICE, John. *Osmaston Road.* 1881-1949. Born in Stoke-on-Trent, he worked at Grimwades, Copelands and for thirty years at Doulton, Burslem, before becoming decorating manager at Osmaston Road in December 1945. He worked on the plates which were presented to H.R.H. Princess Elizabeth on the occasion of her marriage. Each plate centre was a view of Derbyshire comprising a fine brown print coloured and signed J. Price.

PRINCE, Edwin. *King Street.* One of the last of the painters apprenticed at the old Nottingham Road factory. A good landscape painter who was obviously influenced by the chief landscape painter at the old factory, Daniel Lucas. After the close of the works in 1848 Prince worked in London. Since the Bemrose Volumes have been donated to the Royal Crown Derby Museum Trust it has been possible to correct and update the biography of this painter. A notice of his obituary appeared in January 1896 which clearly stated that he painted for Sampson Hancock (q.v.) whilst in retirement at Overstrand, Cromer, Norfolk, and these items were sent to King Street for firing (a similar story to Lucien Boullemier (q.v.)).

Prince had certainly been one of the best landscape painters to have worked at the Nottingham Road factory and on its closure he was employed as a painter on glass for the Wales glass manufactory in Newcastle upon Tyne from about 1855 to 1875. This would suggest that most pieces decorated and signed for Sampson Hancock would date from about 1880.

A fuller discussion of Prince's work appeared in the catalogue of the exhibition 'Painters and the Derby China Works' held between March and June 1987 at the Victoria and Albert Museum. (See illustrations pp. 18 and 23.)

RADFORD, William Henry. *Osmaston Road.* Born 1 September 1855 at Stokes Prior, Worcestershire, and must surely be connected with the Worcester painters of that name. His descendents possess a Derby Crown plate, fully marked and dated 1882. He died at Wolstanton, Staffs., 1933, and was buried at Blythe Bridge. He had married Annie Robinson in 1887. A painter in the early Derby Crown period 1877-80.

William Henry Radford, painter.

RATCLIFFE, Jack. *King Street.* Flower painter who worked for a while at Minton. Was at King Street during the last few years before the take-over. Jack Ratcliffe has been a regular visitor on Open Days in the Royal Crown Derby Museum, and the writers are grateful to him for his personal picture of the King Street factory in his time. Working with Fred Chivers, Edwin Mosley, Arnold Machin R.A., Albert Haddock and Bill Hargreave (qq.v.) had been quite an experience. After the take-over, Jack Ratcliffe left the ceramic world, and worked for Rolls Royce until his retirement when he continued to paint for pleasure and occasionally on commission at his home in Derby. He died in the late 1970s.

Jack Ratcliffe, painter.

RAYWORTH. *King Street.* As stated in the chapter on King Street there is no evidence of him being at King Street and he is remembered for the large number of plaques, mostly on opaline, which have survived.

REDFERN. *King Street.* Gilder working in the 1920s.

REED, T. *Osmaston Road.* Art Director from 1890 to 1926, joining the company in 1890 after working for Mintons. Reed was responsible for all art departments except Leroy's studio. It is interesting to speculate on how well Reed was able to work with Leroy; while Reed's work must have benefited by the presence of Leroy, the younger man must surely have felt daunted by such a dominant character as the celebrated Leroy (see Chapter 9). Whatever their relationship, Reed attended Leroy's funeral in 1908. Mary Lomas (William Litherland's great niece) recalled meeting Reed in 1906, when she was a young girl, and remembers how impressed she was by his presence. Reed's work has not been without its critics; it is clear, however, that he was well able to cope with designs for general relase. After all, this was the man that designed 'Mikado' in 1894 (Cassidys alone had imported ten million pieces of this pattern on various wares by 1958), and the Royal Crown Derby Museum has on loan at present, designs, sketches and watercolours which demonstrate his creative talent. However, Reed was not thought suitable for the current market during the difficult years of the later twenties and he left the company in 1926.

REMNANT, C. Mentioned in W.H. Brock's notebook, left in 1899.

ROBINSON, Phillip I. *Osmaston Road.* Born at Stoke-on-Trent in 1914. He attended Malvern College of Art in 1930, Burslem School of Art in 1936 and the Worcester College of Art in 1937 becoming Professor of Free Fine Arts there in 1938/9. He became Art Director of Royal Crown Derby in 1940, later holding the position concurrently with that of Managing Director and Chairman. He left Osmaston Road in 1961 to set up the Abbeydale factory at Duffield.

ROE, J. Mentioned in W.H. Brock's notebook, leaving 1913.

ROGERS, J. *Osmaston Road.* A gilder at Osmaston Road, who is recorded as having assisted Jack Dale and George Hemstock (qq.v.) to gild the special service presented to H.R.H. The Duke of York and Princess May of Teck on the occasion of their wedding in 1893. This service was exhibited in the Royal Crown Derby Showrooms (now the Museum) and also at the Derby Art Gallery on 28 October 1893. The cost was recorded as £160.

James Rouse sen.

ROUSE, Charles. *Osmaston Road.* Son of James Rouse, sen. (q.v.). He was a gilder, became head gilder late in the last century and was succeeded by George Hemstock (q.v.) early in the present.

ROUSE, James, jun. *Osmaston Road.* Worked at Osmaston Road, it is said, in a room by himself, but little authenticated work has been seen. The portrait plaque of his father (see above) which now hangs in the Royal Crown Derby Museum, is signed by him. (See illustration p. 96.)

ROUSE, James, sen. *Nottingham Road, King Street, Osmaston Road.* To this fine man and painter goes the distinction of being the only painter to have worked at all three Derby factories. James Rouse was the son of a gardener, who was well known in the town of Derby as a successful cultivator of auriculas, anemones, tulips, heaths and other flowers. Young James was born in 1802 and was later apprenticed, at the Old Nottingham Road factory, to Robert Bloor. According to Haslem, James Rouse was called upon to decorate three large vases, known as 'Long Toms'. He painted all round the bodies with a solid mass of flowers intermingled with a little fruit, and the manner in which he executed these gave Bloor some pleasure, but came as a surprise to his workmates, who had certainly underestimated the talent of their young colleague. The centre vase in the set was 25 in. high and the side pieces 21 in. He left Derby about 1826 to work for a short time in the Potteries. After this he was engaged by the Coalport factory, and he remained to execute much fine work for John Rose who was head of the enterprise.

Although flowers were Rouse's speciality he painted, fruit, figures, animals and landscapes. Haslem also informs us that Rouse was responsible for many of the best exhibits shown by Coalport at the International Exhibition in 1851 and also again in 1862. Rouse, he stated, was responsible for much of the Sèvres style painting and was fortunate enough to have worked with William Cooke who excelled in this soft manner of painting. Rouse left Coalport in about 1871 to return to the Potteries, where he worked chiefly at Cauldon Place for Ridgway. Later for three or four years he worked on metals in Birmingham, giving great satisfaction.

In 1875 Sampson Hancock (q.v.) asked Rouse to return to Derby to work at his King Street factory. James Rouse was of great value to Hancock, being able to paint anything required. However, in October 1882 Rouse left King Street to take up an appointment at Osmaston Road. Although in his eighty-first year, he quickly showed the management that the quality of his work was not at all impaired by his age. Painting on plaques, as well as useful ware, his subjects were again varied. A glance at the listed patterns will show the variety of his work executed at Osmaston Road. Haslem also tells of the demand for Rouse's work coming from America. James Rouse had almost completed the beautiful floral reserves on the Gladstone service when, sadly, a paralytic stroke restricted his working career. He died in February 1888. (See illustrations pp. 21, 74 and 104, and plates 2, 3, 15, 20 and 23, pp. 19, 48, 51 and 54.)

ROUSE, William. *Osmaston Road.* Another son of James Rouse (see above) who worked at Osmaston Road as a painter.

ROWLEY, George. *Osmaston Road.* A flower painter who worked at Osmaston Road at the beginning of this century and whose work is sometimes signed. He is recorded as having left in 1908.

SADDINGTON, Jack. *Osmaston Road.* Was apprenticed at Osmaston Road as a gilder in 1898 and left in 1943. (See illustration p. 242.)

SCHOFIELD, F. *King Street.* Was working about the time of the take-over in 1935, at King Street, as a flower painter.

SCOTT, Alan. *Osmaston Road.* Appointed Resident Designer in November 1962. Attended West Hartlepool College of Art and later the post-diploma course on advanced pottery design at the College of Ceramics, North Staffordshire College of Technology.

SHARP, Samuel. *King Street.* A founder-partner in the King Street factory, whose name is used in mark No. 2. Was formerly a potter at the old Nottingham Road Factory.

SHIRLEY, Mrs. *Osmaston Road.* Came to Osmaston Road about 1880 and worked closely with Thomas Hough, for whom she designed two patterns and executed the decoration throughout herself. She had been left a widow with six children. She died in 1905 whilst she was still working, aged 72. Recorded by W.H. Brock as groundlayer.

Shufflebottom, modeller.

SHUFFLEBOTHAM. *King Street.* A modeller at the King Street factory in the early days, who according to John Haslem, 'had no mean ability' in the art of modelling flowers for application to ornamental wares. He also says that Shufflebottom was dead by 1876.

SMART, S. Mentioned in W.H. Brock's notebook, left 1894.

SMITH, A. Mentioned in W.H. Brock's notebook, leaving 1911.

SMITH, George. A painter in the Derby Crown period to whom patterns were allocated in the Osmaston Road pattern books.

W.N. Statham, painter.

STATHAM, W.N. *Osmaston Road.* Hailed from Matlock where he was not only a churchwarden for many years but also wrote a history of Matlock Church. As the Osmaston Road chief landscape painter of the very early Derby Crown period his name is mentioned in the pattern books but his signed work is rare. His granddaughter has in her possession a fine miniature of her father painted by Statham. After leaving Osmaston Road he ran a successful photographer's business in Matlock and it is interesting to note that he also sold Crown Derby and other china. He taught for a time at Riber Castle, and amongst designs he executed were the Matlock war memorial and the oak pulpit in the parish church. Born 1863, died January 1940. (See plate 21, p. 51.)

STEPHAN. *King Street, Osmaston Road.* A modeller whose name is often mis-spelt. Believed to have been a descendant of the famous Derby modeller Pierre Stephan who modelled the original set of elements still in production today. He is recorded by Haslem as having worked at King Street.

Edward Swainson, modeller, seen here at work on 'Seated boy with book'. Note the pair of figures on the bench and see plate 6, p. 33. *Courtesy Mr. M. Newbold*

William Stephan entered an agreement on 30 August 1876, for two years to act as 'Designer and Artificer for Pottery Models and Shapes', though according to Haslem Stephan was dead by 1876. (See plate 18, p. 50.)

STEVENSON, G. A Derby draper who was financially interested in the King Street factory from 1859-66.

STORER, H. *Osmaston Road.* A Derby Crown period flower painter, designed pattern no. 1155.

SUTHERLAND, F. Painter mentioned in W.H. Brock's notebook, left 1893.

SWAINSON, Edwrd. *King Street.* This modeller was born in 1866 and began to work at the King Street factory c.1880 and completed a very long stay at the works, finally retiring in 1935 when the works was bought by Royal Crown Derby. He had modelled before many distinguished visitors including the royal family when they visited the King Street Exhibition at Wembley in 1924. The illustration above shows him at work on a traditional Nottingham Road figure of a boy holding a book. See Twitchett, *Derby Porcelain,* colour plate 73, for a Nottingham Road example which derives its source directly from Meissen. (See illustration p. 228.)

SWAN, Samuel. *Osmaston Road.* Modeller who worked in close contact with Thomas Hough (q.v.) and who executed some animals and fine baskets in Parian body.

TABOR, W. Mentioned in W.H. Brock's notebook, leaving September 1914.

TAILLANDIER, P. *Osmaston Road.* The Osmaston Road Minutes Book records the arrival of P. Taillandier from Coalport, early in 1894. He is said to have been a descendant of the Sèvres floral artist of the same name. As he came to Osmaston Road to assist Désiré Leroy (q.v.), it is possible that he too was apprenticed at the famous French factory. His painting is very fine but he was at Derby for a short period only. (See illustrations pp. 134, 200 and 201.)

TAYLOR, Joseph. *King Street.* He was apprenticed on leaving school at the King Street factory, and worked there as a potter throughout his life. Born in Derby,

Edwin Trowell.

he married Edith Le Lacheur and died in 1916. (See illustrations pp. 14, 16 and 228.)

THOMAS. W. Derby Crown period painter, subjects unknown.

TOWNSEND, G.W. *Osmaston Road.* Gilder mentioned in the Osmaston Road pattern books, in the later Derby Crown period.

TROWELL, Edwin. *Osmaston Road.* Born in 1869 in Derby, he was apprenticed to the Derby Crown Porcelain Company in 1882, aged thirteen. It was soon noticed that he had great skill as a landscape painter, most certainly influenced by Count Holtzendorf (q.v.). He attended art classes at night school, and by the age of fifteen, through the illness of James Rouse sen. (q.v.), he was given a chance to assist with the Gladstone service. Trowell said he was called to the Art Director's office to be asked, 'Do you think you could manage?' Without

Rare photograph given to the Royal Crown Derby Museum by Mr. Heseltine, grandson of George Hemstock, and depicting from left to right, Fred Turvey, decorating manager c.1920, Albert Haddock, one of the finest gilders of this century, John Porter Wale, head painter, Charles Nichlinson gilder, George Hemstock, head gilder, and Jack Saddington gilder. Taken at Osmaston Road circa 1919.
Courtesy Royal Crown Derby Archives.

hesitation came the reply, 'Yes.' He related that for weeks he worked alone. However, there is no other evidence that Trowell painted the pieces of the service (see Appendix VI), but he is mentioned as having completed one of the replicas, and to have painted the floral reserves, with James Platts painting the landscape. Is it possible, therefore, that a few pieces from the Gladstone service were painted by young Edwin?

Despite the success that awaited him, he left to join a Lancashire hospital to take the certificate of the Medical and Psychological Association of Great Britain and Ireland. The Derby Crown Porcelain Company discovered where he was and offered him tempting terms to return. Having by then won his certificate and the heart of the deputy matron, whom he married in 1895 at the age of twenty-six, he rejected them. Although in Derby he is remembered as a fine landscape artist, in fact he made his career in the hospital service, and said in defence of the workhouse system: 'Their [the inmates'] life was certainly not so bad as some would have it. They were treated with respect and, for the period, their standard of living was reasonably good.' The Trowells were master and matron of several hospitals from South Wales to Hemel Hempstead where they arrived on November 31st 1902. It would appear that they retired to the Isle of Man in 1923 where Edwin painted the local scenery. He was widowed in 1944, but by 1954, when he was interviewed by the press, he had married again and was happily living with his second wife. He had been a prominent Mason and had returned to Hertfordshire to live in Boxmoor. (See illustration p. 143, and plate 24, p. 54.)

WALE, John Porter. *Osmaston Road.* Born Worcester 1860, and was employed at Worcester until 1877 when he joined Edward Phillips and William Litherland at Derby. His versatility led him to become head painter. He designed numerous patterns and his influence continued until his death in January 1920. The Royal Crown Derby Museum now possesses a wealth of his watercolours most delicately executed with natural colouring. See illustration above and pp. 123, 139, 155 and 158.)

WENCKER. *King Street.* A German flower painter working at King Street, shortly before the take-over in 1935.

T. Wilkinson, modeller.

Charles Newbold Wright,
painter and gilder, c.1923.

WHITEHEAD, V. Mentioned in W.H. Brock's notebook, left 1899.

WILKINSON, Tom. *Osmaston Road.* Modeller at Osmaston Road and still working in the late fifties aged seventy. Concerned with the services made for the Sheiks of the Middle East, modelling the gigantic rice bowls and tureens. During his long working life at the factory there can be little in which he did not have a hand, ranging from figures to useful items like teapots, etc. (See plate 54, p. 188.)

WILLIAMS, Fred. *Osmaston Road.* Another painter who was allocated many patterns in the Osmaston Road pattern books. Sometimes signed his work with a monogram. Still being mentioned in pattern book 10, but thought to have left in 1895.

WILLINGHAM. Mentioned in W.H. Brock's notebook, left 1900.

WOOD, A.F. *Osmaston Road.* A painter whose floral reserves on vases are often signed. He left the factory in 1918. (See illustration p. 128, and plate 43, p. 121.)

WOOD, Edwin. *Osmaston Road.* Listed as a painter in the 1890s.

WRIGHT, Charles Newbold. *Osmaston Road.* Painter and gilder who worked at Osmaston Road and was allocated more than twenty-five patterns in the Derby Crown period including pattern 962, dessert plate, celadon, ground, birds, spray and flowers by Wright; and 1268, 'Greek' s/s cup and saucer, flowers by Wright. He married Martha Deakin, sister of H.H. Deakin (q.v.).

This Indenture

made the 7th day of September in the year of our Lord one thousand eight hundred and eighty Three BETWEEN Emily Squires of 22 Chetwynd Street in the Parish of St Peters Derby in the County of Derby an Infant of the age of Fourteen years (hereinafter called the said Apprentice) of the first part William Squires of 22 Chetwynd Street aforesaid Father of the said Apprentice (hereinafter called the said Father) of the second part and Henry Litherland and Edward Mc Innes of Derby in the said County of Derby and Potters and Co-partners (hereinafter called the said Masters) of the third part WITNESSETH that the said Apprentice of her own free will and with the consent of the said Father Doth by these Presents put place and bind her self Apprentice unto the said Masters to learn that branch of a Potter's Art or business called Painting and them to serve after the manner of an Apprentice from the third day of September 1883 for the term of Seven years (the usual holidays excepted) from thence next ensuing and fully to be complete and ended during all which term the said Apprentice shall and will faithfully honestly and diligently serve and obey her said Masters as a good and faithful Apprentice ought to do And the said Masters do hereby covenant for themselves their executors and administrators to and with the said Father his executors and administrators that they the said Masters shall and will teach and instruct the said Apprentice or cause her to be taught and instructed in the aforesaid branch of the Potter's Art or business in the best manner they can during the said term And also shall and will find the said Apprentice fair and reasonable work during the said term And also shall and will pay the said Apprentice for her work and services during the said term (the usual holidays excepted) such wages as are hereinafter mentioned that is to say

Three shillings per week for the first year
Four " " " " " " second
Five " " " " " " Third
Six " " " " " " Fourth
Seven " " " " " " Fifth
Eight " " " " " " Sixth
Nine " " " " " " seventh

And the said Apprentice and the said Father do hereby severally covenant and agree with and to the said Masters their executors and administrators that the said Apprentice shall during the said term honestly and faithfully serve her said Masters and well and truly perform the Conditions and Agreements herein contained on the part of the said Apprentice to be done and performed And that the said Apprentice shall not nor will during the said term become or be a party to or concerned or concurring in any Agreement or proceeding commonly called or resembling a Turn-out by or between any journeymen or other workmen And in case there shall be any Turn-out and the said Apprentice shall be concerned in or shall encourage the same or otherwise not obey the reasonable commands of her said Masters then the said Masters be at liberty to put an end to and determine this Indenture and to cease to teach or instruct the said Apprentice during all or any part of the then residue of the said term And further that if during the continuance of the said term any number of workmen employed by the said Masters shall withdraw from their Manufactory in violation of existing Agreements so as to prevent the general business of the said Manufactory or the said branch thereof from being carried on and the same is thereby not carried on or if the said Masters shall consider it advisable to suspend the carrying on of their said business or of the aforesaid branch thereof and shall so do then and in either of such cases and so long as the said business or the said branch thereof shall not be carried on shall be suspended as aforesaid the said Masters shall not be liable or called upon to pay any wages to the said Apprentice. And the said Apprentice is hereby expressly authorised and allowed during the time or times the said business or the said branch shall cease to be carried on as aforesaid or shall be suspended as aforesaid to employ her self in any other manner or with any other person for her own benefit. And the said Father doth hereby further agree with the said Masters that he the said Father shall and will find and provide the said Apprentice with sufficient meat drink washing lodging clothes and all other necessaries at all times during the said term In witness whereof the said parties have hereunto set their hands and seals the day and year first above written.

Signed sealed and delivered by the above-named

Emily Squires	Emily Squires
William Squires	William Squires
Henry Litherland	Henry Litherland
Edward Mc Innes	Edwd Mc Innes

L.S.

Signed in the presence of Henry Lea

15 WOMEN ENAMELLERS AND GILDERS AND ANONYMOUS PAINTERS

In the early days at Osmaston Road some of the workpeople were recruited from Stoke-on-Trent but many more were trained at Derby — gilders, enamellers and burnishers as well as painters, all of whom played a tremendous part in laying the foundations of quality for which the works soon became famous.

Women were employed as gilders or enamellers working on the well known Imari patterns which were produced in so many designs that they prove impossible to list. This work called for artistic skill and a great deal of discipline in order to copy accurately the works patterns which were always in evidence, and which were the yardsticks used by the supervisors who were checking not only quantity and quality but also style. If a girl's or woman's work did not look as much like the works pattern as was thought possible it was cleaned off and had to be re-painted without extra payment. This type of work was never signed, although each gilder or enameller had a small mark, either a numeral, or perhaps an initial, which they used to mark the base of the work purely for the purpose of identification when the work reached the finished warehouse. This practice, used in the eighteenth and nineteenth century, is still used today; however there is no key to this code, the marks having been used and repeated after workpeople have left or retired. Many of these women gilders and enamellers worked at Osmaston Road for fifty years and in some cases longer. The training of the apprentices was thorough and long; they did in fact, on joining the company, sign an indenture (see illustration opposite) stating that they agreed to work for seven years. The practice ceased in 1891.[15] A list of enamellers employed by the company since the war is shown as Appendix IV.

The burnishing of the Imari and other patterns was again carried out by women and girls, the only exception being one or two of the Special Productions where it is clearly stated that the burnishing and chasing was to be done by a specified senior male artist and/or gilder. The fact that burnishing was the final manufacturing process demanded a high degree of care in the operation. At the beginning of the century as many as thirty burnishers were employed and several stayed to complete fifty years' service with the company.[16]

Working at the same time as the male painters listed in the previous chapter, and to whom specific patterns were allocated, were perhaps fifteen or twenty male painters in a separate department, and with a foreman. From these two rooms came quantities of hand painted dinner, tea and dessert ware, together with some vases, all of which were unsigned. The same high degree of skill and artistry was apparent in this work and many of the paintings of floral and other subjects were worthy of a signature.

Miss M. Townsend, enameller and gilder.

15 B. Bill, P. Band, M. Gerrard, K. Hemstock, F. Gerrard, E. Davey and M. Winterson are just a few of the gilders who were working at the beginning of the present century. Likewise among the enamellers were Miss Broughton, C. Bennett, B. Barker, J. Midgely, W. Watkin, and many more.
16 N. Gothan, G. Parker and M. Murray being amongst that number.

16 DESIGN

In July 1883 the following piece from Dr. Dresser's 'Art of decorative design' appeared in *The Artist:*

> 'The advice which I must give to every designer is to study carefully exactly what is required, before he proceeds to form his ideas of what the object proposed to be created should be like, and then to diligently strive to arrange such a form for it as shall cause it to be perfectly suited to the want which it is intended to meet.'

He goes on to say that on all rounded forms such as cups and vases, all ornaments should be of an extremely simple character and grouped so as not to suffer by being foreshortened. Certain laws of perspective should be understood in designing for all objects of this kind; on flat surfaces the design should by no means represent anything which might be interpreted into a right and wrong way up; for instance, when in use most of a plate's decoration is more or less covered. Plates should, therefore, receive but little ornament, and that should be of a radiating quality; figures, landscapes seem unnaturally placed — especially large heads and portraits. Dr. Dresser stressed that in most examples of the best work, these principles were fundamental.

The extent to which the Derby factories fulfilled Dr. Dresser's criteria for good design, readers may determine for themselves from the examples of wares given in this book. That the Derby factories understood the laws of perspective, even on curved objects, cannot be in doubt. We see examples of the necessary radiating quality on plates, particularly in the running rose patterns. However, all those subjects which Dr. Dresser warned against as unsuitable for plates, namely figures, landscapes, flowers and portraits, were meat and drink to Crown Derby. Large heads were also used; the boy's head by James Platts (see plate 22, p. 51) is particularly compelling in design.

Certainly Derby wares are highly decorative and thus might not please Dr. Dresser, although they usually met with the approval of contemporary commentators. *The British Mail,* 1881, writing on the China Works stated:

> 'From the SHOWROOM [now the Museum] we proceeded to the STUDIOS of M. LANDGRAFF [*sic*] and Count Holtzendorf, to whom the proprietors have committed the artistic interests of the Works. Here we inspected many exquisite designs for plaques — birds, flowers, etc., being freely introduced. The DESIGNING DEPARTMENT also contained many beautiful conceptions, if we may so term them, not yet worked out, but which will doubtless in due time be put forth to raise higher the reputation both of the artists and of the Works.'

The early death of Landgraf in 1882 (see p. 230), is likely to have been the motivation for the appointment of Richard Lunn on August 2nd that year. He retained the position of Art Director until 1889. Lunn was accused by some directors of being only good at elaborate and costly wares. A report in the *Derbyshire Times,* September 1883, talks of the visit to the works of the celebrated painter, Whistler, who was so taken with the wares, ground laid in such subtle hues, that he considered they required no further embellishment. He was, however, informed that the British art-patron likes his porcelain highly ornamented. Nor was Whistler's taste shared by his fellow Americans who greatly appreciated the extreme richness of the wares. American support for what was then the most modern major china works in Europe is underlined by such orders as that from the Cincinnati Museum of Art for various vases, plates and cups. The items were shipped from Liverpool to New York for transportation to Cincinnati in 1886. The bill from the retailers, Buckley and Co., of Birmingham, is dated February 2nd 1887, and is still held by the museum.

The New York Times, December 26th 1882, mentions a visit to the China Works of 'the Jersey Lilly', Mrs. Langtry, and states: 'One of the specialities which finds particular favour abroad and of which the Company is very proud is the "Persian Ware" decorated with raised gold, the colour of which is remarkably pure.'

Lunn was succeeded by T. Reed and it was during his period as Art Director that Désiré Leroy came to Derby. Antoinette Feÿ-Halle criticises his work, in particular a blue ground vase decorated in white enamel, as being heavily gilded and showing 'how little British taste evolved in the last thirty years of the nineteenth century. Gilding was now far too heavily applied.'[17] Miss Halle's remarks would have found little support amongst Leroy's contemporaries. The skills which he had acquired through his working period at Sèvres were appreciated both at the time and by collectors ever since. In December 1906 *The Pall Mall Magazine* accurately predicted that his work would be worth its weight in gold. Leroy was able to use colours in relation to each other that none of his contemporaries attempted. Occasionally later artists have tried to emulate his skills and have failed miserably. The late Sèvres productions often lose their jewelling; it is seldom, if ever, that one finds jewelling missing from any piece which Leroy made for Royal Crown Derby.

Reed, meanwhile, was broadening the scope of the Imari type patterns and increasing the use of printing as additional decoration on wares. Some patterns were entirely printed and merely framed by a single 22 carat gold line. One such pattern, 'Mikado', was designed by Reed and became one of the most popular ever created by Royal Crown Derby. Cassidy's distributed ten million pieces of the pattern in Canada alone, and the event was celebrated by a commemorative bowl. Other blue and white patterns included 'Wilmot', 'Victoria' and 'Peacock'. The leading engravers of these patterns were Isaac Smith, H. Short, who too worked for the company for more than fifty years, and Walter Lowndes, one of Short's apprentices who later become a successful silversmith.

In 1927 H.T. Robinson became chairman of the Company, and in 1931 was instrumental in bringing in Donald Birbeck as successor to T. Reed (Robinson and Birbeck had previously worked together at Cauldon). There is no extant evidence that Birbeck handpainted any pieces himself, but his watercolour interpretations of birds and animals were the source of inspiration to modellers such as Arnold Mikelson. The scope of his talent is demonstrated both in the designs for the celebrated service got up for an Indian Prince shown on pp. 90-94, and in the colour plates shown on pp. 209, 212, 213 and 216.

The accusation is levelled at the Company from time to time that they only make traditional items and that their output is derivative. However, *The Magazine of Arts,* 1884, commented 'they have not been content to remain mere plagiarists in porcelain.' 'The Billiards Player' (plate 17, p. 50) was made circa 1880 by Herbert Warrington Hogg without using traditional base or support. In the 20th century, Tom Wilkinson's 'Anna Ahlers', the actress from the art deco period,

17 *Nineteenth Century European Porcelain,* Antoinette Feÿ-Halle and Barbara Mundt, Trefoil, 1983.

kept the china works in vogue (see plate 54, p. 188), and indeed, some small platinum bordered cups, recently purchased for the Museum, are dated as early as 1933 and demonstrate that the Company was in the forefront of modern design.

Today the company produces a most popular series of paperweights of animals, birds and fish. The Classic Collection, four figures named Penelope, Athena, Persephone and Dione (see plate 62, p. 227), were created by the Design Director, Jo Ledger, and modeller, Robert Jefferson, in 1986. When the Prime Minister, Margaret Thatcher, visited Royal Crown Derby on January 29th 1986, she gave the series an enthusiastic reception, saying that she found them 'stylish' with 'flowing line, movement and marvellous facial expressions'. Another recent series is the 'Royal Cats', the first four models are titled 'Abyssinian', 'Siamese', 'Persian' and 'Egyptian', each cat wearing the headgear of the royal houses of these ancient kingdoms. They too are the artistic creation of Robert Jefferson. See plate 61, p. 226.

The work of the museum is now paramount in encouraging the study of the history of Royal Crown Derby. The conservation of designs and wares from the past life of the factory is a present inspiration to today's designers, who whilst working in a modern idiom are yet aware that they are working within a proud and highly skilled tradition.

Appendix I Review of the past decade at Royal Crown Derby

Over ten eventful years have passed since the very hot night in June 1976 when the first edition of *Royal Crown Derby* was launched at the Penta Hotel in South Kensington. In 1984, Betty Bailey, the book's co-author, retired from her position as deputy curator at the Royal Crown Derby Museum, and Natalia Wieczorek was appointed in her place.

Extensive renovations have been made to the Osmaston Road china works, which has now been operating for one hundred and ten years, the longest continuous period of any of the three Derby China Works. The façade of the building has been completely refaced. In 1986 the museum was closed for complete refurbishment. The many improvements included a small lecture and exhibition room, a new archive room with additional storage space, a new office for the curator and a spacious and elegant foyer, with purpose designed cabinets to display the current productions, and with smaller demonstration exhibits showing such things as the history and development of traditional patterns. The autumn of 1987 saw the opening of a room devoted to the King Street factory as part of the museum complex, where it is hoped the importance of this factory, as the direct link with the original china works, may be fully demonstrated. Objects on display there include Sampson Hancock's working stool and an 'Old Japan' plate painted and signed by him. A mug has been given by Mrs. Elizabeth Rochfort-Boyd which was specially commissioned by her father, Howard Paget the owner of the King Street factory. He gave it her as an inducement to drink up her milk when she was a small girl — a pattern of fishes is revealed at the bottom when the mug is empty. The Paget teaset with the zeppelin mark (see p. 20) is also on view.

The museum is open daily, Monday to Friday, except for holidays, and it is, therefore, advisable to check that the museum is open before making a visit. 'Open days', which the curator and his deputy have now been running since 1972, provide a wealth of exchange of information and documentation between the museum and people from all over the world. On 'open days' which are held on the first Tuesday of the month from 10 a.m.-4 p.m., members of the public, be they dealers or collectors, or indeed anyone with an interest, may come to discuss a particular piece, which need not necessarily be of Derby manufacture.

A new society 'The Derby Porcelain International Society' has been formed to study and promote the history of china and pottery in the City of Derby and its environs. The first major event staged by the Society was the Loan Exhibition at the Royal Academy during the Burlington House Fair in September 1985.

1986 saw the bi-centenary of the death of William Duesbury, the man who had raised the Derby China Works to international fame and set the standards for succeeding proprietors to maintain, and a series of events was organized to celebrate his life. On November 2nd (the date of Duesbury's funeral) a service of thanksgiving was held in Derby Cathedral, attended by the Lord Lieutenant of Derbyshire, Col. Peter Hilton, Viscountess Scarsdale (dressed in 'Scarsdale Yellow'), the Mayor and Mayoress of Derby together with other civic dignatories from the City and County, members of the Derby Porcelain International Society and many of the employees at the china works or their descendants, including Frank Duesbury, who has since given a shaped vase and cover to the museum. During the service a Derby figure of St. Thomas and a new Kedleston vase were placed on the altar table.

The service of thanksgiving for the life of William Duesbury, held at Derby Cathedral on 2nd November, 1986.

The service was followed by a party at Osmaston Road where a unique collection of Derby coffee cans, all with Imari or Japan style decoration were on show. These had been collected by John Twitchett over the last decade, with examples from as far afield as New York, Montreal and Toronto. The collection dates from 1800 and includes items from all three Derby China Works.

A series of three lectures was given as part of the bicentenary celebrations: 'Duesbury and the town of Derby at his Time' by Roy Christian; 'William Duesbury the Man' by John Twitchett; and 'William Duesbury — the Productions' by Judith Anderson. An exhibition entitled 'Painters and the Derby China Works' was mounted at the Victoria and Albert Museum and demonstrated the ability of the Derby painters to keep abreast of the new fashions and techniques of their times.[18] The exhibition is to be staged in Toronto in October 1988, and John Twitchett is conducting a lecture series.

An article by John Twitchett giving a detailed account of William Duesbury was published to coincide with the bi-centenary by *Ceramics,* Issue 5, August 1987. A five petal commemorative tray was issued (see illustration), and a porcelain plaque honouring Duesbury is to be placed in the cathedral.

Special productions since the publication of the first edition of *Royal Crown Derby* include a presentation casket to celebrate the bi-centenary of American Independence in 1976, given by the Queen to President Ford, a replica of which

18 'Painters and the Derby China Works' by John Murdoch and John Twitchett, exhibition catalogue, Victoria and Albert Museum, March-June 1987.

Royal Crown Derby five petal tray commemorating William Duesbury, and issued during the bi-centenary year. Duesbury who brought international fame to Derby through his china works at Nottingham Road, died on 30th October, 1786.

is in the Museum. The Queen's silver jubilee in 1977 was commemorated with a basket of traditional shape, displaying the royal coat of arms, and again a replica may be seen in the Royal Crown Derby Museum. In 1986 Her Majesty Queen Elizabeth, the Queen Mother, was presented with some yellow ground coffee cans and saucers, bearing her cypher, to mark the launch in Govan shipyards of the *Norsea*. To celebrate her eightieth birthday, Royal Crown Derby presented Her Majesty with a small set of four 'Talbot' shaped yellow ground dishes painted with her residences, the Royal Lodge, Windsor; the Castle of May, Caithness; Birkhall, Aberdeenshire; and Clarence House, London.

In January 1986 the Prime Minister, the Rt. Hon. Margaret Thatcher, visited the Royal Crown Derby China Works (see p. 249 and illustration overleaf).

Among the major gifts to the Museum in the last ten years was a bequest of china by the late Molly Barratt, daughter of Robert Barratt who had adorned many urns and dessert services with flowers and landscapes with his talented brush. The china had been treasured by her father and includes the rare scent bottle illustrated on p.108. Such gifts demonstrate the warmth of feeling of the workforce, past and present, to Royal Crown Derby.

It was an 'open day' in the summer of 1985 which led to the most generous gift of the 'Bemrose Volumes' to the Museum by Mr. Thomas St. John Wood and his daughters, Mrs. Lynda Beldon Wood and Mrs. Gail Lowry, in memory of his wife and their mother, Mrs. Doreen Gratton Wood. The Bemrose volumes which had descended to the Wood family through Charles and Louise Bemrose, consist of drawings and watercolours, papers, photographs of such artists as Billingsley,

The Prime Minister, the Rt. Hon. Mrs. Margaret Thatcher visiting Royal Crown Derby, and seen here decorating a plate, pattern 1128.

Pegg and Webster, and correspondence including letters relating to china purchased by the royal family. The volumes were the principal exhibits at the Victoria and Albert Museum exhibition staged as part of the Duesbury bi-centenary celebration (see p. 250).

The purchase of the William Pegg Sketch Book of 1813 for the museum, was of major importance as previously only fragments of his work had been seen. This book has been exhibited in London twice, and is now on permanent exhibition at the Royal Crown Derby Museum where the archive collection also includes the Bemrose volumes, many designs by Leroy, and, of course, all the Derby pattern books. Every effort is made to update information, and research gathered from the archives is published from time to time. Unfortunately a lot of the material is too fragile to be made available to the general public.

The outstanding gift of the past decade must be that of Mr. Ronald Raven, the internationally acclaimed surgeon, who specialises in the treatment of cancer. He

Her Royal Highness the Princess of Wales unveiling the commemorative dish to celebrate the opening of the Ronald William Raven Room in the Royal Crown Derby Museum Complex on Thursday December 10th 1987. The princess is seen with Mr. Ronald Raven (left) and Mr. Stuart Lyons, chairman of Royal Crown Derby (right).

is giving his remarkable collection of Derby wares to the museum. The size of the gift necessitated the setting up of a trust to ensure that the collection could be suitably housed and the resulting 'Ronald William Raven Room' was officially opened by Her Royal Highness the Princess of Wales on 10th December, 1987. Mr. Raven has supplied furniture and personal effects so that the room reflects his personality. Part of his collection has been made available, and is already on display during Mr. Raven's lifetime, a most generous gesture. The rest of the collection will later be given to the Museum, thus completing the collection in the Ronald William Raven Room.

Appendix II Marks and Year Cyphers found on decorated wares

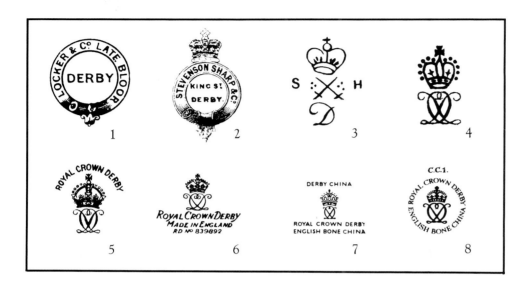

1 King Street 1848-1859
2 King Street 1859-1866
3 Standing for Stevenson and
  Hancock 1863-66
  Standing for Sampson Hancock
  1866-1935

4 Osmaston Road 1877-1890
5 Osmaston Road 1890-1940
6 Osmaston Road 1940-1945
7 Osmaston Road 1964-1975
8 Osmaston Road 1976

The following three marks are sometimes added to King Street productions 1916-1935 and as such are helpful in dating.

For William Larcombe 1916-

For Larcombe & Page 1917-34

For Paget c.1934

This crossed 'P' mark was based on 'Pug' and 'Peg' the pet names used by Paget and his second wife.[19]

After the take-over of the small King Street factory, the Royal Crown Derby China Works occasionally used the S & H mark: it should be realised that this right had been purchased along with the works in 1935. However, the Osmaston Road potting was mostly lighter and of better quality although it is true to say that both works maintained a high standard of decoration.

Marks nos. 4, 5, 7 and 8 carry, usually below the mark, a cypher referring to the year in which they were decorated.

Mark no. 5 from 1891 has the word 'England' in a vertical position at the side, and from approximately 1921 until 1964 'Made in England', horizontally beneath it.

Normally the mark is over glaze in red, but sometimes appears in other colours. With regard to under glaze marks mark no. 4 appears in black without year cypher, and mark no. 5 in dark green. This of course means that a piece marked under glaze may have been decorated at a later date and thus would prove the exception to the rule.

19. The telegraphic address for King Street was BCM/PUG!

1880	1881	1882	1883	1884	1885	1886	1887	1888	1889	1890	1891
1892	1893	1894	1895	1896	1897	1898	1899	1900	1901	1902	1903
1904	1905	1906	1907	1908	1909	1910	1911	1912	1913	1914	1915
1916	1917	1918	1919	1920	1921	1922	1923	1924	1925	1926	1927
1928	1929	1930	1931	1932	1933	1934	1935	1936	1937	1938	1939
										I	II
1940	1941	1942	1943	1944	1945	1946	1947	1948	1949	1950	1951
III	IV	V	VI	VII	VIII	IX	X	XI	XII	XIII	XIV
1952	1953	1954	1955	1956	1957	1958	1959	1960	1961	1962	1963
XV	XVI	XVII	XVIII	XIX	XX	XXI	XXII	XXIII	XXIV	XXV	XXVI
1964	1965	1966	1967	1968	1969	1970	1971	1972	1973	1974	1975
XXVII	XXVIII	XXIX	XXX	XXXI	XXXII	XXXIII	XXXIV	XXXV	XXXVI	XXXVII	XXXVIII

Derby year cyphers (believed to be correct to within one year). The 'V' Mark of 1904 is accompanied by the word 'England'; that of 1942 the words 'Made in England'. Similarly in respect of the 'X' Marks of 1901 and 1947. Between the 1940s and 1950s the year cypher mark was mostly omitted on wares which were often marked in green or pink.

Extract from a notebook, showing potting marks from July 1883 to December 1890 used at the Osmaston Road factory. It is believed that capital letters were used from 1890-1900. After this the month and year were impressed on biscuit ware.

Appendix III 'Forty years at Royal Crown Derby' by Brenda Bentley

Brenda Bentley.

Opposite:
Past employees of Royal Crown Derby. Top left: Dave Harrison, presser. Top right: W. Colley, dipper. Bottom left: A. Harrison, dish presser. Bottom right: T. Kirk, Caster.

I was born at Melbourne, South Derbyshire in 1932, my maiden name being Parnham, and began and indeed completed my education in that lovely small town. Not everyone knows that it gave its name to Melbourne, Australia, and was the birthplace of Thomas Cook of travel fame.

Most girls have their dreams and I had thought of myself doing secretarial work and certainly had no aspirations to decorate china. Like so many young girls of my time, my mind was made up for me, difficult as that may seem to the younger generation today, by my father who was very aware of the job difficulties of the time. Royal Crown Derby were asking for gilders and enamellers and I very soon found myself brought to Osmaston Road, travelling by bus during December 1946. You may well imagine my apprehensive feelings in this quite new and 'foreign' environment. The town of Derby seemed a very big and frightening city. I said very little but was to be taken on as an apprentice gilder according to the arrangements made between mother and the China Works.

On 2nd January, 1947 I was sent off in good time to be punctual for my first day's work, and arriving, somewhat scared, was ushered into one of two groups of girls. I found myself in the group of enamellers; this mistake worried me but soon was forgotten because of the pleasure of working with colours. Gilding with 22 carat gold was to me dull and boring. This was my initiation into my ceramics career, which in later years, in spite of the usual 'ups and downs' was to give me much job satisfaction. We girls, like our predecessors, went through the training period using red enamel to smother, not only the wares, but of course ourselves!

An early creative job was to paint the pink roses in 'Derby Posie' and the mind boggles to think that the celebrated W.E.J. Dean, known in the factory as Billy Dean, was required to do this type of work towards the end of his career, because of the wartime conditions. At one time the men were called upon to decorate the birds and we girls would only be allowed to paint the beautifully modelled flowers applied to the bases. These Royal Crown Derby flowers have always been special and indeed Cheryl Tatler now continues in this fine art of modelling applied flowers to decorate figures, birds, boxes and to become part of the range of jewellery. The mention of jewellery reminds me that as young girls our wages were not high, but we would save up and buy a brooch and earrings set of pastel colour and with our professional sense of colour and our painting talents we would cold-colour paint these sets each time a new colour was required to complement a new dress or outfit.

When I started working at the China Works, the hours ranged from 8am to 6pm Mondays to Fridays and 8am to 12.30pm Saturdays. About 10am somewhat dubious beverages arrived in the work-room and were usually drunk through thirst rather than for pleasure. The mid-day break was mainly to eat our own sandwiches brought from home, although there was a contraption which would bake potatoes, and a small room served in place of a canteen. How things have changed! Today, of course, Royal Crown Derby has a fine canteen ably run by Vicky and her girls.

We are often asked what we think about whilst decorating. I well remember that prior to the works dance we girls would sit with our hair in curlers, but our heads covered with scarves — a factory rule. These occasions were looked forward to and were held at the Midland Institute. Bus loads of soldiers would be invited to our function and usually we would be invited back to theirs. The Second World War

Girls in the decorating department working on pattern 1128, c.1920.
Royal Crown Derby Museum Archives

provided no shortage of soldiers and a good deal of fun was had by all. To amuse ourselves whilst working we had a girl who sang solos (soprano) and she would also entertain the gilders! Poems and descriptions of the latest film at the local cinema were given, this being the age of the Hollywood filmstar with all the glamour and escape it created. The other girls would make sure that the performers' work was kept up to prevent losses in wages. What better experience for me when I became Supervisor of the decorating department!

Summer could bring its problems, but here again the practical Midland girls made large paper hats from the waste from the lithographers department and subsequently we looked more like nuns. The added heat came from the glass roof and windows as light is essential to decorating. To cool our feet we filled large tureens with cold water and thus we had foot-baths! When Winter came we had hot plates from the kiln discreetly placed in our jumpers. In those days, I remember with amusement, the manager would walk through the department in his shirt-sleeves in Winter, but would always be oddly wrapped up in suits in Summer.

At times naturally work could be boring though we were never allowed to drop our standards of quality, but there were always visits of famous people and, indeed, exciting Royal visits. One Royal visit in particular reminds me that I was sent home to Melbourne, by the supervisor, to fetch more flowers. My mother was very proud indeed when I returned to the China Works with roses, almost the trade mark of Derby China, for the visit in 1948 of Princess Elizabeth, who was to become our much loved Queen. Over the years I have worked on many Royal items during my long career, but I remember the set of plates done for Her Majesty Queen Elizabeth, the Queen Mother, and had the great pleasure of meeting and talking with her. A visit by Lord Snowdon comes quickly to my mind; a young colleague, deaf but by no means dumb as her father would always say, was spoken to by Lord Snowdon, and after I had pointed out her handicap to him, he immediately waived away the media, and with his inimitable feeling for his fellow being, spoke to her in sign language with his hands. In the early days at the Works I could never have envisaged a visit to Buckingham Palace when called upon to deliver some of our famous wares.

The original mode of packing china for transportation was by barrel and these

Royal Crown Derby group photograph on the retirement of Mary Murray, one of the fine burnishers at Osmaston Road. Brenda Bentley is seated right. 30th March 1973.
Royal Crown Derby Archives

were not changed for the cardboard cartons until my time. Some of the hoops would be acquired by the girls to decorate the benches for impending weddings; it was the custom to raise two shillings per head and to get a half tea set in white. I still have mine.

We all make mistakes and surely I was no exception when, as Supervisor, I collected biscuit blue instead of the mauve enamel used in decorating colour 'Aves'. The result was a complete disaster the other colours gleaming, but oh dear! the substituted mauve was more akin to cement.

On works tours, in the early days, visitors would often pick up items still wet and not fired, but nowadays there are warning notices.

My forty years at the internationally renowned Crown Derby Works have enabled me to span the changing techniques, and to see lithography brought to very high standards. I drew some of the first designs to be lithographed. Other items decorated by me were plates, sporting tankards and, of course, figures. It would be foolish of me to say that I had enjoyed every moment of my career, but on reflection I am pleased to have had the satisfaction of watching young girls become competent and reach the high standards which are required at Osmaston Road, and to have been one of the many who have had the experience of working at what is probably the most famous China Works in the world.

Appendix IV Enamellers employed since the Second World War

List supplied by Brenda 'Pip' Bentley. Unless otherwise stated the enamellers listed are women.

B. Bentley	1947	1987	K. Wood	1969	1980
S. Kimsey	1947	present	L. Brown	1970	1973
J. Gould	1948	1960	P. Hardy	1970	1975
Mr. H.C.G. Jacob	1951	1959	L. Payne		
Mr. W.G. Jacob	1952	1956	(née Hilliard)	1970	1979
J. Grifiths	1955	present	H. Dudley		
M. Townsend	1957	present	(née Prince)	1970	1981
J. Kimsey			Y. Harper (née		
(née Brown)	1958	1970	Brearly, later		
B. Riley	1960	1964	Freestone)	1970	1981
J. Doyle	1960	1968(?)	L. Purdy	1971	1976
M. Mason	1961	1969	V. Akers	1971	1979
Mr. T. Bramfitt	1962	1964	J. Wilcockson	1971	1980
L. Tristram	1962	1967	C. Windridge	1972	present
C. Jackson	1962	1971	J. Aston		
P. Webb	1963	1970	(née Taylor)	1973	present
L. Johnson	1965	1970(?)	V. Akers	1974	1979
C.M. Pell	1965	1970	S. Whitbread		
S. Scott	1965	1972	(née Tivey)	1974	1981
C. Komaniki	1966	1971	J. Roome	1976	present
M. Waldon	1968	1970	L. Holmes		
S. Beardsall	1969	1972			

Appendix V　　List of Chairmen and Directors 1875-1988

CHAIRMEN

1877	W. Litherland	1925	E. McInnes	1964	Lord Poole, P.C., C.B.E., T.D.
1883	J. McInnes	1927	H.T. Robinson		
1897	Wm. Bemrose	1932	H. Taylor	1968	W.T. Gill
1908-9	Samuel S. Bacon	1937	H.T. Robinson	1972	J.G. Bellak
1910	E. McInnes	1953	P.I. Robinson	1983	Sir Richard Bailey, C.B.E.
1911	Samuel S. Bacon	1958	O.A.J. Ling	1987	S.R. Lyons
1913	H. Litherland				

DIRECTORS

1877	Ed. Phillips	1929	G.W. Leech	1960	G. Paletz
1877	Wm. Bemrose	1929	J.A. Robinson	1960	W. Inch　*Deputy Managing Director*
1878	Henry Bemrose	1931	Mrs. K.O. Robinson	1961	J. Frost
1878	Charles Newton	1931	W.E. Wootton	1962	F.W. Miller
1879	Walter Evans	1932	Col. Harry Clive	1964	A.G. Ellis
1879	Henry Evans	1932	C.T. Birbeck	1964	R.S. Weightman, O.B.E., T.D., J.P.
1879	F.I. Robinson	1935	C.M. Brunt		
1880	Henry Litherland	1936	A.E. Greenland	1968	J.G. Cliff
1880	E. McInnes	1937	Capt. J. Blower	1968-85	A. Rigby
1881	Henry Litherland ⎤ *Joint Managing*	1940	P.I. Robinson　*Managing Director*	1968	K.M.D. Mills
1881	E. McInnes ⎦ *Directors*	1940	Harry Joyce	1971-85	W. Fisher
1883	John Litherland	1953	C.F. Osborn	1973-79	T.G.A. Birks
1888	Samuel S. Bacon	1953	H.C. Gittoes	1979-85	A.M. Harvey
1903	C.F.E. McInnes	1954	Mrs. K.O. Robinson	1982-85	M.H. Worthington
1908-9	Wm. Bradshaw Litherland	1955	E.J. Peake	1985	J.W. Ledger
1904	Wm. Pepper	1955	P. de Waller	1985-87	S.R. Lyons
1924	W.B. Litherland	1956	O.A.J. Ling	1985	H.M.T. Gibson
1924	A.N. McInnes	1960	A.T. Smith　*Managing Director*		

H.T. Robinson

Appendix VI The Gladstone Dessert Service: A contemporary report

The deputation of Liberal Working Men consisted of the Executive Committee, which included Mr. W.G. Norman, chairman, Mr. Henry Mosley, treasurer and Mr. William Strangeway, secretary. On Saturday December 22nd, 1883, the presentation to Mr. Gladstone took place at Hawarden Castle.

It is interesting to note the details of the central scenes, all finely painted by Count Holtzendorf:

Four high Comports
View All Saints
Derby from Exeter bridge
The Stepping Stones, Hathersage
The Straits, Dovedale

Four low Comports
The Peak Cavern, Castleton
The Black Rocks (Stonnis), Cromford
Dale Abbey
Derby Free Library

Plates
Four Wye views
Monsal Dale
Chee Tor
Derwent Edge
Hartington village
Hardwick Hall
The Terrace at Haddon Hall

Bakewell Street scene
The Peacock at Rowsley
Wingfield Manor
Chatsworth (two views)
High Tor, Matlock
Eyam
The Silk Mill, Derby

Complete Service 26 pieces.
The deputation was introduced to the Prime Minister by the two Members for the Borough, Sir William Vernon Harcourt and Mr. Alderman Roe.

The Response
The speech is given in full to enable historians and students to have an insight into the sociological aspect of the ceramic industry at the time of the presentation.

'With respect to that tribute, that splendid tribute, which a very short investigation shows me is worthy of the best periods of the remarkable manufacture which now supplies a marked portion of your city — with respect to that tribute, I gratefully accept it, not as having any relation to the measure of my deserts, but as having relation to that unbounded liberality of estimation with which, as I well know, it is the practice of the people of this country to recognise and acknowledge whatever attempts are made by public servants to confer advantage upon their country. Your good wishes and prayers on my behalf I accept with equal absence of reserve. With respect to that eulogy which you have been pleased to pronounce, friendship is proverbially partial, and no amount of self-love could possibly induce me to believe that the partiality of friendship in advance of what justice requires or warrants has not been conspicuous on this occasion; but notwithstanding, I look upon that eulogy and I receive it in the same manner as I receive your beautiful service of china — not as exhibiting the due measure of any performance of mine, but as exhibiting the generous estimate in which goodwill and honest effort are regarded by my countrymen. The matter that presents itself to me connected with your porcelain manufacture, offers me a subject on which I should have real pleasure in dilating if the occasion were one for much detailed remark. But there are two points on neither of which I need detain you long, and on which I will venture to speak in connection with the porcelain manufacture of this country, and with the porcelain manufacture of Derby in particular. In the first place, it is to me a matter of singular interest to observe that to England has been allocated a peculiar, and, I think you will say with me, a very high office in connection with porcelain manufacture. It is quite true that the countries of the Continent, and Saxony in particular, preceded you, as the distant East had preceded them, in the production of porcelain; but the porcelain that was produced in Germany and France was produced by dint of Royal subventions, by means of pecuniary aid granted after all out of the public purse, granted by public authority, and, therefore, proceeding from public sources. We have all of us had enough experience in questions of the kind to know the meaning of that. It received subsidies out of the general taxation and wealth of the respective countries. It was England that first of all placed the manufacture upon a sound basis. Even that splendid manufacture of Chelsea was, you know very well, maintained by a grant — a very honourable and creditable grant — of £800 a year from a member of the Royal Family, the Duke of Cumberland. As I have always understood, it was the withdrawal of the grant that caused the manufacture of Chelsea to decline and die, but it was given to two cities of this country — to Worcester and Derby — to found the production of porcelain upon the principles of free and independent commerce. Not a farthing, so far as I know, was ever received by you in the way of public subvention, nor, unless I am much mistaken, was it received at Worcester. I need not say that when Wedgwood — a name most illustrious in the history of English commerce — came into the field, he, in the same manner, disclaiming every public aid of that kind, was content to appeal to the native and genuine resources of combined industry, intelligence, and skill, and it is upon that sound and permanent basis, and not upon the uncertain ground of accidental help derived from collateral sources of a fictitious character, that the porcelain manufactury of this country has stood from that time onwards, and will, as I trust, long continue to stand. Standing as it does on that basis, it is remarkable — and I think I am justified in what I am about to say — that undoubtedly in the last century England took a very high place in porcelain manufacture, but in the present century certainly the relative place of England appears to me to be higher still, and I believe it is not too much to say — I do not think I am indulging in arrogance or national vanity when I say — that at the present moment England stands at the head of the porcelain producing countries of the world. There is one other word I will say on this subject, and it is this. I regard this manufacture with the greatest interest. For very many years I have had a great love of porcelain. I think that they are entirely mistaken who consider its production merely as a branch of industry, or merely as a branch of skilled industry; it is likewise a branch of art — a branch of art in which the principles of fine arts are applied to an industrial purpose. Now, in my opinion, the thing that we want most in regard to material progress is, not to assist those who labour in escaping from labour to what is sometimes very roughly and inaccurately called head work — for there are no less independent members of the community than those who do the lowest description of what is roughly and inaccurately called head work — what we want is to elevate labour; we want to refine labour; we want to lift labour more and more into regions and upon the level of refined production. There is there, depend upon it, an unbounded field before you. There is no limit to the field that opens in that way. I am not jealous of foreign supply. I have to reflect that out of two loaves of bread that you eat one is foreign. At the same time, with regard to the supply of labour of the highest class applied to the production of objects that are beautiful as well as useful, I must confess that I should be very glad to see the day when we would be less dependent upon foreign supply, and when we should be able to count upon an ample and abundant amount of the very highest and most refined in every description of industrial art drawn from our own soil, drawn from our own population. I need not say, therefore — you will understand me at once when I say — with what interest I regard a pursuit like yours, because it has that tendency in the most direct and efficient manner, and brings out qualities of which there is an inexhaustible store in the English nature and character, and which merely want opportunity, and consideration, and practice to give to you, as English artisans, the very highest place, I believe, among the nations of the world with respect to beautiful as well as useful productions. I will not trouble you further upon that; but will only repeat, that, although I knew that the greatest pains and the greatest liberality would be exhibited by you in presenting a worthy example of the Derby porcelain manufacture, I must say that the beauty of that which you have placed on the table fairly surpasses all my expectations.'

It is known that apart from the sample plate, illustrated on p. 74, there are in a private collection four replicas and duplicates, one of which is illustrated in colour, plate 23, p. 54. Two others are also by James Rouse Sen., and Count Holtzendorf, but one is by neither of these men. The landscape is painted by James Platts and the floral panels by Edwin Trowell. The gilding on this plate was executed by H. Hickman.

The letters reproduced opposite give confirmation that only 17 duplicates or replicas were made, of which the above four plates (now in a private collection) form a part.

Extracts from Letter Book **256**

December 16/93.

THE DESSERT SERVICE

which was presented to Mr. GLADSTONE by the WORKING MEN of DERBY in 1883.

consisted of eighteen plates and eight dishes. The ground-colour is rich Mazarine Blue, with painted Posies in oval medallions by JAMES ROUSE. In oblong medallions are the initials W.E.G., one letter in each of three medallions. In the centre of each piece is a Derbyshire Landscape, painted by HOLTZENDORFF.

Some extra Plates were done by the same artists of which those now purchased by Henry Boden Esq. are the last; no more will be made. The others were disposed of as follows:—

    1. Mr. Hawkins, Bournemouth.
    1. Messrs Davis Collamore & Co. New York.
    1. Messrs Osler, London
    1. Mr. H.G. Stephenson, Manchester
    2. Mr. Wm Litherland, Liverpool
    1. Mr. Phillips, Exeter.
    1. Mr. Wenworth Wass, South Norwood.
    1. Mr. Henry Heath, Newcastle.
    2. Mr. Henry Boden, Derby.

                W. Litherland
                Mang. Director.

254

16 Decr 93

Dear Sir,

I am much obliged by your favor enclosing cheque value thirty pounds, in payment for the six dessert plates — The Gladstone Dessert Service is now a matter of History, as far as the China Works are concerned, as these six plates are the last, and no more will be done —

I am pleased for you to have the Trial Plate of the Service, as it is very interesting, on a/c of the subject painted on it.

I think the enclosed will give all the information you ask for — I also send you a copy of the Pamphlet which has a description of the Service, in case you have not one by you —

                Yours faithfully
                M. Litherland

Henry Boden Esq
The Friary
Derby

Bibliography

Blacker, J.F., *The ABC of Collecting Old China,* London Opinion Curio Club, 1908.

Jewitt, L., *Ceramic Art in Great Britain,* Virtue & Co., 1878.
A revised and expanded edition of the nineteenth-century sections, by Geoffrey A. Godden, was published by Barrie & Jenkins, London, in 1972.

Godden, Geoffrey A., *Victorian Porcelain,* Herbert Jenkins, 1961.

Haslem, John, *The Old Derby China Factory,* George Bell, 1876.

Twitchett, John, *Derby Porcelain,* Barrie and Jenkins, 1980.

Twitchett, John, and Sandon, Henry, *Landscape on Derby and Worcester Porcelain,* Henderson and Stirk, 1984.

Twitchett, John, and Murdoch, John, *Painters and the Derby China Works,* Trefoil 1987.

Wallis, A., and Bemrose, William, *The Pottery and Porcelain of Derbyshire,* Bemrose, 1870.
The present authors have been able to refer to Wallis & Bemrose's own copy, which contains much unpublished material.

Modern ceramic historians, with the benefit of research in the last twenty-five years, have found certain inaccuracies in the nineteenth century works and it is felt necessary to warn students that great care should be taken to check information taken from them. This does not mean that all information should be regarded as inaccurate; in fact the works should form a valuable addition to any ceramic library.

Acknowledgements

I would like to thank the Royal Crown Derby Porcelain Company and in particular Mr. Stuart R. Lyons, chairman, and the Hon. Hugh Gibson, Managing Director, for their help and support for this project. Thanks are due to Miss Ann Linscott, Head of Public Relations and to her department, especially John Morton; Mr. Arthur Rigby and Mr. John Bate, executives in charge at the Osmaston Road China Works; Miss Natalia Wieczorek, my former deputy curator; the guides and indeed all the workforce who have supplied information for this book, especially Mrs. Vicky Williams; the late Mrs. Alice Williams and Mrs. Elizabeth Rochfort-Boyd for the information about Francis Paget; and Mrs. Margaret Sargeant who only recently joined us as Museum secretary.

The principal photographers have been Michael Ryan, of Long Handborough, Oxfordshire, always ready to go into action at the drop of a hat, and Hubert King of W.W. Winter of Derby, who also never failed me. I should also like to thank all the other photographers who supplied their work for this and the previous edition. Finally it would be impossible for me not to mention David Holborough and Roy Beeston of David John Ceramics whose patience and tolerance were often stretched; and Brenda 'Pip' Bentley for taking 'the lid off' the enamellers department during her forty years at the China Works. This edition would not have been possible but for the understanding of my publishers, the Antique Collectors' Club of Woodbridge.

John Twitchett

Index

The Antique Collectors' Club

The Antique Collectors' Club was formed in 1966 and now has a five figure membership spread throughout the world. It publishes the only independently run monthly antiques magazine *Antique Collecting* which caters for those collectors who are interested in widening their knowledge of antiques, both by greater awareness of quality and by discussion of the factors which influence the price that is likely to be asked. The Antique Collectors' Club pioneered the provision of information on prices for collectors and the magazine still leads in the provision of detailed articles on a variety of subjects.

It was in response to the enormous demand for information on "what to pay" that the price guide series was introduced in 1968 with the first edition of *The Price Guide to Antique Furniture* (completely revised, 1978), a book which broke new ground by illustrating the more common types of antique furniture, the sort that collectors could buy in shops and at auctions rather than the rare museum pieces which had previously been used (and still to a large extent are used) to make up the limited amount of illustrations in books published by commercial publishers. Many other price guides have followed, all copiously illustrated, and greatly appreciated by collectors for the valuable information they contain, quite apart from prices. The Antique Collectors' Club also publishes other books on antiques, including horology and art reference works, and a full book list is available.

Club membership, which is open to all collectors, costs £15.95 per annum. Members receive free of charge *Antique Collecting,* the Club's magazine (published every month except August), which contains well-illustrated articles dealing with the practical aspects of collecting not normally dealt with by magazines. Prices, features of value, investment potential, fakes and forgeries are all given prominence in the magazine.

Among other facilities available to members are private buying and selling facilities, the longest list of "For Sales" of any antiques magazine, an annual ceramics conference and the opportunity to meet other collectors at their local antique collectors' clubs. There are over eighty in Britain and more than a dozen overseas. Members may also buy the Club's publications at special pre-publication prices.

As its motto implies, the Club is an amateur organisation designed to help collectors get the most out of their hobby: it is informal and friendly and gives enormous enjoyment to all concerned.

For Collectors — By Collectors — About Collecting

The Antique Collectors' Club, 5 Church Street, Woodbridge, Suffolk